Praise for
Meals That Heal Inflammation by Julie Daniluk

"Julie makes adopting an anti-inflammatory diet an easy-to-navigate and delicious journey. This book is a fantastic resource for anyone looking to improve their health from the inside-out. A must-read." —Leslie Beck, R.D., bestselling author of *The Plant-Based Power Diet and Globe and Mail* columnist

"A mega guidebook and cookbook in one. . . . [Y]ou don't have to have a stomach issue (or be wildly obsessed with anti-inflammatory foods) to enjoy this book. The meals themselves are worth cooking up for mind, body and inner health!" —*LavishlyNatural.com*

"[Daniluk] shows you how to shift your diet to one that includes healing foods that also taste great. . . . *Meals That Heal Inflammation* takes on inflammation and empowers you to eliminate it from your body through proper nutrition and exercise." —*Diets in Review.com*

"Peppered with useful tips. . . . If you suffer from inflammation and its associated pain, or know someone who does, *Meals That Heal Inflammation* could be the best book you buy all year." —*alive* magazine

"I can't decide whether to give this book to my doctor or put it in my kitchen. Maybe I'll do both. . . . Daniluk makes such a convincing case for eating well, I actually believe her when she says she now craves blueberries over chocolate cake." —*Vitality*

SLIMMING
MEALS THAT HEAL

Lose Weight Without Dieting, Using Anti-inflammatory Superfoods

JULIE DANILUK, R.H.N.

HAY
HOUSE

HAY HOUSE, INC.

Carlsbad, California • New York City
London • Sydney • Johannesburg
Vancouver • Hong Kong • New Delhi

Published and distributed in the United States by: Hay House, Inc.: www.hayhouse.com®
• *Published and distributed in Australia by:* Hay House Australia Pty. Ltd.: www.hayhouse.com.
au • *Published and distributed in the United Kingdom by:* Hay House UK, Ltd.: www.hayhouse
.co.uk • *Published and distributed in the Republic of South Africa by:* Hay House SA (Pty), Ltd.:
www.hayhouse.co.za • *Published in India by: Hay House Publishers India:* www.hayhouse.co.in

Image credits: Page vi: Tim Leyes; Pages 21, 26, 49: Leanne Chan; Page 81: Jessica and
Nick Ortner

The author of this book does not dispense medical advice or prescribe the use of any
technique as a form of treatment for physical, emotional, or medical problems without
the advice of a physician, either directly or indirectly. The intent of the author is only to
offer information of a general nature to help you in your quest for emotional and spiritual
well-being. In the event you use any of the information in this book for yourself, the
author and the publisher assume no responsibility for your actions.

Library of Congress Control Number: 2014932646

Tradepaper ISBN: 978-1-4019-4570-1

17 16 15 14   4 3 2 1
1st Hay House edition, May 2014

Printed in the United States of America

CONTENTS

DEDICATION AND GRATITUDE

I dedicate this book to the seekers, the builders, and the conscious souls who trust that nature can return their body to wholeness. I also dedicate this book to the healers who act as the fulcrum to activate the wellness that is within every person's destiny.

My husband, Alan Smith, wore every hat in the creation of *Slimming Meals That Heal*. From conception to final edit, he has been the granite that provides the foundation to triumph. He managed the recipe testing and food styling, advised the flow of the chapters, and edited alongside me till the wee hours of the night. I love you.

My sister, Lynn Daniluk, took care of everything at Daniluk Consulting so I could carve out time to write SMTH. Her recipe revisions and suggestions were huge contributions. The greatest gift of all is how she consistently gauges and infuses integrity into our business with the precision of an archer. Thank you for being my chief champion.

My fellow nutritionist Cynthia Macmillan has been such a loving and inspiring assistant, copyeditor, recipe beautifier, and reference finder. Her mastery of language elevated SMTH, and her friendship elevated my experience as a writer and nutritionist.

Alex Freemon, editor of SMTH for the Hay House edition, who meticulously elevated the text. Kudos to Louise Hay, Reid Tracy, and the rest of the amazing Hay House family for their support of the important message that food is a powerful tool for healing. It is such an honor to be part of a community of extraordinary conscious authors.

My literary agent, Rick Broadhead, is a kind sage: I am always amazed at his tireless commitment when it comes to ensuring that an author's needs are met. He is the hardest-working agent in the business, and I am so lucky he encouraged me to become a writer over a decade ago.

My brother and yoga instructor, Shambunata (Steven Daniluk), gives me endless hours of joy, calm, and self-reflection. He is able to pluck stage fright out of my heart and doubt from my mind with the precision of a Jedi knight!

To the researchers and experts I interviewed, or who made written contributions: Cheryl Reifsnyder, Leanne Chan, Jason Tetro, Marc St. Onge, Bryce Wylde, Josie Driver, Brent Bishop, Chance Woods, Jennifer Nelson, Jessica Ortner, and Jennie Brand-Miller, M.D. They all helped to investigate and clarify information. They say it takes a village to raise a child; this book is a literary baby that my community helped to shape.

My mom, Elaine, and I have taken turns being both the caretaker and patient as we discovered our own personal prescription with food. Mom took me off all refined food when I was seven years old to rectify my ADHD. I radically changed her diet to heal her body at the age of 65. We both transformed our health 52 years apart and are reminded that the miracle of healing is just a meal away!

My father, Neil, lives in a state of constant contribution to others. One of the greatest gifts he ever gave me was to model how to celebrate work by doing something so enjoyable that you would do it for free. His excitement to help with my book tour is a glowing example of the joy he imparts to the process of putting "your shoulder to the wheel."

To my amazing group of copyeditors, proofers, and recipe creators/ testers: managing editor Deirdre Molina, copyeditor Linda Pruessen, proofreader Liba Berry, Karen Rolfe, Sarah Britton, Holly Klamer, Kaydn Gangnier, Hannah Arthurs, Fiona McCarthy-Kennedy, Victoria Mirski, Linda Smith, Paz Etcheverry, Taevan Gangnier, Zora DeGrandpre, Margaret Reffell, Joan Morris, Jodi Graham, R.H.N., Jackie Santos, R.H.N., Ilona Napravnik, Myriam Llano, R.H.N., Jo-Ann Blondin, Angela Gruenthal, CNP, Larysa Osmak, B.Ed., M.A., R.H.N., R.B.I.E., Melanie Cornacchia, and Bev Szandtner, R.H.N. Without you this book would still be a pile of sauce-soaked scraps of paper in my test kitchen. I am so grateful to my co-host, Chef Ezra Title, who provided some special "Healthy Gourmet" dishes.

To my expert advisors: Dr. Zoltan Rona, Eric Sanderson, Kate Kent, Daniela Rambaldini, Dr. Kate Wharton, and Dr. Patricia McCord. Your opinions and research give this book depth and a wider perspective.

To my supporters: Marc St. Onge and Pamela Andrews with Ascenta Health, Deane Parkes and Brenda Parkes with Preferred Nutrition, and Mike Fata and Kelly Sanderson with Manitoba Harvest Hemp Foods. Your support of my book tour has allowed me to bring this healing message to a much wider audience, and I am so grateful for our shared vision of a healthy planet.

PREFACE

In 2011, I created the definitive guide to understanding inflammation and its link to chronic disease. I wanted to educate readers on how inflammation was affecting their health, and how food is the most powerful healer available to us. To do that, I wrote *Meals That Heal Inflammation*—a book that explains in detail the causes and effects of the body's inflammatory response. I also provided recipes so readers could learn that delicious, healing food belonged in their kitchens and their lives.

After the book was released, I was overjoyed by the hundreds of e-mails I received from readers who found their painful symptoms were going away. By eliminating inflammatory choices, people reported their arthritis pain was down, skin conditions cleared up, depression lifted, and swelling disappeared. What's more, I received hundreds of testimonials from readers who tried the MTHI plan and lost weight without dieting. Based on that response, I decided to take the concepts that were in the original book and put the focus on weight loss, which is a concern for so many of us today. I began to develop a new meal plan called *Slimming Meals That Heal*, and saw great results: my nutritional coaching clients went on to lose 25, 45, even 100 pounds.

When I first met her on *The Marilyn Denis Show*, 52-year-old Marg Stahlbaum was not able to walk up a flight of stairs without pain. During her first nine months on the SMTH plan, she went from 295 to 194 pounds. Marg says she loves that the SMTH plan is flexible and works with her busy life. As Marg's swelling went down she regained full mobility, increasing her ability to take on extensive exercise for the first time in years. Within 4 months of starting the program, she ran her first 5-kilometer race. However, what she says has made her happiest is a renewed self-confidence that she shares with her children and grandchildren.

In his wildly successful book, *Wheat Belly*, Dr. William Davis inspired a grain-free revolution by focusing on the fattening influence of wheat. He explained how wheat is more inflammatory when a person is intolerant or allergic to its complex protein, called gluten. In a similar vein, *Slimming Meals That Heal* examines the relationship between food allergies, inflammation, and weight gain. SMTH deepens the reader's understanding of how food can hurt or heal. Expanding on MTHI, I've covered topics such as the cleansing and healing powers of superfoods and techniques that directly reduce cravings. You'll learn how to boost metabolism and balance hormones with a five-step plan that will assist in you reaching what I call your "vitality weight"—the natural, balanced weight where you're healthy and thriving and have energy to burn!

What many scientists and researchers are now beginning to appreciate is the role inflammation plays in weight gain. For starters, inflammation can make you resistant to certain hormones, in particular to insulin, a hormone secreted by the pancreas. Excess consumption of carbohydrates causes your cells to become resistant to insulin. During insulin resistance, the pancreas tries to compensate by producing more of the hormone. Thus, inflammation causes the pancreas to exhaust itself, sort of like a machine that is never turned off, and become a super-mega-duper insulin-producing factory. And insulin not only reduces blood glucose levels, it also makes you gain weight.

Inflammation also makes you resistant to leptin, a hormone that is secreted in adipose (fatty) tissue and promotes satiety. As a result, when you experience abnormal inflammation you have a greater chance of suffering from huge food cravings.

An excess of fat tissue leads to a higher production and secretion of the pro-inflammatory compounds called adipokines, which recruit immune cells that release nasty reactive oxygen species (ROS). The result is major tissue damage (especially in the adipose tissue), pain, and internal swelling that ultimately contribute to obesity-related diseases. The association between inflammation, obesity, and even diabetes is so strong that it is known as the "inflammation-diabesity" connection (obesity + diabetes = diabesity).

For your health and your weight, the best foods to eat are whole foods. One of the biggest advantages of eating whole, unprocessed foods is that you get the harmony of all of their nutrients together, the way nature intended. These critical nutrients keep your immune system strong and protect you from disease—single vitamins and minerals in supplement form are isolated and do not have the same beneficial effect.

In sharp contrast, eating processed foods exposes you to preservatives, dyes, and chemicals that have been linked to a higher incidence of ADHD, asthma, and immune imbalances. Processed food is also too high in salt, sugar, and trans fats.

When whole grains are refined, the bran and the coat of the grain are often removed. Dozens of nutrients are lost, though artificially adding a few back on actually emboldens manufacturers to call the product "enriched."

With all of the extra fat and sugar in processed foods, calories add up quickly. The natural fiber in many vegetables, fruits, and grains fills you up without empty calories. Scientists estimate that eating 25 to 40 grams of fiber a day is ideal for optimal health. People who eat mainly processed foods get fewer than 10 grams of fiber a day. Cellulose, an insoluble fiber in plants, speeds up the elimination of waste, absorbs toxins, softens the stool, reduces hunger, and improves bowel disorders.

Another key to a healthy diet is variety. If you're busy, you may be tempted to rely on convenience foods made mostly of white rice, pasta, and bread. The great news is that cooking healthy meals at home doesn't have to be overly complicated or cost more! For instance, beans, whole grains, and produce are much cheaper than pre-packaged processed foods.

The recipes in *Slimming Meals That Heal* focus on vegetables—you need 10 servings of veggies a day for true sustained health. The average North American eats less than three. Including two to three servings of fruit will help to reduce your sweet cravings.

Fruits and vegetables also contain phytochemicals such as flavonoids and carotenoids. These natural compounds in plants work as antioxidants, which protect your cells against damage.

WHAT CAN YOU EXPECT?

This book is divided into three parts. Part I explores the scientific research that demonstrates the connection between obesity, inflammation, and emotional eating. We also look at how removing food allergies can lead to naturally balanced weight. By eating anti-inflammatory foods, you reduce the stress on the organs and glands responsible for making your hormones.

Part II outlines the five-step slimming plan that leads to effortless weight balance. It focuses on the anti-inflammatory food chart, clearly outlining the importance of avoiding processed meat and refined carbohydrates. These acid-forming foods create an inflammation response that leads to premature aging and disease. Fruits and vegetables are alkaline, which raises the pH of the body, reducing the incidence of inflammation. Many studies covered in SMTH have found that a diet rich in healthy foods like fruits and vegetables is associated with a reduced risk of cardiovascular disease, many types of cancer, and type 2 diabetes. The solution to easing inflammation and losing weight without dieting is to embrace wholesome, healing food.

Part III contains a menu plan that spotlights the top slimming superfoods in over 120 healing recipes. You'll enjoy widely known superfoods (such as blueberries, cacao, hemp, and pomegranate) and less common ones as well (lacuma, mesquite, and maca). *Meals That Heal Inflammation* took much inspiration from East Asian and Indian cuisines. After you establish that you do not have a nightshade vegetable intolerance, you may enjoy the Mediterranean flavors in *Slimming Meals That Heal*. I've included tomatoes and red peppers as optional ingredients in this book's recipes so that the recipes are both satisfying to the palate and naturally low in calories.

So let's get started. As the ancient Greek playwright Aeschylus wrote, "There is advantage in the wisdom won from pain." As you regain your full vitality, you will relish the understanding that your health is your wealth.

PART ONE

THE SCIENCE OF WEIGHT LOSS

"The truth will set you free, but first it will piss you off."

—GLORIA STEINEM

CHAPTER 1

WHY DIETS DON'T WORK

WHY DO DIETS FAIL?

How many diets have you tried? In 2007, Traci Mann and her research team at UCLA did an exhaustive review that included 31 studies of popular diets. Mann concluded that calorie restriction garnered very short-term weight loss, with up to 66 percent of dieters gaining back more weight than they lost.

The trouble with a diet is that it ends. That is, there is a fixed moment when the "healthy" eating stops and the "normal" or old eating pattern resumes. This is why the SMTH plan can make a breakthrough. Instead of putting you on a restricted diet, it works with you to develop a new normal. What if your new food choices left you so deeply satisfied that there was no need to eat the foods that harm you? What if new comfort foods also healed your tissues, allowing your body weight to establish its natural set point?

There are three main reasons that diets fail:

1. The diet is sold as a "fix."

Most people experience diets as a temporary state. You are willing to put up with temporary shortages and the torture of watching your favorite food be served to others in order to squeeze into a dress for a wedding or a swimsuit for your vacation. But then you lose motivation, and the weight comes back.

SMTH Solution: Let go of the concept of dieting once and for all. Break out of food prison and embrace a lifelong health strategy that I call not a diet but a "live-it." Explore oodles of new foods from different countries to expand your choices instead of limiting them. Give yourself all the time you need to get used to new habits and then build on them. For example, you could take a cooking class, try a new cuisine next time you're out, or experiment with new fun snacks.

2. The diet is too strict, and you end up binging on "forbidden" foods.

A diet that restricts a major food group (e.g., a low-fat or low-carb diet) ends up eliminating all your comfort foods. After all, you wouldn't gain any benefit from restricting a food you weren't eating to start with, right? So when life gets rough, you fall off the wagon. You might last a few months and lose weight, but boredom and deprivation will eventually drive anyone to break out of their food prison. It is unworkable to forgo all treats forever—our brains are hard-wired to seek pleasure.

SMTH Solution: Enjoy healing versions of your favorite recipes, such as the chocolate pudding, bread, crispy onion rings, and sorbet found in this book. For those occasions when you don't have time to cook, health food stores stock some tasty alternatives. Ensure that you eat proteins, fats, and carbohydrates in healthy amounts to combat cravings. By timing your treats and understanding that you will have another treat tomorrow, you avoid overeating and binging.

3. Hormonal challenges.

At 30 years of age, everyone's metabolism begins to slow down. If you have a family history of low thyroid function or a history of extreme dieting with big swings in weight, your body may become stubborn and hold on to weight even when you restrict calories. If you binge, your body naturally stores extra fat in case you decide to go back on another "diet." This vicious cycle makes it harder and harder to lose weight and keep it off.

SMTH Solution: The good news is you can shift your hormones and break through the weight plateau that you're stuck on right now. By embracing a "live-it" that is fun and sustainable, you can expect to lose one to two pounds a week—and it will stay off because your new way of eating supports hormonal balance. As well, by enjoying some movement (dance, yoga, rehab exercises), you can rev up your fat-burning engine to burn more calories per hour.

If you are tired of strict, depriving diets, I invite you to join me in my "live-it." You'll boost your mood, reduce pain, and reach your vitality weight. Your vitality weight is not a number on a scale or a measurement dictated by society. Your vitality weight is found when you have reached balance and you feel content and happy in your body. Your body will start to love you and allow you to accomplish extraordinary things.

DO YOU HAVE A LOVE/HATE RELATIONSHIP WITH FOOD?

If you find yourself relishing your next bite and then loathing the guilt of your latest indulgence, you're not alone. The latest prediction is that 51 percent of the world's population could be obese by year 2030. I want to share with you my personal story. For those who've read my first book, some of the details may be familiar, but I want to emphasize here how my relationship with food once had me on a fast track to inflammatory weight gain.

MY STORY

I think my parents are superheroes. When I was seven, my mom figured out that food allergies were at the root of my health problems. When she took me off sugar, red dye, and artificial preservatives and flavors, I blossomed overnight. I slept eight hours straight for the first time in my life. I was able to focus in school, and my grades improved dramatically. As long as I stayed on a natural diet, I was a transformed kid.

I was happy, calm, and confident until I discovered my secret passion: cookies and ice cream. When I turned 16, I went back to eating refined foods as a way to rebel. Despite how horrible I felt after eating foods I was allergic to, I found myself unable to stop. I would live on a strict diet of carrots and tofu, and then I would binge on a whole pint of ice cream, a box of peanut butter cookies, half a loaf of toasted bread with sugar and cinnamon, and sometimes rice squares to top off a 3,000-calorie binge that would last less than an hour! I would eat and eat until the food would just come back up. I did not know then that this behavior was called bulimia. At the time I thought I was the only one on the planet who ever ate this way. This secret ritual continued for years. I tried to do it only when I was at home alone, and I would hide the evidence.

But one day my sister caught me in the washroom throwing up, and we had a fight that I will never forget. I now understand that this tough love was the first crack in the veneer of my attempt to become perfect. I am forever grateful that she forced me to see that I was suffering from a real illness.

The effects of bulimia eventually took their toll. My teeth started to lose their enamel from all the sugar and stomach acid. (The only teeth that do not have major cavities are my two front teeth!) My stomach lost its ability to digest my meals correctly. Even when I ate something healthy, if it contained a bit of something that didn't agree with me, I had to fight to keep it down.

Because my stomach became very weak from years of abuse, I started to have more bouts of food poisoning (which happens when the pH in the stomach is not low enough to kill off bacteria or mold in food). Although my sister tried to help me, I found it hard to slow down my bulimic episodes because I didn't know how to replace my only coping mechanism. Food had become my drug of choice, one that helped me forget any emotional pain.

When I decided to go to theater arts school, there was a huge pressure to be thin. So my ritual continued. I would sometimes pass out in acting classes because my blood sugar was a roller coaster. What I didn't understand back then was that although I got rid of most of the food I ate, the damage to my pancreas was already done.

I didn't receive any formal help for my eating disorder until I met acupuncturist and therapist Kate Kent about a knee injury. After only a few minutes she said, "I hope you don't mind me being forward, but do you have an eating disorder?" I was stunned; the only person who had ever confronted me was my sister. "How could you know my darkest secret after only 10 minutes?" I asked in awe. Kate simply replied, "I danced for years and know the signs."

I started two months of tough therapy with Kate where I learned to express my true feelings and draw boundaries with people. I was able to dissect the reasons for my self-abuse with food. I slowly started to assemble a toolbox of other coping methods that helped me heal. Now I'm offering these tools to you in *Slimming Meals That Heal*.

With Kate's help, I discovered joy and compassion as my blood sugar finally balanced. My desire to be fully engaged in life started to outweigh the few moments of pleasure I got from tasting something I was allergic to. I also learned that I could make treats that didn't cause allergic reactions, so now I have my cake and eat it too.

By listening to my intuition about food and learning which foods were nourishing, I became a more conscious and caring person. My greatest hope is that I can help others find that escape from food prison.

We all have different challenges we face when it comes to our relationship to eating. When you are feeling low or confused or tired or fed up, I invite you to imagine receiving help. Sit in a quiet place and visualize a healer who is a source of power and inspiration to you. Imagine a cord, connecting you. Receive their wisdom, their strength, and their confidence. There is nothing to fix because you are not broken. You are evolving and learning major lessons with every bend in the path.

Think about the caterpillar—it turns into a butterfly only when it struggles to burst out of the cocoon. As soon as a caterpillar is done growing, it forms itself into a chrysalis. Within the chrysalis the old body parts of the caterpillar undergo a remarkable metamorphosis to become beautiful. If you cut open the cocoon too early, the butterfly dies. You have to let the butterfly strengthen its own wings against the restraint of the cocoon.

I deeply appreciate the path I have taken. By struggling out of my own cocoon of illness, I have found wings that I never conceived possible. You are ready to burst out and fly. I'll meet you up there.

SLIMMING MEALS THAT HEAL—THE UNTOLD STORY OF INFLAMMATION AND WEIGHT GAIN

Depending on how many decades you've been alive—and how many of those decades you've spent trying to control your weight, you've probably seen many diet fads come and go. The 1990s had the low-fat revolution, the cabbage soup diet, and the lemonade cleanse, to name just a few. The 2000s had the high-protein, low-carb obsession. You may even remember the high-protein, low-carb thing going around in the 1970s as well.

One of the basic principles that well-meaning health practitioners have promoted for years is that weight loss always comes down to calories in versus calories out—that whether you eat a balanced, health-promoting diet of vegetables, fruit, whole grains, and lean protein or a bunch of processed junk, as long as the calories are right, you'll lose weight. This book contradicts that long-held belief. Not only should you eat a healthy, whole-foods diet because it boosts your energy and reduces your risk of disease, you should also do so because a calorie is not, in fact, just a calorie.

The reason that all calories are not equal comes down to the simple (and sometimes complex) differences in the way calories from different sources react inside your body. The way you process the calories in avocado, beets, or celery is far, far different from the way you process the calories in high-fructose corn syrup and margarine.

In this book, you'll discover that the missing piece to your dieting and weight-loss puzzle comes down to inflammation. As recently as the late 1990s, nutrition scientists began to discover ties between the markers for inflammation and weight-related conditions like metabolic syndrome, diabetes, heart disease, and obesity. Later studies began to reveal the causal relationship between persistent inflammation and being overweight or obese, in addition to added risk for all of the diseases that go along with obesity.

Of course, some inflammation is part of a normal, healthy immune response to invaders. When you come into contact with a virus, bacteria, toxin, or allergen, your body launches its immune defense mechanisms. One of these mechanisms is inflammation. As a part of the normal immune system response, the purpose of inflammation is to heal injured or infected tissues. This is known as acute, or short-term, inflammation. However, the natural inflammatory process becomes harmful when the immune system doesn't appropriately shut off these tissue-rescuing mechanisms. What results is a chronic state of inflammation. Chronic, or long-term, inflammation can manifest as a variety of diseases, including cancer.

INFLAMMATION: THE FOUR "I"S

The root causes of chronic inflammation fall into four basic categories: injury, infection, irritation, and imbalance. When any of these four factors persist, the affected tissues can't heal. The result is a persistent chronic inflammatory state.

You can address all of these factors and heal—or prevent—chronic inflammation with a live-it food plan. The solution lies in supporting your immune system. Let's take a closer look at each of the four categories.

Injury: Physical and/or Emotional

Physical injuries—like topical wounds, gastrointestinal ulcers, or twisted ankles—are obvious sources of inflammation. Injured tissues are usually healed through a healthy, acute inflammatory response. However, when physical injuries aren't allowed to heal properly (for example, if you aren't able to take the appropriate amount of time off from your busy schedule to heal and convalesce), it's likely that the inflammatory reaction won't end appropriately.

Instead, the immune system cells responsible for creating and sustaining inflammation may just carry right on fighting. This means the damaged tissues won't be repaired, and, even worse, the ongoing inflammation can cause further tissue damage. Chronic inflammation is especially common in vulnerable areas like joints, which often sustain injury from a fall or from sports.

When you're young and very active, your body tends to heal and rebound rather quickly, although boredom and impatience can make it difficult for anyone with an injury to wait for it to fully heal. The site of any injury that isn't allowed to heal properly—regardless of an individual's age or fitness level—will be weakened and vulnerable as a result of a poorly controlled inflammatory process, making the area prone to chronic inflammation in the future.

In contrast to physical injuries, emotional injuries are less obvious, and, to a certain extent, less respected. Old stigmas about emotional health are slowly fading, but people still tend to have difficulty understanding that emotional lows aren't just "all in your head," or something that you should just "get over." Your emotional well-being plays a significant role in your ability to fight off illness, the amount of physical pain you experience, and even your chances of dying prematurely.

It's still largely the social norm to ignore your emotional traumas. While it's important not to dwell on past hurts and perceived transgressions, it's equally important to acknowledge the impact that psychological tribulations have on your physical health. To achieve balance, you'll need to acknowledge the sources of your pain and identify problems for the sake of working through them and bringing them to a healthy resolution. I highly recommend seeking out a health professional who will work with your needs.

If you're still not convinced that emotional difficulties share the same playing field as physical symptoms when it comes to your health, consider the emerging field of psychoneuroimmunology (PNI). This medical discipline investigates the fascinating connection between the mind, the nervous system, and the immune system.

PNI research indicates that your thoughts and emotions can profoundly affect the chemistry of your body. Production of pro-inflammatory messengers called cytokines influences a whole spectrum of diseases that are normally associated with age, such as cardiovascular disease, type 2 diabetes, arthritis, osteoporosis, and certain types of cancers.

Ultimately, if you want to heal inflammation, you must address the root causes of physical and emotional injuries in addition to making wise food and lifestyle choices. Whole-body healing is a key element in supporting immune system health and reducing inflammation. While holistic healing corrects imbalances and helps heal existing pain and dysfunction, holistic living helps prevent imbalances and reduces your risk of developing disease and dysfunction in the future.

In fact, this is such an important part of healing that I devoted an entire chapter of this book to emotional healing. Stress reduction and positive coping techniques such as exercise, traditional arts, and meditation are essential to heal chronically inflamed tissues. The combined principles of healing what's already gone wrong and preventing future ills are at the heart of my live-it philosophy.

Infection: Topical and/or Internal

Pathogenic (aka disease-causing) infections strongly trigger the immune system to launch an inflammatory response. This relationship is simple to understand because inflammation is the primary first responder sent out to protect your body from unwanted invaders such as bacteria, viruses, funguses, yeasts, and other parasites.

Among all infections, topical infections are usually easiest to notice because they occur on the surface of the skin, feel painful to the touch, and have the annoying tendency to bump into every available surface—constantly. They're also relatively easy to treat compared with internal infections because you have direct access to the site of infection. You can apply anti-parasitic and antiseptic medicines right on the wound, and you don't need any special tools to monitor how well it's healing.

On the other hand, internal infections may be less obvious—especially if they're low-grade. However, even low-grade infections will cause inflammation—you just may not notice that your body's engaged in a fight. It's likely that you won't feel noticeable symptoms that an infection or illness has become more serious or widespread. The most common internal infections enter the body through the digestive system, respiratory system, or the blood.

Some internal infections can be acute and immediately noticeable—even severe. One example of such a fast-acting pathogen is food poisoning. Food poisoning is a broad term for acute health problems that result from food or drink. People with a weak or sensitive digestive system can be more vulnerable to food poisoning because they have lower levels of stomach acid and digestive juices, reduced intestinal immunity, damage and inflammation in the gastrointestinal tract, or inadequate intestinal microflora.

Microflora is a term that generally describes the species of plants or bacteria and other microorganisms in a specific environment or host. Intestinal microflora consist of both beneficial organisms, like certain species of bacteria and yeast known as probiotics, and other organisms that may cause no harm when present in small numbers but that have the potential to become pathogenic under certain circumstances.

You may have seen probiotics added to a number of food products such as yogurt, probiotic-infused beverages (e.g., kefir or Amazake), sauerkraut, and the beneficial cultures added to fermented vegetables. These products can be a healthy addition to diet if you tolerate the other ingredients, but the dose is often much weaker than the medicinal doses found in a probiotic supplement. Probiotics are essential because they help to digest food; increase nutrient absorption; contribute to immune defense against harmful microorganisms; and synthesize certain vitamins, including folic acid, vitamin B12, and vitamin K. Even though probiotics permanently reside in your intestines, your food and lifestyle choices will affect how well they thrive. All the culprits that have the potential to directly damage your intestinal lining may also affect the health of your probiotics.

At the other end of the spectrum from probiotics, the pathogenic microflora that can exist in your intestinal tract include parasites such as certain species of harmful yeasts, fungi, and bacteria like *E. coli.*

Food poisoning is far more common than we'd like it to be because it's nearly impossible to completely avoid exposure to pathogens and parasites. It's important that you support your immune system with healthy eating patterns to ensure that you are equipped to fight off the effects of food poisoning in the event that you do come into contact with food-borne pathogens. In *Meals That Heal Inflammation,* you'll find more information about common food pathogens and the ways you can prevent food poisoning.

Irritation: Toxins and/or Allergens

First of all, what is a toxin? Originally, the term *toxin* was defined as a poisonous or venomous substance produced by, or derived from, an organism that causes disease when present in low concentrations in the body. The modern definition also includes man-made substances and other irritants present in the environment that can damage cells.

Interestingly, not all toxins have noticeable detrimental effects to all individuals. For example, you may be able to metabolize and eliminate a particular toxin quickly, which may prevent it from causing the significant or noticeable cell damage that it would wreak on someone else. However, all toxins can trigger inflammation, and cell injury will result from constant or long-term exposure to irritants like radiation, asbestos, alcohol, heavy metals, pesticides, drugs, tobacco smoke, and free radicals. When your immune system is exposed to a toxin, it responds with inflammation to eliminate the intruder—even at the cost of killing some of your own cells.

Not all toxins arise from external sources. Your body and resident intestinal microflora inevitably produce metabolic waste every day. For example, there is waste that arises as a by-product of digesting food. These waste products need to be eliminated rapidly to prevent accumulation. The effectiveness with which your body detoxifies itself is determined by the health of your organs of elimination—your liver, kidneys, lungs, large intestine, and skin. If you have weaknesses in one or more of these organs, you'll be more susceptible to a buildup of toxins. Furthermore, long-term exposure to toxins sustains inflammation and runs contrary to the goal of reducing inflammation as a way to mitigate disease and pain.

Allergies are very similar to toxins, in that your body identifies as a toxin a food or environmental substance that may be harmless to most people. Just as your immune system would fight off the intrusion of a pathogen or toxin, it creates an inflammatory response against the allergen that can range from a mild rash to anaphylactic shock. Left unchecked, these responses may even contribute to the development of autoimmune diseases.

As outlined in *Meals That Heal Inflammation,* there are five major sources of food allergies. Among them are weak digestion, stress, and toxic load. A person may have weak digestion for several reasons, including stress, poor food choices, overeating, and imbalanced intestinal microflora. All of these factors can cause damage and subsequent inflammation in intestinal tissue.

Choosing healing foods, such as those recommended in the live-it food plan, can help restore your intestinal health, improve your immune function, and decrease the number or severity of your allergies.

Note: If you have numerous or severe allergies, I recommend that you work closely with a health practitioner to resolve them. Look for a reputable doctor of naturopathic, Ayurvedic, or Traditional Chinese medicine.

Imbalance: Nutritional and/or Hormonal

People living in economically developed countries have easy access to an abundance of food, and yet many people suffer nutritional deficiencies. Although most people aren't deficient in calories, there are often deficiencies in nutrients like omega-3 fats, trace minerals, and vitamins.

A nutritional deficiency deprives your body of the materials required for healthy cell metabolism and proper tissue repair. Conversely, an excess of any single nutrient can result in an imbalance that doctors call "toxicity." Either kind of nutritional imbalance can lead to various disorders, including hormone disturbances, a strained immune system, and chronic inflammation. For example, an adult who is deficient in vitamin D will eventually experience impaired immunity and calcium absorption, progressive demineralization of the bones, and bone pain. And yet vitamin D is one of the most likely of all vitamins to cause toxic reactions if intake is excessive. Prolonged intake of vitamin D at levels of 10,000 IU or more can result in excessively high levels of calcium in the blood (hypercalcemia), possibly leading to calcification of the soft tissues of the kidney, heart, lungs, and blood vessels.

Hormonal imbalances can also be strong instigators of disease and inflammation. Unfortunately, since hormones tip out of balance slowly, clinical diseases linked to hormone imbalances may show up in blood work much later than the point when you start to experience symptoms, or your imbalance may seem completely asymptomatic even after a disease condition is deeply established. As an example of how difficult it can be to identify an imbalance, consider the "normal" range of thyroid stimulating hormone (TSH) in a laboratory blood test. Your lab results won't fall outside the typical range unless they're below 0.5 µIU/mL or above 5 µIU/mL. The top end of the range is 1,000 percent higher than the bottom end of the range.

The answer to the question of how hormones start to shift out of balance in the first place can be complicated, but there are a few salient factors that can deeply impact your endocrine organs. These include:

- Food choices
- Lifestyle, especially daily schedules, sleep quality, and routines
- Habits such as exercise, cigarette smoking, and alcohol and drug intake
- Stress—physical and emotional
- Prescription hormones and oral contraceptives
- Radiation and heavy metals
- Environmental toxins, particularly xenoestrogens
- Certain pathogenic infections

As you examine this list, you'll notice that many of the factors influencing hormone health are within your control. That's great news! The live-it food plan can guide you in tackling the first issue: food choices. Later on in *Slimming Meals That Heal*, we'll take a deeper look into the food choices that best support healthy hormone balance.

DON'T DIET, LIVE-IT!

You've already read that *Slimming Meals That Heal* is different from other "diets" because it places an emphasis on understanding the causes and effects of inflammation as they relate to what you eat, your weight, and your overall health.

The reason most diets fail is because self-imposed, temporary food restrictions feel unbearably and unsustainably restrictive. Right away, you'll be able to separate *Slimming Meals That Heal* from all of the rest because it's not a diet at all. Instead, it's a "live-it" food plan.

If you're reading this book straight through, you will encounter the term *live-it* quite often, so let me carefully define it here at the start. What's a live-it? Quite simply, it's a way of living and eating that supports total-body health by relying on whole, healing foods. Unlike many diets—which often emphasize a temporary regimen that is focused on what you have to minimize, give up, and cut out of your normal eating pattern—a live-it emphasizes the bounty of choices that are available direct from nature.

Slimming Meals That Heal eliminates the need to count calories and will help you conquer your cravings by offering a delicious new way of eating. This new approach will vanquish the specter of inflammation that's been looming over you as you've struggled with your weight. You'll feel so fantastic from eating these nurturing foods that you'll finally be able to live it up! You'll feel a renewed sense of energy and, most important, you'll recover from any nutritional imbalances you may have.

Another difference between the usual "diet" and *Slimming Meals That Heal* is that this isn't a one-size-fits-all solution. There's no single, perfect healing diet that suits everyone. You're an individual on the inside as well as the outside. If you think about food allergies alone, it's easy to see that everyone has different needs. A food that may nourish and heal one person may be harmful to another. Similarly, you are unique in the way you metabolize foods and in your specific nutritional needs.

All around the world, people have come to accept pain as a normal consequence of aging, but it doesn't have to be that way. Pain is often a sign of tissue inflammation, which can be remedied—either through prevention, intervention, or a combination of the two. Many of the "normal" symptoms of aging may be tied to reversible immune responses and tissue damage. As you'll discover over the next few chapters, you don't have to live with inflammation and pain indefinitely. And you don't have to struggle with calorie counting and failed weight-loss attempts for one more day.

Welcome to juicy vitality!

*"After I was diagnosed with celiac disease,
I said yes to food, with great enthusiasm . . .
I vowed to taste everything I COULD eat,
rather than focusing on what I could not."*

—SHAUNA JAMES AHERN

CHAPTER 2

HOW ALLERGIES CAUSE WEIGHT GAIN

Does your morning snack trigger an energy crash? Does lunch leave you feeling bloated and sluggish? Your symptoms might be caused by food allergies or intolerances. These reactions can be set off by almost anything—from certain types of protein or sugar to chemical additives. Both allergies and intolerances can set off complicated chain reactions that make it difficult or impossible for you to lose weight.

Most people think of weight loss only in terms of calories: burn more calories than you eat and the pounds will come off, right? Unfortunately, it's not that simple. Food is supposed to give you energy, but foods you are allergic to or intolerant of can harm you. Food reactions set off a domino effect that alters the chemistry of your digestive system, the levels of good and bad bacteria in the gut, blood sugar levels, and hormone levels. The combination can trigger an immune system response and system-wide inflammation, which, in turn, can affect your ability to reach and maintain a healthy weight.

FOOD ALLERGY, FOOD INTOLERANCE—WHAT'S THE DIFFERENCE?

It's easy to get food reactions confused, especially since the terms sound similar. On the surface, the symptoms of food allergies and intolerances can look pretty similar too. The difference in how your body reacts to the food in question lies at the cellular level.

A food allergy is exactly what it sounds like: an allergic response to food. Usually, it's a response to one part of the food, called an allergen, which is most often a protein. Allergens in food can still cause reactions after they have been cooked and after they've gone through your digestive tract. Just like allergic reactions to pollen or bee venom, allergic reactions to food can range from mild and annoying all the way to life-threatening. According to the US Centers for Disease Control and Prevention, 90 percent of food allergies come from dairy, peanuts, soy, wheat, shellfish, fish, and tree nuts. The recipes in both *Meals That Heal Inflammation* and *Slimming Meals That Heal* use alternative ingredients to minimize exposure to common food allergens. The only allergens that are rotated into the plan are ones known to have anti-inflammatory benefit. These include fish and tree nuts like walnuts and hazelnuts. If you suspect you have an allergy to these foods, it is important to keep them off the menu.

An immune system reaction is composed of two equally important aspects: the adaptive response and the innate response. The *innate immune system* consists of cells and proteins that are always present and ready to mobilize and fight microbes at the site of infection. The *adaptive immune system* is called into action against pathogens that are able to evade or overcome innate immune defenses. Food allergies trigger your adaptive immune system. You can think of the adaptive immune system as sending out a sort of elite assassin squad: it develops defensive cells that are targeted to a specific food "invader." These defensive cells, called B-lymphocytes, have a very specific allergen target and specialized weapons called antibodies with which to cope with the food assault.

A food intolerance, on the other hand, has symptoms that can develop more slowly. Intolerance may result from your inability to digest or get rid of something you've eaten. It may also involve your immune system, but unlike an allergy, food intolerance activates your body's innate immune system. If the adaptive immune system is the elite assassin squad of immunity, then your innate immune system is more like the ground troops, guarding against any and all attacks. These innate immune system troops aren't deployed to fight specific targets, but they can call into play some of the same types of antibody weapons as the adaptive immune system.

Food intolerances can cause serious symptoms that aren't technically considered allergies, but that doesn't mean they aren't serious—only that your body doesn't develop specific defensive cells that target particular "invaders."

Sometimes it's difficult to tell whether you're allergic to a food or having a different type of reaction. Food hypersensitivity is an umbrella term for any reaction to a food that others can eat safely, and it includes both allergies and intolerances.

ALLERGEN ATTACK! HOW YOUR BODY FIGHTS INVADERS

In order to understand why your body's reactions to different foods can sabotage your weight-loss efforts, we need to take a closer look at exactly how the body responds to these foods. Since allergies and intolerances trigger different physical responses—at least at the outset—we'll look at allergies first.

Here are some key terms you'll read about in this chapter:

- **Antibodies:** Immune system targeting agents that identify and neutralize foreign antigens such as those found on bacteria, viruses, pollen, and food particles
- **Antigens:** Proteins or polysaccharides (carbohydrates) that trigger the production of antibodies; also called allergens
- **Histamine:** A messenger that increases blood flow, increases the permeability of the blood vessels, and can potentially cause smooth muscle contraction and pain

- **Mast cells:** Storage cells for histamine and other chemical messengers, which they release into the surrounding tissue on contact with their target antigen.
- **Basophils:** A type of white blood cell that has similar functions to a mast cell but circulates freely.

The immune system is designed to protect you: it puts your body on red alert and redirects resources to heal an injury or fight infection. When your immune system is responding to an actual threat—such as foreign bacteria or a poisonous substance—all of these physical reactions can help you destroy or eliminate the invader. Increased blood flow to an area allows white blood cells and other defensive substances to reach the invader quickly. Increased blood vessel permeability lets immune system cells move out of the blood into the tissue itself, where they can surround and destroy the target. If the "invader" is in your gastrointestinal (GI) tract, vomiting and diarrhea help your body to eject the offender before it can cause any damage.

If you eat a food you're allergic to, immune cells in the gastrointestinal tract perceive that food as a harmful invader. The first time you eat it, you might not have any symptoms, but your body starts gearing up to fight the invader should it return. It activates cells to make antibodies (specifically IgE antibodies; you'll learn more about the different types of antibodies in the next section). These antibodies attach to mast cells and basophils, "arming" them so they can respond immediately if the target antigen ever creates a bond. The next time your body detects the food, an allergic reaction usually begins within five to thirty minutes.

Mast cells are found throughout your body, but especially in the tissue of the nose, throat, lungs, skin, and gastrointestinal tract. Basophils are usually found in blood, but will also collect in tissues inflamed by an allergic reaction, where they can help repel the invader. When they encounter their target antigen, they release massive amounts of chemical messengers that affect the surrounding cells and tissues, creating inflammation.

MAST CELLS

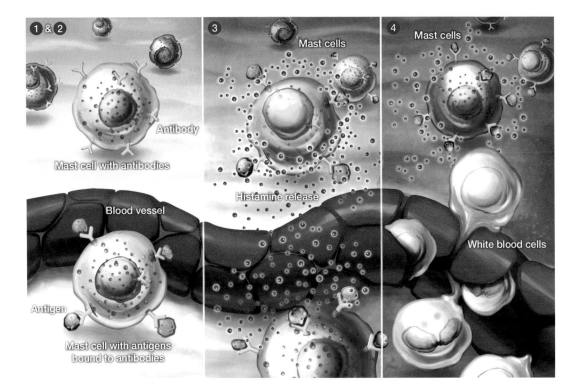

1. Antibodies that will recognize the specific antigen bind to mast cells in the body tissue.
2. If the mast cells encounter their target antigen, the antibodies latch onto it.
3. This triggers the mast cells to release histamine and other chemical messengers into the surrounding tissue.
4. Histamine increases blood flow to the area and makes blood vessels more permeable. This enables white blood cells and other invader-fighters to reach the area quickly and enter the tissue.

In the short term, the adaptive immune system is very good at protecting you from potentially dangerous invaders, but imagine what happens if you eat an allergen day after day. Your body remains in permanent attack mode. The temporary measures that are so useful for getting rid of harmful bacteria and other invaders can begin to harm your system as well. For example, let's look at how long-term release of histamine affects your body.

HISTAMINE, ALLERGIES, AND WEIGHT GAIN

When a mast cell is activated, a massive amount of histamine is released into the surrounding tissue. As it reaches different types of cells and tissues, it turns on different types of defense systems. These, in turn, trigger changes that result in obvious allergy symptoms such as hives, swelling, itching, breathing problems, vomiting, diarrhea, and abdominal pain.

What might not be as obvious is that these changes also affect your metabolism, your weight, and how you store fat. Your body has a host of different responses to an invader. You can imagine them like the individual strands in a complex spiderweb: as soon as something bumps up against one pathway, all the others are affected as well.

Histamine acts directly on the surrounding blood vessels to increase blood flow and blood vessel permeability. These changes help defensive cells and chemicals to reach the area quickly and move into the tissue, where they can destroy invaders. In the process, fluid moves out of the bloodstream and into the tissue. The area swells as liquid builds up in the spaces between cells, filling with toxins, waste products, and dead cells produced by the immune reaction. Normally, the body clears out the fluid and waste products once the threat has been eliminated. If you are exposed to the same food allergen day after day, however, your body never gets the chance to recover. Fluid builds up, making you feel thick and bloated, and adding pounds to the scale.

If you take antihistamines to combat your allergy symptoms, they may also trigger weight gain. Recent research showed that people who take prescription and over-the-counter antihistamines tend to weigh more, have larger waist circumference, and have higher levels of circulating insulin.

Histamine has indirect effects as well. It stimulates production of additional hormone messenger molecules, called prostaglandins, to cause a local inflammatory response. These messengers make nearby pain receptors more sensitive. You are less likely to adhere to an exercise plan if you are in pain, which makes it even tougher to keep your weight at a healthy level.

You need a way to break the cycle or an allergic reaction will just keep getting more and more powerful. That's where cortisol comes into the equation.

CORTISOL

Cortisol synthesis increases during an allergic reaction because of this hormone's role in counteracting the inflammatory activity that histamines set in motion. That's not all cortisol does, though. Cortisol is known as the "stress hormone" because it helps to prepare your body to survive danger. In the process, it affects nearly every tissue and organ in your body.

One of cortisol's tasks is to maintain a ready source of energy—in the form of glucose—in the bloodstream, so it activates enzymes in the liver that churn out glucose. Cortisol reinforces the effect by making your cells less sensitive to insulin, which is responsible for clearing sugar out of the bloodstream. Cells that are insulin-resistant are unable to absorb circulating glucose, instead keeping it available for a fight-or-flight response. This is great if you need to flee a hungry bear, but not so useful if the only "danger" is a food you're consuming. Since your body doesn't actually need that extra energy, the circulating glucose overload is eventually stored as fat. Meanwhile, your glucose-starved cells continue to send hunger signals to your brain in an attempt to get much-needed energy.

High cortisol levels are associated with depression, which can also cause metabolic changes that predispose you to obesity. Stress-induced cortisol surges have also been shown to cause cravings for high-calorie foods, especially sweets. This can lead to overeating and weight gain, particularly if cortisol levels remain high. In extreme cases, long-term exposure to high levels of cortisol may cause eating disorders and addictions.

When cortisol levels remain elevated, the blood sugar spike creates long-term changes in your metabolism. The pancreas pumps out insulin in response to high blood sugar, but since cortisol makes cells insulin-resistant, even more insulin is produced. Eventually, the pancreas may not be able to keep up with the increased demand for insulin, which is one reason high cortisol is thought to cause type 2 diabetes.

As well, cortisol increases the synthesis of the fast-acting stress hormone adrenaline. Like cortisol, adrenaline increases blood sugar levels by causing additional sugar release into the blood, as well as by making insulin less effective. This may explain why you get a rush when you eat a food you are allergic to. Could you be seeking an adrenaline rush from cookies and ice cream, just to land flat when the adrenaline wears off?

With elevated cortisol levels, the amount of fat stored around your mid-section increases, and this "central fat" is associated with increased risk of heart disease and type 2 diabetes. Central fat is especially sensitive to the fat-storage effects of cortisol. And the stored fat secretes additional cortisol, creating a fat-storage snowball effect.

Cortisol contributes to weight gain, and weight gain then contributes to a condition known as leptin resistance. Leptin is a hormone that signals your brain when you have enough energy stored, making you feel full rather than hungry. For reasons that aren't fully understood, obesity disrupts normal leptin signaling, setting you up for a cycle of more and more weight gain.

THE CORTISOL TRAP

Cortisol creates a self-perpetuating cycle: it changes your metabolism, which increases cortisol production while making your cells more sensitive to the hormone, resulting in even more metabolic changes. Your body stores more abdominal fat, which is also linked to metabolic disorders such as high insulin, insulin resistance, and glucose intolerance. All of these, in turn, can increase cortisol levels even more. On top of that, cortisol production becomes higher in those who are obese. In the long term, high cortisol levels can lead to fatigue, hypertension, osteoporosis, decreased immunity, cravings, addictions, and more. Is it any wonder that this hormone is linked to weight gain and obesity? Following are some of the body changes that arise from the cortisol trap.

Inflammation

It's obvious that allergic reactions trigger inflammation, but what you may not know is that fat tissue also contributes to inflammation. Fat tissue, or adipose tissue, produces inflammatory messengers. As the amount of fat in your body increases, so does the number of inflammatory molecules circulating through your system—triggering cortisol synthesis and all its downstream effects.

Less Effective Digestion

Another of cortisol's effects is to direct resources away from your digestive tract, resulting in less efficient digestion and less efficient absorption of essential nutrients. At the same time, inflammation in your gut also decreases your ability to absorb nutrients from the foods you eat. As a result, you may lack a specific vitamin or mineral, even if it's in your diet, simply because your damaged digestive tract is not able to absorb it.

Changes in Gut Permeability

Your intestinal cells create a protective barrier in your digestive tract. Leaky gut syndrome, or intestinal hyper-permeability, occurs when your digestive lining is damaged by toxins, parasites, allergies, yeast, pathogenic bacteria, and certain medications (e.g., painkillers). When this happens, substances such as undigested food can leak through the gut lining and create what's called an initiate immune response.

In turn, more foreign proteins entering your bloodstream can increase the potential for autoimmune disorders. An autoimmune disorder occurs when the immune system mistakenly attacks and destroys healthy body tissue. In celiac disease, the immune system attacks cells in the intestinal lining, damaging the finger-like villi and their ability to absorb nutrients. Other autoimmune disorders include Hashimoto's thyroiditis, multiple sclerosis, anemia, rheumatoid arthritis, and lupus.

What we're just starting to understand is that you can reduce excessive gut permeability by avoiding food allergies. New studies are in development that demonstrate the power of allergy avoidance and its potential for balancing the immune system.

HEALTHY GUT VS. LEAKY GUT

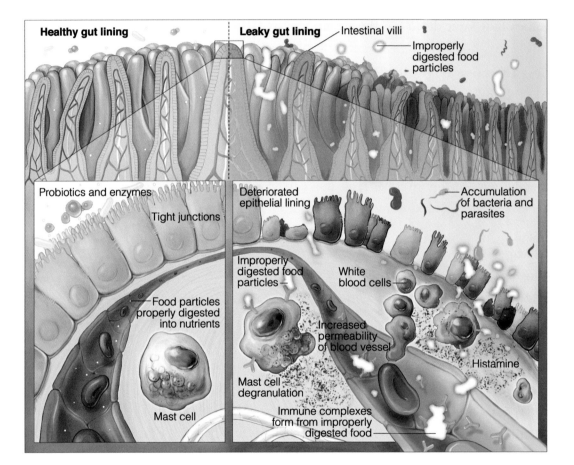

Healthy gut lining

Leaky gut lining — Intestinal villi

Improperly digested food particles

Probiotics and enzymes

Tight junctions

Food particles properly digested into nutrients

Mast cell

Deteriorated epithelial lining

Accumulation of bacteria and parasites

Improperly digested food particles —

White blood cells

Increased permeability of blood vessel

Histamine

Mast cell degranulation

Immune complexes form from improperly digested food

Changes in Gut Bacteria

Changes in gut permeability can lead to changes in the makeup of gut bacteria and an increase in bacterial toxins in the bloodstream. These toxins have been shown to cause inflammation, insulin resistance, and weight gain in mice. Research suggests that these toxins may cause weight gain in humans as well.

FOOD INTOLERANCES AND CONDITIONS RELATED TO FOOD ALLERGIES

Food intolerances make up the majority of the unpleasant food reactions people experience. They result when your body can't break down or eliminate certain molecules found in food. This isn't a "specific" immune response, but some of the same defense pathways are activated. Food intolerances may activate an immune response, flooding your system with histamine. They may decrease the efficiency of your digestive tract, leaving nutrients for normal gut bacteria and yeast, which multiply in response, triggering inflammation. The mechanisms your body uses for allergic and intolerant reactions overlap in multiple places, which is why differentiating between types of food sensitivities can be a challenge.

Let's look at some of the specific foods that may cause a reaction that affects your body weight.

Wheat and Gluten Sensitivities

Celiac Disease

Gluten is a very common sensitivity. *Gluten* comes from the Latin word for "glue" because it's what makes dough stretchy and elastic. It's actually made up of two types of proteins—gliadins and glutenins—that are uniquely toxic to the human digestive system. Gluten is found in wheat, kamut, spelt, rye, and barley, and even trace amounts are enough to cause a reaction in some individuals. This means that gluten-sensitive people often have to avoid foods, such as oats, that are processed in the same facility as wheat and other gluten-containing grains. Oats contain a similar complex protein to which many people are sensitive, so there are no oat recipes in SMTH.

One of the most severe types of gluten sensitivity is known as celiac disease, a disorder in which the body treats gliadin as a harmful invader. Cells in the intestinal wall break down gliadin and "present" different parts of the protein to immune cells. This process normally makes it easier for immune cells to identify invaders and produce targeted antibodies, but in this case the immune system acts as if the intestinal cells presenting gliadin are guilty by association, making autoimmune antibodies to those cells as well as to gliadin itself. Autoimmune antibodies destroy cells lining the intestinal tract. The ongoing immune attack causes extensive inflammation and damage to the intestinal wall, interfering with the body's ability to absorb nutrients. If a person with celiac disease continues to eat gluten-containing foods, the intestinal wall can be so severely damaged that it can no longer absorb nutrients, leading to severe malnutrition.

Celiac disease is generally diagnosed by the presence of specific IgA antibodies that attack the tissue of the intestinal lining (autoimmune antibodies) and an intestinal biopsy to confirm damage to the intestinal lining. These methods will only reliably identify celiac disease while someone currently has gluten in their diet because the immune system stops making autoimmune antibodies in the absence of gluten. For this reason, most people who have celiac disease will find that their intestines begin to heal once they change to a gluten-free diet.

Celiac disease may cause digestive symptoms such as bloating, cramps, chronic diarrhea, constipation, vomiting, or weight loss. However, adults are less likely to have digestive symptoms and more likely to have symptoms that are harder to connect to a digestive disorder, such as anemia, fatigue, bone or joint pain, arthritis, depression, itchy skin, or even seizures. Some adults will appear to have no symptoms at all. However, the ongoing intestinal damage can cause long-term health problems ranging from malnutrition to liver disease and increased risk of intestinal cancer.

Although researchers estimate that celiac disease affects approximately one out of every 133 people, the disease can cause such varied symptoms that many sufferers remain undiagnosed for 10 or more years.

Gluten Intolerance

Until recently, celiac disease and wheat allergy were the only gluten-related health problems recognized by most physicians. However, it's become clear that many people (up to one in 17) who don't have celiac disease or detectable antibodies to wheat still react to wheat products in their diet. These people are gluten sensitive: that is, they don't produce the autoimmune antibodies characteristic of celiac disease, but their bodies nevertheless treat wheat proteins as toxic.

Like celiac disease, gluten sensitivity can cause such a wide array of symptoms that it can be difficult to diagnose. In addition, there seems to be more than one type of gluten sensitivity. Recent research published in the *American Journal of Gastroenterology* looked for the existence of wheat sensitivity in patients who didn't have celiac disease and tested negative for anti-wheat IgE antibodies. They found that about 75 percent of wheat-sensitive patients in their study were also sensitive to other foods, such as milk, and just 25 percent were sensitive only to wheat. Those with multiple food sensitivities had symptoms that were more similar to those of allergic patients than those with celiac disease, even though they didn't test positive for IgE antibodies. (This can be a significant barrier to weight loss, as people may continue to eat gluten grains due to their negative test result even when they suffer from symptoms.) Those who were sensitive only to wheat had characteristics that could suggest they were pre-celiac. For example, there are some people who may test negative on a blood test today, but then test positive in the future when more damage to the gut lining has occurred. You may decide that it is most important to avoid gluten if you feel it is causing symptoms rather than waiting for the immune system to react with antibodies. Many people choose to go through the medical process of getting a celiac diagnosis, as it is possible to get subsidies for gluten-free food. The downside in following the medical process is that you must continue to eat gluten, potentially causing further damage. The upside of going gluten free immediately is you can start healing and losing weight now by listening to your gut!

Gluten and Weight Gain

It may be that the variation in symptoms of celiac disease and gluten sensitivity is caused by the immune system reacting to gluten and other wheat proteins in a variety of different ways. The gliadin component of gluten inhibits cell growth in the laboratory and can cause cell death. In animal studies, gliadin causes release of zonulin, a protein that increases intestinal permeability. Zonulin is also found in humans. It is expressed at high levels during severe episodes of celiac disease and is released in response to gluten in the intestines of both people with celiac disease and those without.

In addition to gliadin, wheat contains wheat germ agglutinin (WGA), a plant protein that acts as a natural insecticide. Like gliadin, WGA is toxic to cells in laboratory tests. At lower, nontoxic concentrations, it causes intestinal cells to relax their links to one another, which increases intestinal permeability. This effect was observed at WGA concentrations similar to those that occur in the human digestive tract.

Small amounts of WGA also cause intestinal cells to secrete inflammatory messengers, which can further increase intestinal permeability. Additionally, it activates the white blood cells that are brought into the intestines during the inflammatory response.

Wheat Addiction?

Celiac disease and gluten sensitivity can lead to weight gain in many of the same ways that other food allergies do—that is, by triggering inflammatory pathways and activating histamine, cortisol, and other hormones that can contribute to weight gain. However, wheat also appears to cause weight gain by making you crave the very wheat-containing foods your body treats as toxic.

When gluten is digested, a morphine-like compound dubbed an exorphin results. Exorphins, short for exogenous morphine-like compounds, are sometimes called "food hormones" because they are similar to endorphins—the morphine-like hormones your body produces naturally. The "exo" in exorphin reflects the fact that exorphins originate outside your body, whereas endorphins are made inside your body.

Endorphins are found primarily in the brain, where they bind to opiate receptors—the same receptors bound by opiates such as morphine, heroin, and codeine. When activated, these receptors can trigger feelings of euphoria, happiness, sleepiness, or decreased pain. Compounds that bind opioid receptors tightly—like morphine and heroin—cause strong reactions and can be addictive.

Naturally produced endorphins create these effects on a milder level. For example, your body produces opioids naturally in response to pleasurable foods such as sweet and high-fat treats. The "buzz" created by eating foods that trigger opioid production can contribute to weight gain all by itself, as everyone who has gained a few extra pounds during the holidays will know! Eating sugar also decreases pain sensitivity, another characteristic of opioids, in both rats and humans. Long-term exposure to sugar makes people less sensitive to morphine, suggesting that the brain develops something like a tolerance for sugar the same way it develops a tolerance for morphine. When a food leads to the production of additional "food hormones," the pleasure of eating that food can be magnified. Of course, this only works if your body actually absorbs the food hormone. In many cases, the food hormone also needs to cross the protective barrier that separates the brain from the bloodstream in order to reach those pleasure-inducing receptors. Research has demonstrated that gluten exorphins are absorbed into the bloodstream in mice. Not only that, gluten exorphins also cross the blood-brain barrier, creating changes in behavior, learning, and pain processing. It's worth noting that conditions such as depression, seasonal affective disorder (SAD), stress, and eating disorders are often associated with food cravings due to alterations in the body's endogenous opioid peptides. Changes in these natural opioids can change the number of or activity levels of opioid receptors, and those changes may make you more susceptible to the effects of exorphins.

More research is needed before we will fully understand how exorphins interact with the brain. However, evidence is mounting that gluten-derived exorphins act similarly to the endorphins your body produces in response to sugar—causing pleasure, cravings, and, over the long term, changes in the way your body processes all types of opioids.

Lactose Intolerance

One common cause of food intolerance is the lack of a particular enzyme. Take lactase, for example. This enzyme is normally found in the gut, where it breaks down the milk sugar called lactose into glucose and galactose so that they can be absorbed in the small intestine. If you're missing lactase, your body can't break down lactose. Instead, lactose continues through the digestive tract, where your normal gut bacteria breaks it down, producing gas in the process. Lactose provides a handy supply of nutrients for gas-producing bacteria and yeast in your gut. The gas causes symptoms such as bloating, abdominal pain, cramping, and diarrhea—a condition known as lactose intolerance. If you're lactose intolerant, you're not allergic to lactose: your body simply can't digest it.

Toxic Substances

Food intolerance can also occur when your body identifies some food—or part of a food—as toxic. Your body goes on the defensive: vomiting, diarrhea, headaches, and other symptoms are the result of the body's attempts to neutralize and eliminate the perceived threat.

This sort of intolerance is often cause by chemicals or compounds added to food as preservatives or to enhance the food's taste or color. Artificial additives such as MSG (monosodium glutamate), food coloring, BHA (butylhydroxyanisole), BHT (butylhydroxytoluene), parabens, and mineral oil can cause reactions that include headaches and rashes. Sulfites, which are found naturally in some foods but are also added to dried fruits, smoked meats, and other foods as a preservative, can cause breathing difficulties, particularly in people with asthma.

Some foods naturally contain high amounts of biogenic amines such as histamine, tyramine, phenylethylamine, or tryptamine, which can cause headaches or nausea. Tyramine has also been shown to trigger migraines in those sensitive to it. Salicylates, found naturally in foods such as currants, oranges, curry, and paprika, as well as in aspirin, can cause nasal and gastrointestinal symptoms. Histamine is found naturally in some aged cheeses, and eating foods containing too much histamine can cause hives and swelling. And then there are other foods—like strawberries, tomatoes, and chocolate—that can trigger histamine release when you eat them in large quantities if you are sensitive to them. In fish like tuna and mackerel, which contain large amounts of histamine, bacteria contamination can cause scombroid poisoning.

Food Intolerance and Irritable Bowel Syndrome
If you have frequent bouts of abdominal pain or cramping, or problems with constipation, diarrhea, or both, you may be one of 10 to 20 percent of people suffering from irritable bowel syndrome (IBS).

IBS is a collection of symptoms that arise when the gut stops working the way it normally would. It may move material through more quickly than usual, resulting in diarrhea. It may move more slowly than usual, causing constipation or allowing gas to build up in the intestines. IBS can have many different causes, including brain-gut signaling issues, impaired gut movement, stress or depression, and bacterial overgrowth.

People with IBS have a higher than usual rate of food sensitivities. In one study of patients with IBS, those who ate gluten had significantly worse symptoms than those who did not.

Other research has shown that many people with IBS are sensitive to fermentable carbohydrates: fermentable oligosaccharides, disaccharides, monosaccharides, and polyols (FODMAPs). FODMAPs include small carbohydrates such as lactose (milk sugar), fructose (found in many fruits, high-fructose corn syrup, and table sugar), and sorbitol (found in some artificial sweeteners), all of which are poorly absorbed by people with IBS. Unabsorbed carbohydrates are fermented by gut bacteria, creating gas, which, in turn, can cause flatulence, bloating, abdominal pain, diarrhea, and other GI symptoms.

Many people with IBS find that a low-FODMAP diet can help with IBS symptoms. However, because FODMAPs can have prebiotic effects (prebiotics are carbohydrates that feed both good and bad microbes in the gut), it is important to identify the specific carbohydrates that trigger IBS symptoms. Another diet that may be helpful for people with IBS is the GAPS (Gut and Psychology Syndrome) Diet created by Natasha Campbell-McBride, M.D. The GAPS Diet is based on the Specific Carbohydrate Diet developed by renowned American pediatrician Dr. Sidney Valentine Haas. If you suffer from attention deficit hyperactivity disorder (ADHD), depression, or other mental illnesses, check out Dr. Campbell-McBride's book *Gut and Psychology Syndrome: Natural Treatment for Autism, Dyspraxia, A.D.D., Dyslexia, A.D.H.D., Depression, and Schizophrenia*.

IDENTIFYING FOOD ALLERGIES AND INTOLERANCES

Everywhere you turn, it seems, you can find tests claiming to help you identify food allergies, sensitivities, and intolerances. Take care when choosing your approach to identifying food sensitivities because not all of these tests are created equal. Some have no evidence backing their claims; others will identify such a broad range of "reactive" foods that it makes it overwhelming to understand how to prioritize which foods you should avoid.

Identifying a food allergy or intolerance will have long-term benefits for your health and well-being, but it is not a quick or easy process. A reputable physician, nutritionist, or naturopathic practitioner won't simply run a few tests: he or she will look at your medical history and your current symptoms and use that information to choose specific tests to perform, such as skin prick testing, assessing IgE and IgG levels for specific foods, or a food elimination/challenge. Below is an explanation of the different types of tests available, what they test for, and how reliable they are.

Tests for Food Hypersensitivities

The B cells in the immune system produce antibodies (Ab) that are also known as immunoglobulins (Ig). Their job is to identify and neutralize foreign objects such as bacteria and food allergens. There are a number of different classes of immunglobulins that take on different tasks (e.g., IgA, IgE, and IgG). It's important to note that levels of antibodies in your system will naturally fluctuate, so it's possible to test negative for a specific food antibody on one day and test positive another day.

Serum IgE Antibody Testing

Expert panels in both the United States and Great Britain agree that the most accurate way to identify a food allergy is to test your blood levels of IgE antibodies against specific foods. This is a very effective test, but it will show only immediate food allergies—that is, allergies that cause a reaction as soon as you come into contact with that food. To catch delayed food intolerances and hypersensitivities, combined testing methods are necessary.

Skin Prick Allergy Testing

Although skin prick testing can help you and your physician identify foods that might be causing an allergic reaction, this test by itself isn't enough to diagnose a food allergy. For instance, skin prick testing is only about 75 percent accurate for identifying wheat allergies. Wheat has enough similarities to other grasses that a positive prick test for wheat might mean you have hay fever but no sensitivity to wheat. A negative test result is believed to be 95 percent accurate in predicting the absence of a specific allergy, but it is important to check for intolerances.

IgG Antibody Testing

The National Institute of Allergy and Infectious Disease lists allergen-specific IgG testing as an unproven procedure. However, it is important to keep in mind that this is for the diagnosis of IgE-mediated food allergies. IgG antibody testing is one of the key ways to identify celiac disease, which does not involve IgE antibodies. IgG antibody testing may be helpful in identifying food intolerances, which also do not involve IgE antibodies. For instance, several studies showed that IgG testing could help identify foods that caused symptoms in some patients with IBS. In another study, IgG testing helped patients with chronic migraines to identify foods that triggered their symptoms.

IgG testing can be particularly helpful when you are trying to identify foods causing mysterious symptoms. For example, I used to eat a great deal of almonds because of their high nutritional value. After IgG testing, I discovered that almonds were the culprit of my recurring mild cough. After I cut almonds from my diet, my respiratory system dramatically improved.

Allergen-specific IgG testing can help you to identify potential food intolerances, but for a final diagnosis, it's critical that you gather other information as well. Think of IgG testing as a way to point you toward potential problem foods. The food elimination and challenge test, explained on page 90, will help you pinpoint which of those foods is causing your symptoms.

Salivary IgA Testing

Researchers have shown that anti-gliadin IgA antibodies can be detected in the saliva of children with celiac disease, and some studies suggest salivary IgA testing may be helpful in the diagnosis of other food hypersensitivities as well. However, salivary IgA testing has not been shown to be a reliable method for testing.

Breath Testing

Fructose and lactose intolerance can be identified by means of a test for breath hydrogen. When lactose, fructose, or other carbohydrates are not digested properly, their fermentation by gut bacteria produces methane and hydrogen. These gases escape through the lungs and can be measured using a breath test, usually for hydrogen. This type of test is relatively sensitive and accurate, but both false-positive and false-negative results do occur.

Food Diary

Diagnosing a food allergy or intolerance can be tricky both because people can react to foods in so many different ways and because those symptoms can be caused by many conditions other than allergies and intolerances. Your first step in identifying potential food sensitivities is to start keeping a detailed diary of the foods you eat and your symptoms. Keeping a food diary will help you and your health care provider make a connection between a specific symptom and a specific food or ingredient. It is easy to keep track of your menu choices by noting the time and amount of each food consumed and how you feel after you eat it. There are also great downloadable applications such as myfitnesspal.com that will help you track how many nutrients you are getting from your food selections.

Double-Blind Placebo-Controlled Challenge

The gold standard for identifying food allergies is to completely eliminate the allergy-causing food long enough for your system to recover, then "challenge" yourself by eating the food and see if your symptoms recur. This is trickier than it sounds, though, because of the placebo effect—the ability of our minds to trick us into feeling better because we think we've gotten rid of the offending food, even if we haven't really identified the underlying cause of our symptoms. The ideal way to identify food hypersensitivities is to completely eliminate the food from your diet, then eat a cracker (or some other food item) that may or may not have been prepared with that food. Neither you nor the person testing you would know whether you had eaten the food you were testing until after your symptoms had been measured. This is known as a double-blind challenge because it avoids bias (and the placebo effect) by keeping everyone involved "blinded" to the food you're being served until after the results are in.

You may want to consider having a friend assist you with a blind challenge at the end of your elimination phase of the *Slimming Meals That Heal* plan. Keep in mind that people sometimes reintroduce wheat and feel fantastic because it initially stimulates the "feel-good" chemicals in the brain. They then dismiss the need to keep it out of their diet moving forward, even though they may start experiencing symptoms in a day or two. Be mindful to watch for the crash after a food challenge by keeping a diary of symptoms for up to 72 hours after eating a test food. My nutritionist friend Joy McCarthy said, "Remind yourself that eating 'well' today will feel even better tomorrow when you wake up feeling awesome!"

Food Elimination and Challenge

In *Slimming Meals That Heal,* you will be minimizing food allergens for the next 8 to 12 weeks. On page 90, there is a full explanation on how to do a proper food challenge by reintroducing one new test food at a time after the full rest period. I think this is the hardest step because you'll want to jump back to your favorite "craving" foods. But it's important for you to stay committed to a slow introduction; it can take up to 72 hours for an allergic or intolerance reaction to occur, and you need at least 3 days between separate food tests. After you've tested a food, you need to give your immune system and hormones a chance to balance out again. The process is slow but the rewards are priceless. I have hundreds of testimonials from people who are pain free and losing weight without restricting calories. Read on to discover delicious substitutions for every food you crave!

A young student asked the master, "You never lose your balance. What is the secret?" O Sensei, the founder of Aikido, replied, "No, I am constantly losing my balance. My skill lies in my ability to regain it."

CHAPTER 3

THE HORMONE HEIST: THE LINKS BETWEEN HORMONE HAVOC, INFLAMMATION, AND WEIGHT

Hormones act as chemical signals, communicating and influencing virtually every physiological process. Your body makes about 70 major hormones, and they have the power to signal for inflammation, reproduction, hunger, satiety, energy levels, and most every other function we need to survive. The inflammation at the root of chronic disease, weight gain, and obesity is very often the result of hormonal imbalances.

The interplay of inflammation and hormonal imbalance leads to a very sticky kind of weight gain. I've worked with people who have "tried everything," and who can't seem to get rid of stubborn fat or else continue to gain weight. The strategies I outline in SMTH work to reduce appetite cravings and regulate mood changes to naturally balance weight without dieting.

It is becoming the norm for people to think hormonal imbalances are just part of being human—up to 70 percent of women deal with premenstrual syndrome (PMS), and men may lose up to 1.5 percent of their testosterone production per year after the age of 30. The good news is that these hormonal imbalances are avoidable and treatable when you shift your focus to living an anti-inflammatory lifestyle.

Here are the main culprits of hormone disruption, based on the latest research:

- Disruption to normal biorhythms from inadequate rest as well as excessive exposure to computers, cell phones, television, and any other form of electromagnetic fields (EMFs). Biorhythm disruption decreases the output of progesterone, an important hormone.
- Diets that include hormone-treated products. For example, eating dairy from cows injected with milk-stimulating hormones (a practice that is legal in the US but banned in Canada) affects the balance of sex hormones in your body.
- Excessive alcohol intake, which burdens your liver and impairs its ability to break down and safely convert certain hormones, especially estrogens and testosterone.
- Prescription drugs, many of which directly affect hormone production—for example, oral contraceptives and hormone replacement therapy (HRT). Others indirectly affect circulating levels of hormones by inhibiting the liver's ability to break them down.
- Groundwater contamination from birth control pills, prescription drugs, and hormone replacement therapies.
- Nutrient deficiencies, especially vitamin B6 and magnesium. These nutrients are necessary for metabolizing estrogen and other hormones in the liver.
- Excessive caloric intake. When your body carries excess fat, one consequence is that it converts various steroids to estrogens.
- Chemicals known as xenobiotics or xenoestrogens found in plastics, pesticides, food additives, and many common household products can affect normal hormone levels. Some xenobiotics promote the release of pro-inflammatory cytokines like TNF-α. These substances are the matches

that light the fuse of inflammation. In MTHI, I explained that these pro-inflammatory cytokines—the lit matches—set the stage for free-radical tissue damage and for the pain that is so characteristic of chronic inflammation. Some of these substances also contribute to insulin resistance, diabetes, and obesity. The link between many chemical toxins and obesity is so strong that it has been coined as "chemobesity" by some researchers.

END-O-CRYING

Many women going through perimenopause and menopause are estrogen-dominant, meaning the ratio of estrogen to progesterone is skewed toward an over-balance of estrogen. The resulting weight gain and water retention are evidence of out-of-whack estrogen. Physical changes are only part of a miserable story that includes mood swings, depression, and all-too-frequent binging on "comfort foods." During menopause many women also become deficient in the very vitamins and minerals that can help reduce inflammation—vitamins like B6 and minerals like magnesium and zinc. These nutrients support the liver as it tries to clear out extra estrogen and the xenobiotics we are all exposed to. The liver is working so hard to clear all the toxins that it uses up its stores of these critical nutrients.

Seventy-five percent of all autoimmune disease happens to women. Inflammation caused by hormonal imbalance could be a key reason why women suffer more pain than their male counterparts. On the other hand, when the balance of all the reproductive hormones is normal, estrogen can actually have an anti-inflammatory effect for the brain and the cardiovascular system.

Estrogen dominance can affect men too, causing decreased sperm count, baldness, the development of breasts, and weight gain. Men with high levels of estrogen may also have enlarged prostates, which can potentially lead to prostate cancer.

The following chart will help you understand the nutrients that can have a positive impact on your hormone balance. Foods that contain these substances, as well as healthy fats, fiber, vitamins, and minerals, can be very beneficial in reducing prostate enlargement, PMS, and perimenopausal and menopausal symptoms. And remember, the recipes in the *Slimming Meals That Heal* plan are chock-full of all these nutrients!

NUTRIENTS THAT IMPACT HORMONES

NUTRIENT	WHAT IT DOES	WHERE IT'S FOUND
BIFIDOBACTERIUM	A bacteria (probiotic) that lives mostly in the large intestine. Bifido prevents the colonization of unfriendly bacteria and yeasts in the colon that make estrogen dominance worse.	Fermented products such as miso and lacto-fermented veggies, including vinegar-free sauerkraut (finely shredded cabbage fermented with beneficial bacteria); also available in supplement form.
B VITAMINS	Important for the proper functioning of liver detoxification enzymes and for energy-producing reactions. Vitamin B6 helps the liver metabolize excess estrogen. Choline, folic acid, and vitamins B2, B6, and B12 support estrogen-sensitive tissues and promote overall wellness.	Algae, avocado, beans, eggs, meat, peas, seeds, and whole grains; if needed therapeutically, a supplement of B-complex and additional key B vitamins (e.g., B3 and B6).
BORON	Increases synthesis of estradiol (good estrogen) and decreases calcium excretion; helps prevent postmenopausal osteoporosis by stopping the activation of the enzyme caspase-3, which can initiate the programmed cell death of new bone cells.	Almonds, apples, asparagus, cabbage, carrots, figs, grapes, peaches, prunes, raisins, and strawberries.
BRASSICAS (CRUCIFEROUS VEGETABLES)	Contains protective substances called dithiolethiones, indoles, and isothiocyanates that help prevent disease and fight cancer; also a good source of the hormone-balancing nutrients vitamin C, folic acid, carotenes, and fiber.	Bok choy, broccoli, Brussels sprouts, cabbage, cauliflower, Chinese cabbage, collards, horseradish, kale, kohlrabi, mustard greens, radish, rutabaga, turnip greens, and watercress.

NUTRIENT	WHAT IT DOES	WHERE IT'S FOUND
CALCIUM	Menopausal women may need greater amounts of calcium due to lowered levels of estrogen. Estrogen protects the skeletal system by promoting the storage of calcium in bones and protecting against osteoporosis.	Almonds, asparagus, beans, blackstrap molasses, broccoli, dark leafy greens (e.g., spinach, kale), figs, salmon, seeds (especially sesame), and tempeh.
FIBER (SOLUBLE AND INSOLUBLE)	Fiber binds to estrogen derivatives (from the liver) and encourages excretion of excess estrogen through the stool. According to a Tufts University School of Medicine study, women on high-fiber diets excrete two to three times more estrogen in their bowel movements than women who eat a diet low in fiber and high in fat.	Whole, unprocessed foods; nuts and seeds, including flaxseeds and chia; raw and cooked vegetables; and fruit, legumes, and whole grains.
FLAVONOIDS (VITAMIN C AND HESPERIDIN)	Vitamin C and other phytonutrients (including bioflavonoids such as hesperidin, rutin, and quercetin) help promote liver detoxification of excess estrogen. Vitamin C and hesperidin have been shown to relieve hot flashes.	Amla (Indian gooseberry), berries, broccoli, Brussels sprouts, cauliflower, citrus fruits, kale, kiwi fruit, kohlrabi, mango, papaya, peas (especially raw and from the pod; e.g., snow peas, sugar peas), pineapple, and sweet potato.
MAGNESIUM	Eases symptoms of irritability, anxiety, mood swings, and insomnia; also helps the bones absorb calcium and raises HDL (good cholesterol). Magnesium also reduces premenstrual symptoms and menstrual cramps. In a double-blind trial using only 200 mg of magnesium per day for two months, women reported a significant reduction of several symptoms related to PMS caused by estrogen dominance, including fluid retention, weight gain, swelling of extremities, breast tenderness, and abdominal bloating.	Almonds, cashews, halibut, spinach, pumpkin seeds, lentils, avocados, figs, raw cocoa beans, escarole, quinoa, teff, kale, kelp, and hemp hearts; also available in supplement form.

NUTRIENT	WHAT IT DOES	WHERE IT'S FOUND
OMEGA-3 FATS	Help reduce inflammation, blood pressure, and depression; slow heart rate; balance hormone production; increase metabolism; reduce fat storage; promote liver detoxification and bowel regularity; ease menstrual cramps; and protect women and men from some hormone-sensitive cancers.	Coldwater and deep-sea fish; anchovies, herring, mackerel, and sardines; supplemental fish oil should be sustainable and tested for heavy metals. Algae, echium, flax, hemp, chia, and sancha inchi seeds are good vegetarian sources but must be consumed along with vitamin B6, magnesium, and zinc.
VITAMIN E	A powerful antioxidant; helps reduce inflammation, promotes liver health and function, protects cells and cell membranes from free-radical damage, maintains cardiovascular health, relieves hot flashes, and alleviates vaginal dryness. A randomized trial testing the effects of vitamin E supplementation found that 105 breast cancer survivors (who were experiencing at least two to three hot flashes daily) showed an improvement in symptoms when taking vitamin E.	Asparagus, avocado, brown rice, egg yolks, lima beans, nuts, peas, seeds, and sweet potatoes; also available in supplement form (make sure to use supplements labeled as containing "mixed tocopherols").
LIGNANS	Lignans—specialized plant substances—may decrease hot flashes and vaginal dryness. Lignans are metabolized into phytohormones, which help to balance hormones, decrease the activity of excess estrogens, and displace xenoestrogens. Plant lignans also decrease reabsorption of estrogens and testosterone from the colon. A recent study of 21 women found that when they ate 4 tablespoons of ground flaxseed every day for six days, their hot-flash frequency was cut in half. Additionally, the participants reported improved mood, reduced muscle pain, fewer chills, and less sweating.	The best food sources of lignans include gluten-free grains and raw seeds (e.g., hemp seeds, chia). Fruit and vegetables such as broccoli and berries contain modest amounts. Flaxseeds and sesame seeds are among the richest sources of lignans. To experience the therapeutic benefits of lignans, buy whole flaxseeds, grind them fresh in a coffee grinder, and sprinkle them on cereal or salads.

ARE CRAVINGS ALL IN YOUR HEAD?

Cravings are not just in your head. You may think that if you have enough willpower, you should be able to reason yourself out of eating, but the craving is stronger than your mind. The root of your cravings can be traced to your brain chemistry. Health expert Bryce Wylde explains:

One of the driving forces underscoring the obesity epidemic is our brains' uncanny ability to seek out and detect micronutrients in the food we eat. We're overweight not so much because we can't stop eating as much as our brains don't want us to stop eating until our bodies get the ideal amount of nutrients. When the brain detects refined carbohydrate—an immediately available source of high-calorie, low-nutrient food—it will instruct the body: "unless you're going for a run right now, store that for a rainy day, and when the stomach has made room, consume more in order to achieve the nutrient status we need." Responsibility for monitoring calorie input, energy, and nutrient levels falls to the brain. And, since the brain is the smart organ, it won't stop sending an eat signal until it is sure the body is satisfied for micronutrients.

Self-control also has a lot to do with your brain's dopamine levels. You may find it impossible—no matter what you try—to ignore the command to eat more, even when you're sure you should be satiated. That is because over-eating causes a significant loss of dopamine receptor activity in the brain. In other words, many people are overweight because of low dopamine or insensitivity to dopamine.

Dopamine is a neurotransmitter involved in producing the feelings asso-ciated with pleasure. When large amounts of dopamine are present in your brain, you feel good and may even experience a little "high." The natural ten-dency when experiencing a state of "feeling good" is to seek out more of it and work to sustain it. And so begins the cycle driving us to sustain our feelings of pleasure through the intake of food. Paradoxically, it appears that the same motivating force that keeps us alive, left unmonitored, can also lead to our own undoing, through obesity and its related illnesses.

Since research has proven that overeating over the long term causes a depletion of the dopamine receptors in our brains, this in turn leads to an increase in the very same feelings and emotions that led to overeating in the first place. Consequently, when you're overweight, you will have to eat more food to receive the same quantity of those feelings of pleasure than a more slender person would from eating a significantly smaller portion of food.

A SAD BRAIN EATS FOR COMFORT

Think of serotonin as the "satisfaction chemical" in your brain. Normal serotonin levels are extremely important for helping you feel satisfied with your eating plan so that you can achieve weight loss. When your brain is producing enough serotonin, your appetite shuts off before you overeat. You feel good, and you lose weight more easily. It is not that serotonin itself makes you lose weight; feeling satisfied and having your mood elevated just helps you to eat less. If you have ever overeaten to make yourself feel better, you may have been reacting to low serotonin levels. As the song says, ". . . can't get no satisfaction!"

When your serotonin level is low, your body will crave carbohydrates throughout the day. The problem is that you're likely to satisfy that craving with the wrong kind of carbohydrates and sabotage your weight loss. That is why I recommend, in the SMTH program, that you start your day with protein and vegetables. Enjoy fruit and root vegetables to ensure your carbohydrate cravings are satisfied and that you get the nutrients you need.

Hormonal imbalances affect your mind, personality, and behavior just as much as they affect your physical self. As a result, these imbalances may manifest as chronic inflammatory mental conditions such as depression, memory loss, Alzheimer's disease, dementia, anxiety, attention deficit hyperactivity disorder (ADHD), and attention deficit disorder (ADD).

ARE YOU AN ADRENALINE JUNKIE?

I love to jump out of planes and scuba dive with sharks, but did you know that you don't need to take part in any risky behavior to deplete your adrenal glands and create inflammatory weight gain?

The adrenal glands are two walnut-sized glands that sit on top of your kidneys and make adrenaline, noradrenaline, and cortisol. They make you feel alive and excited, but they also cause you to feel anxious and stressed out when levels reach too high. Your adrenals are exhausted by any stressful situation at work or home, by eating refined food, by taking in too many stimulants (coffee, tea, and chocolate), and from lack of sleep. Your pancreas, gut, and liver are directly affected by these factors, causing chronic inflammation. The thyroid can also become unbalanced from stress, and this leads to even *more* problems with fatigue, energy, mood swings, and weight gain.

Here's a brief overview of the connections between the stress response from the adrenal glands and its negative effects on the other glands in the body:

- Adrenal hormones influence insulin release to free up energy when you feel the need to flee from a stressful event. That is one way that stress can contribute to diabetes and weight gain; if cells can't respond normally to insulin and blood sugar, they just turn that sugar into fat!
- Adrenal stress reduces the conversion of thyroid hormones that control your metabolism, causing you to slow your fat-burning engine.
- Stress literally messes with you head! Adrenal stress disrupts the hypothalamic-pituitary-adrenal (HPA) axis. The HPA axis is a complex network of interactions between the hypothalamus, the pituitary, and the adrenal glands that regulates things such as temperature, digestion, immune system, mood, sexuality, and energy usage.

- Adrenal stress promotes autoimmunity by weakening the immune barriers of the GI tract, lungs, and blood-brain barrier. If immune barriers are breached by food allergens, the immune system overreacts, and you can develop autoimmune diseases—such as Hashimoto's or rheumatoid arthritis.

- Adrenaline and cortisol cause changes in the digestive system, like sudden loss of appetite, heartburn, nausea, and stomach pains. Stress also causes inflammation throughout the digestive system, which leads to aggravation of the digestive tract and affects the assimilation of nutrients. Over the long term, stress can actually cause chronic digestive problems like irritable bowel syndrome and stomach ulcers.

- Adrenal stress causes reproductive hormonal imbalances. Cortisol is one of the hormones released by the adrenals during the stress response. Prolonged cortisol elevations, caused by chronic stress, decrease the liver's ability to clear excess estrogen from the blood.

The good news is that many of the anti-inflammatory foods in the SMTH plan rebuild the adrenals and return the hormones to harmony.

UNDERSTANDING HORMONES

This following chart takes a look at the messengers that play a large role in your ability or inability to lose weight.

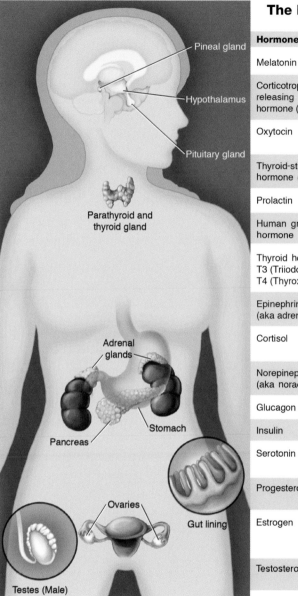

Pineal gland

Hypothalamus

Pituitary gland

Parathyroid and thyroid gland

Adrenal glands

Stomach

Pancreas

Ovaries

Gut lining

Testes (Male)

The Hormones of Weight Loss and Gain

Hormone	Released from	Action
Melatonin	Pineal gland	Promotes sleep
Corticotropin-releasing hormone (CRH)	Hypothalamus	Controls temperature, hunger, sleep, stress adaption
Oxytocin	Pituitary	Bonding, pleasure, muscle contractions
Thyroid-stimulating hormone (TSH)	Pituitary	Stimulates thyroid to produce T3 and T4
Prolactin	Pituitary	Reduces fat metabolism
Human growth hormone	Pituitary	Stimulates body fat breakdown
Thyroid hormones T3 (Triiodothyronine) T4 (Thyroxine)	Thyroid and body cells	Metabolism, energy, temperature
Epinephrine (aka adrenaline)	Adrenal glands	Increases anxiety, strength and sugar metabolism
Cortisol	Adrenal glands	Increases stress and, carbohydrate storage
Norepinephrine (aka noradrenaline)	Adrenal glands	Converts glycogen to glucose, suppress appetite
Glucagon	Pancreas	Breakdown of body fat
Insulin	Pancreas	Increased storage of fats
Serotonin	Digestive lining	Appetite suppressant, anti-anxiety, antidepressant
Progesterone	Ovaries Adrenal glands	Feel-good brain hormone
Estrogen	Ovaries Adrenal glands Fat cells	Supports brain, bone and fertility
Testosterone	Testes Adrenal glands	Builds muscle/burns body fat

49

Messenger: Adrenaline (aka Epinephrine)

Role: Adrenaline is a hormone produced in the adrenal glands and is released when a fight-or-flight response is needed for survival. This fight-or-flight response is necessary to give a brief increase in energy, and, in some cases, strength, so you can either fight something off (like an intruder in your house) or run away (if you're in danger). Adrenaline increases heart rate, opens air passages, increases blood pressure, raises blood sugar, and breaks down fats for energy. These are all needed to provide adequate fuel for fight or flight.

What happens when out of balance? If adrenaline is constantly being released, it can elevate blood sugar and fats in the blood. It can also increase anxiety and insomnia.

How to balance: Try high-intensity resistance exercise (e.g., weighted squats, rowing, and biceps curls). Get plenty of sleep and consider relaxation methods to help reduce stress. Eat balanced meals with fiber, protein (lean meats, fish, and seeds), and fat to help stabilize blood sugar levels.

Messenger: Beta-Endorphin

Role: Beta-endorphin is a neurohormone that is released from the pituitary gland in the brain. It is a chemical responsible for feelings of pleasure and euphoria and for relieving pain. Because of this, it is very addictive. Beta-endorphin plays a role in glucose metabolism and insulin secretion, and may even help build muscle and improve immunity.

What happens when out of balance? Consuming sugar can trigger the release of beta-endorphin, causing a temporary "sugar high," but it is short-lived and causes a crash soon after.

How to balance: The more you exercise, the more beta-endorphin gets released and the longer it stays elevated. This accounts for the "high" felt from exercising—beta-endorphin stimulates euphoria and increases pain tolerance. Increase high-intensity training (HIT) with weight training that focuses on performing quality repetitions.

Messenger: Cholecystokinin (CCK)

Role: Cholecystokinin is a hormone that is secreted by cells in the small intestine. It stimulates the release of digestive enzymes from the pancreas and helps keep the food in your digestive tract moving along. In animal studies, a rise in CCK is always followed by a large reduction in food intake. This effect is usually short-term, with peak effect about 30 minutes after a meal. Sustained high levels of CCK may suppress appetite for extended periods of time.

What happens when out of balance? If you have insufficient stomach acid, CCK will not be properly triggered, because it's signaled by pre-digestion of food in your stomach. If you suffer from low acid or take acid-blocking medicine, undigested food can pass into the intestines, feeding negative yeast and bacteria and causing an imbalance of intestinal flora and inflammation.

How to balance: CCK can be balanced by thorough chewing of your food and balancing stomach pH. Consumption of sour foods and drinks like lemon juice and vinegar stimulates proper digestion. The presence of essential fatty acids and amino acids from easily digestible protein like hemp seeds is an anti-inflammatory stimulator of CCK. Capsaicin from peppers appears to stimulate CCK, but if you suffer from arthritis, you may want to test yourself for nightshade sensitivity. Pine nuts may also have powerful CCK-releasing power.

Messenger: Cortisol

Role: Cortisol is commonly known as the "stress hormone" and is produced by the adrenal gland. It helps regulate numerous body functions, including blood pressure, insulin release, glucose metabolism, immune function, and inflammatory response. It also plays an important role in the regulation of emotion, cognition, and energy utilization.
During stressful events, cortisol triggers the fight-or-flight response. But as with many emergency systems, the stress response comes at a considerable cost.

What happens when out of balance? When cortisol is too high, it makes quick energy (glucose) by destroying muscle tissue to break down amino acids. Cortisol stimulates cravings for high-carb, high-fat foods. Cortisol will greatly increase blood sugar levels and is always followed by a high-insulin response. If this cycle continues long enough, it can result in insulin resistance. High levels of cortisol suppress immunity, leading to excess inflammation. It can also increase fat storage around your midsection and promote high blood pressure. Vitamin C is used up by the adrenal glands in higher amounts during periods of stress.

How to balance: Stress management is crucial for balancing cortisol. All stress is the same, whether real or imagined, and cortisol is released no matter what you're stressing about. Focus on eating high-quality protein foods with every meal and at snacks. Eat every three hours to maintain balanced blood sugar levels and stay away from inflammatory refined foods. Eat foods that combat inflammation like nuts, seeds, fish, fruits, and vegetables. Vitamin C reduces cortisol, so consume up to 1,000 mg from citrus fruits, papayas, melon, strawberries, broccoli, Brussels sprouts, asparagus, and parsley. Enjoy tomatoes and red sweet peppers if you do not suffer from nightshade sensitivity.

Messenger: Dopamine

Role: Dopamine is a neurotransmitter involved in producing the feelings associated with pleasure and emotional response. Its release causes feelings of reward and supports behavioral reinforcement. This plays a role in cravings, as this "pleasure" hormone can be released when you eat certain foods—sugar, for example. This is why there is sometimes a noticeable rush after eating a lot of sugar; dopamine is sending pleasure signals within the brain.

What happens when out of balance? When dopamine is unbalanced, hunger and cravings increase. Overeating causes a depletion of the dopamine receptors in our brains. Obese people have fewer receptors for dopamine. Because of this, they need to eat more foods that trigger dopamine release, such as those containing sugar, to feel pleasure. When dopamine levels are off, mental fogginess, central nervous system disorder, schizophrenia, and Parkinson's disease risk increases.

How to balance: Consume plenty of high-quality proteins from sources like bison, duck, organic eggs, and fava beans, because dopamine is made from the amino acids phenylalanine and tyrosine. Getting enough sleep is important for balance because neurotransmitters are replenished with deep sleep.

Messenger: Estrogen

Role: Estrogen is a hormone produced, in women, in the ovaries, fat cells, and, to a smaller extent, the adrenal glands. In men, the testes produce small amounts. Estrogen has hundreds of functions in the body—from regulating brain functions to building bones. It may also offer a heart-protective effect; after menopause, women's risk for heart disease increases as estrogen production declines with age.

What happens when out of balance? Unbalanced estrogen levels can lead to a decreased libido, altered brain function, increased risk for heart damage, and weakened bones (in both men and women). High levels in men can lead to an enlarged prostate, diabetes, and a higher incidence of heart disease and cancer. High levels in women can lead to estrogen dominance and reduced thyroid function, irregular periods, infertility, and insomnia. Excessive levels can lead to the suppression and reduced activity of testosterone—leading to a loss of muscle and increase of body fat.

How to balance: Losing weight, limiting exposure to pesticides, balancing nutritional deficiencies, and limiting alcohol intake can all help balance estrogen. Cruciferous vegetables enhance the liver's ability to metabolize estrogen into beneficial metabolites. Cruciferous vegetables include kale, broccoli, cauliflower, Brussels sprouts, arugula, and collard greens. Increase fiber and probiotics to eliminate excess estrogen. If a physician recommends hormone replacement therapy, ask about bio-identical hormones.

Messenger: Glucagon

Role: Glucagon is the antagonist to insulin, and is released when energy stores are getting low. Glucagon is secreted by the alpha cells of the pancreas and is often released after long exercise sessions. Glucagon breaks down liver and muscle glycogen when blood sugar drops to increase blood sugar to normal. It also breaks down fat tissue to release fatty acids for energy, assisting in weight loss.

What happens when out of balance? When insulin is high, it prevents the release of glucagon and fat stores. When glucagon is out of balance, blood sugar levels will be high and muscle tissue will constantly be broken down.

How to balance: Consume protein and essential fats at every meal because these foods help keep blood sugar levels stable. Eliminate highly processed carbohydrates because they spike blood sugar and insulin release. Eat balanced meals every three hours because going long periods without eating can break down muscle tissue.
Exercise in short bursts and regularly so your body can absorb more glucose. Practice stress reduction techniques to keep stress levels as low as possible.

Messenger: Growth Hormone (GH aka Human Growth Hormone)

Role: Growth hormone is released by the pituitary gland to regulate growth, spur tissue repair, speed up fat breakdown, and increase the release of specialized hormones called insulin-like growth factors (IGF). GH is one of the body's most potent fat-burning hormones.

What happens when out of balance? GH helps increase muscle mass after muscles are broken down from resistance training. When levels are off balance, fat burning decreases and muscle building can be limited. An excess of GH can increase the potential for type 2 diabetes and abnormal bone growth.

How to balance: Most GH is released during the first few hours of sleep, so get adequate, undisrupted sleep in a pitch-black room. Engage in regular strenuous exercise, especially resistance training and interval training like dancing, running sprints, and cycling hills. Stabilize blood sugar levels with high-fiber foods. Reduce cortisol levels with deep breathing, meditation, and yoga to balance GH.

Messenger: Insulin

Role: Insulin is secreted by the beta cells of the pancreas when carbohydrates and (to a smaller extent) proteins are consumed and blood sugar rises after a meal. It's best known for bringing sugar from the blood into the body's cells to use for energy or storage. It facilitates the transportation of glucose and amino acids across cell membranes. Insulin promotes fat storage when glycogen reserves in the liver and muscle are sufficient. Without insulin, energy stays in the blood and does not go into the body's cells for energy or storage.

What happens when out of balance? If excess carbohydrates are consumed, insulin levels are elevated and will increase fat storage. Unfortunately, high insulin levels also inhibit the breakdown of stored body fat for fuel. High levels of blood sugar and insulin can cause huge swings in blood sugar, from really high to crashing low. When blood sugar drops, energy levels plummet and hunger is signaled to bring blood sugar levels up. High insulin levels can lead to insulin resistance, excessive belly fat, and type 2 diabetes.

How to balance: Consume protein and essential fats at every meal because these foods help mediate a gradual release of glucose and insulin. Limit refined carbohydrates and eat foods high in fiber, as it can regulate glucose absorption. Eat balanced meals every three hours to keep blood sugar levels stable. Reduce stimulants and alcohol intake because they can stimulate insulin release. Exercise three to five times per week, as it increases the amount of glucose that the cells can absorb. Practice stress reduction techniques (e.g., tai chi, yoga), as stress can increase blood sugar.

53

Messenger: Leptin

Role: Leptin is called the "satisfaction" hormone because its function is to tell your brain when you've had enough to eat. Leptin is produced by fat cells, so the more fat you carry, the higher the level of leptin you produce. It plays an important role in how the body manages food intake and fat storage. Leptin regulates body weight by increasing energy output and decreasing the consumption of food. When levels are high, it signals the brain that no more fat storage is required, and food intake should be limited. Leptin can also decrease cravings.

What happens when out of balance? It would make sense that the higher your leptin levels, the greater your appetite control, but if you are overweight you can develop a resistance to leptin. Therefore, leptin's "message" to the brain to stop eating and increase metabolism is not heard.

How to balance: Don't skip meals or harshly restrict calories because this can cause a slowdown in your metabolic rate. You can increase your responsiveness to leptin by becoming more active and building more lean muscle mass. Multiple studies have reported that leptin levels increased when a moderate dose of zinc was administered. Foods naturally high in zinc are meat, seafood, hemp and pumpkin seeds, and legumes.

Messenger: Melatonin

Role: Melatonin is a hormone secreted by the pineal gland when night falls. Circulating levels trail off during the early morning hours to help us awaken. The importance of seven to nine hours of restful sleep is paramount for reducing cravings and improving metabolism. Melatonin is an antioxidant that can reduce inflammation and increase our life span.

What happens when out of balance? Melatonin is important for the repair and regulation of the immune system. It's also necessary to produce sufficient HGH for the production and repair of muscle tissue. Low melatonin can also decrease vividness and frequency of dreams. Excessive melatonin can suppress thyroid.

How to balance: Getting enough deep sleep is essential for melatonin production. Sleeping in a completely dark room maximizes melatonin release. Consume high tryptophan foods such as poultry, seafood, nuts, and legumes to provide the building blocks to make this hormone. Melatonin is naturally found in cherries, walnuts, ginger, mustard, goji berries, St. John's wort, asparagus, brown rice, mint, olives, cucumber, grapes, sunflower seeds, fennel, and cherries.

Messenger: Noradrenaline (aka Norepinephrine)

Role: Noradrenaline is a neurotransmitter produced in the adrenal glands. It's considered a stress hormone and is released when you perceive a threat; it increases your heart rate and blood pressure in order to escape from the threat. It breaks down glycogen to form glucose, increases mental focus, and opens up the respiratory system in order to give you maximum performance to outsmart or outrun a predator. When in balance, it can increase the breakdown of fats.

What happens when out of balance? If there is too much noradrenaline in the system for long periods of time, it will break down muscle and increase fat levels in the blood. Low levels of noradrenaline maybe an underlying cause of depression and ADHD.

How to balance: Like many other stress-related hormones, noradrenaline can be balanced with high-intensity exercise, avoidance of excessive stimulant use, plenty of sleep, and adequate high-quality protein. Under a health practitioner's guidance, you can also try licorice root, B vitamins, and EGCG (epigallocatechin gallate).

Messenger: Progesterone

Role: One of progesterone's most important functions is in the female reproductive cycle. In women, it's produced by the ovaries and, to a lesser extent, the adrenal glands. In men, small amounts are produced by the testes and adrenal glands. Progesterone can assist in balancing insulin, can work as a diuretic, and helps the thyroid to function more efficiently. It can convert into estrogen or testosterone, depending on your needs. Progesterone can affect the brain and acts as a "feel-good" hormone that can reduce cravings.

What happens when out of balance? Progesterone depletion is now thought to cause many of the menopausal symptoms suffered by women in a perimenopause state. Low progesterone levels can throw off estrogen balance and cause estrogen dominance. Low levels of progesterone can create feelings of anxiety, depression, irritability, and even anger.

How to balance: Progesterone is important for weight loss, as it restores hormonal balance and counteracts the dominance of estrogen in the system. Both nuts and seeds contain certain plant sterols that help promote the production of progesterone in women. Plant sterols are fatty compounds found in raw seeds, avocados, green vegetables, and nuts that encourage the release of appropriate amounts of progesterone. Sufficient intake of vitamin B6 (found in beans, fish, avocados, and spinach) is necessary for the production of progesterone. Bio-identical progesterone can be prescribed by your doctor, but be warned that it may cause a temporary weight gain. Once you adjust to higher levels of progesterone, your body will find its ideal weight. Ask your doctor if bio-identical progesterone would be beneficial. Synthetic progesterone (often called Provera) has been shown to cause side effects, including increased risk of cancer, abnormal menstrual flow, fluid retention, nausea, and depression.

Messenger: Prolactin

Role: Prolactin is produced by the pituitary and is a player in a healthy immune system. It is highest during and after pregnancy and is closely related to growth hormone (aka human growth hormone). This is the hormone that stimulates mammary-gland development and milk production in mammals.

What happens when out of balance? High prolactin levels negatively affect your ability to metabolize fat. When fatty tissue receives signals from prolactin, it reacts by reducing the production of another hormone called adiponectin, which is important for the metabolism of a variety of nutrients.

How to balance: Prolactin is secreted after approximately three hours of continuous melatonin secretion. Adequate, deep sleep is necessary for prolactin balance. The amino acids phenylalanine and tyrosine can help lower prolactin by increasing dopamine levels naturally. Enjoy more protein-rich foods, including beef, fowl, fish, eggs, dairy, nuts, and seeds.

Messenger: Serotonin

Role: Serotonin is a neurotransmitter that carries messages between cells. A natural mood regulator, serotonin makes you feel emotionally stable, less anxious, more tranquil, and even more focused and energetic. Serotonin is nature's own appetite suppressant. This powerful brain chemical made from the amino acid tryptophan curbs cravings and shuts off appetite. It makes you feel satisfied even if your stomach is not full. The result is eating less and losing weight. Serotonin may play a role in reducing the risk of many brain abnormalities like depression, panic disorder, and anxiety disorders.

What happens when out of balance? Low serotonin levels increase carbohydrate cravings and may lead to binging in an attempt to bring serotonin levels back to normal. Low levels of serotonin can also affect mental function and contribute to depression or anxiety.

How to balance: Serotonin is derived from the amino acid tryptophan found in poultry, fish, and seeds. Stress may increase your need for serotonin and cause carbohydrate cravings. Prevent this by shifting protein intake to the early part of the day. Get adequate sleep, as serotonin levels are replenished during sleep. Avoid low-carb diets because glucose is required to assist tryptophan's transport to the brain. Serotonin is made after you eat carbohydrates, when the brain receives extra tryptophan. **Note:** SSRI (selective serotonin re-uptake inhibitor) antidepressants work only on the mood function of serotonin and may interfere with appetite function, causing increased cravings and inability to feel full despite consuming enough calories.

Messenger: Testosterone

Role: Testosterone is a steroid hormone produced by the male testes and, in smaller amounts, by a woman's ovaries, as well as by the adrenal glands of both men and women. Testosterone helps to repair and build muscle tissue as well as burn fat. Balanced levels can improve muscle growth, reduce blood pressure, strengthen bones, and increase energy.

What happens when out of balance? Belly fat is a testosterone buster. Fat contains aromatase, an enzyme that converts testosterone into estrogen. Having extra estrogen floating around your system triggers your body to slow its production of testosterone. Low levels can cause fatigue, irritability, depression, erectile dysfunction in men, low libido in women, aches and pains in the joints, osteoporosis, and loss of muscle tissue leading to fat gain. Excessive levels in women can cause acne, infertility, and polycystic ovarian syndrome. Excessive amounts in men (from supplementation) can cause hair loss and aggression. Stress increases cortisol, which in turn destroys testosterone.

How to balance: Vigorous resistance exercise triggers testosterone. Stick to weightlifting movements that hit multiple muscle groups and limit your rest between sets. After workouts, consume adequate levels of healthy fats, as low-fat diets contribute to low testosterone levels. Examples of healthy fats include avocados, seeds, fish, nuts, and coconut and olive oil. Higher-protein diets may help balance testosterone levels. Foods that nurture testosterone include oysters, hemp hearts, maca root, and stinging nettles because of their high zinc, magnesium, and sterol content. Enjoy wild salmon, as it is a rich source of vitamin D, which supports testosterone production.

Messenger: Thyroid Hormones (T3 and T4)

Role: Thyroid hormones T3 (triiodothyronine) and T4 (thyroxine) play a major role in metabolism. Every cell in the body depends on thyroid hormones to regulate metabolism and use fats and carbohydrates for fuel. These hormones also help control heart rate, weight, body temperature, and muscle tone. T4 is converted to the active T3 (three to four times more potent than T4) within the cells with a selenium-containing enzyme; thus, dietary selenium is essential for T3 production.

What happens when out of balance? When thyroid hormone levels drop in the blood, the pituitary gland produces thyroid-stimulating hormone (TSH), which stimulates the thyroid to produce more T3 and T4. When T3 and T4 levels are off, weight, mental function, body temperature, and energy levels can be affected. There are many side effects of low thyroid levels, ranging from fatigue, depression, weight gain, and hair loss to intolerance and feeling cold. If you have any of these symptoms, you may want to visit your health provider to be tested. Tests to ask for include TSH, total T3 and T4, free T3 and T4, and thyroid antibodies. If you are concerned about thyroid cancer, the tests to ask for include calcitonin and thyroglobulin levels.

Hypothyroidism (when levels are too low) can cause a slow metabolism, making weight loss more difficult. Hypothyroidism is fairly common, with some estimates showing 10 percent of women have low thyroid levels. Some research also indicates that when thyroid levels are mildly elevated, bone mineral density can be affected. When levels are too high (hyperthyroidism), symptoms can include weight loss, nervousness, increased heart rate, and difficulty sleeping.

How to balance: To keep thyroid levels balanced, eat foods rich in selenium and iodine, like Brazil nuts, seafood, sunflower seeds, eggs, quinoa, and seaweed. Selenium is needed to activate thyroid hormones, and iodine is needed to synthesize thyroid hormones. Unbalanced estrogen levels can inhibit thyroid function, and stress can adversely affect thyroid function. Therefore, stress reduction is important to maintain balanced thyroid levels. To promote thyroid balance, drink adequate fluids, avoid excess sugar and processed foods, and get adequate omega-3s in your diet. Studies have demonstrated that avoiding foods to which you have an intolerance (e.g., gluten) is correlated with a reduction in anti-thyroid antibodies.

The herbs guggul (aka commiphora mukul) and ashwaganda promote conversion of T4 to T3. Tyrosine is the amino acid that is the backbone of thyroid hormones. Food sources include fish, chicken, avocados, lima beans, nuts, and seeds.

THE LIVER IS THE ANSWER

Your liver is responsible for metabolizing hormones—including insulin and estrogen. If your liver can't break down these hormones and they stay elevated, you are more prone to gain weight (especially abdominal weight—the dreaded "spare tire") that is *so* difficult to lose. If you damage or burden your liver with alcohol, it will be less efficient at clearing hormones from the blood. This will put you at a greater risk of developing inflammatory conditions such as insulin resistance, obesity, diabetes, and estrogen dominance.

One of the reasons red wine is touted as a potentially beneficial alcoholic beverage is that it is a good source of the powerful antioxidant resveratrol. However, this plant nutrient is also abundant in raw grapes, mulberries, bilberries, blueberries, cranberries, black currants, purple cabbage, red onion, and more. Red wine is *not* the only way to get this potent antioxidant!

Beer drinkers beware as well. Beer elevates levels of prolactin, which encourages growth of breast tissue (even in men), decreases fertility, and increases the risk of developing prostate cancer. Women with elevated prolactin levels are at greater risk of developing breast cancer. Alcohol also depletes vitamins and minerals from your tissues. In particular, it drains B vitamins from your liver, which once again predisposes you to inflammatory conditions.

TAKE CARE OF YOUR HORMONES WITH GOOD FOOD

The stressors in your life can be hard to control. After all, you can't just decide not to work or opt out of childcare or eldercare responsibilities the way you can decide to replace French fries with Jicama Fries on page 234. So, the most practical way to recover from the constant onslaught of stressors is by eating the right foods—foods that nourish your nervous system, adrenal glands, and whole system. You can create a huge difference in your life simply by eating healing superfoods that give your hormones the building blocks they need to achieve balance. Now that we have explored how to balance our hormones, it is time to showcase the most powerful food superheroes and their tasty sidekicks.

57

"I decided to become the CEO of Save My Ass Technologies INC."

—KRIS CARR, CANCER THRIVER, AUTHOR,

MOVIE PRODUCER

CHAPTER 4

THE NUTRITION OF WEIGHT LOSS

Each day your body regenerates more than 70 billion cells. Your red blood cells are replaced every four months, your skin cells regenerate every month, and the lining of the small intestine renews itself every four to six days!

Through your food choices, you have the power to affect the outcome of all that regeneration. The quality of those new cells is reliant on the available building materials.

Remember that inflammation is the body's response to injury, infection, irritation, or imbalance, and the symptoms these conditions cause are redness, soreness, heat, swelling, and/or loss of function. When any four of these factors persist, the affected tissues cannot heal and regenerate properly. We must resolve the infection, remove the irritation, or correct the hormonal imbalance in order to reduce the destruction of cells. The good news is that by following an anti-inflammatory live-it that is high in phytonutrients, amino acids, and essential fatty acids (EFAs), we are able to quench the flames of inflammation and turn on cell repair.

In this chapter, we'll explore the specific nutrients that reduce inflammation, allowing you to lose those stubborn pounds your body holds on to as a response to pain and swelling. We'll start with a look at the amazing powers of superfoods and then break down some essential facts on how carbohydrates, proteins, and fats figure into the larger picture.

THE TOP 25 SUPERFOODS (AND THREE SUPER-ROOTS) FOR INFLAMMATION AND WEIGHT REDUCTION

If we use superfoods as the materials for regeneration, our newly formed cells will be stronger and healthier than the old cells they replace. The following chart outlines 25 amazing superfoods—along with some trusty sidekicks that provide an extra boost.

APPLES
Apples contain a whopping 7 mg of calcium D-glucarate, a phytochemical that plays an important role in liver detoxification and estrogen balance. Apple cider vinegar may slow the release of sugar (from foods) into the bloodstream and help to avoid dangerous spikes in blood glucose. Balanced blood sugar means less inflammation and less weight gain.
Sidekick: Cinnamon and apples are a match made in heaven. Try the Best No-Bake Apple Crumble on page 304 and you will agree.

ARTICHOKES
Artichokes are a fantastic weight-loss food due to their high fiber content. They are also a soothing liver tonic, which helps to bring balance to the hormones. Recent research indicates that extracts in globe artichokes can be isolated and used to increase the amount of mucus that is created by the stomach lining. This mucus protects the stomach lining from the acids that break down our food and prevents the creation of stomach ulcers. Artichokes also possess strong antispasmodic properties for muscle aches and pain caused by tension and muscle spasm. Artichoke extracts have been shown to be as powerful as antispasmodic agents as the often-prescribed pharmaceutical drug papaverine.
Sidekick: Mint Kale Pesto on page 210 tastes great as a dip for steamed artichokes.

AVOCADOS

Avocados have the ability to boost levels of glutathione, a powerful antioxidant that ramps up your immune system, warding off invading pathogens that are an underlying cause of inflammation. Research shows that glutathione plays a key role in the prevention of cancer and heart disease. Avocados are a good source in L-carnitine, which boosts your fat-burning metabolism. They are also brimming with B vitamins, which help to improve your mood, reducing the tendency to overeat.

Sidekick: Lime, some garlic, and a touch of sea salt along with avocado makes a great guacamole! The acid in the lime prevents the avocado from oxidizing and helps to keep it a lovely shade of green. Check out the Key Lime Shake on page 153.

BEETS

Rich in antioxidants, beets contain the highest plant source of betaine at 127 mg/100 gram serving. A study by Greek researchers shows that betaine lowers C-reactive protein levels, a marker of heart disease and chronic, low-grade, systemic inflammation. Beet greens are loaded with magnesium, otherwise known as the relaxation mineral. Studies show that a deficiency of magnesium is associated with obesity and the chronic, low-grade inflammation that goes with it.

Sidekick: Salmon on a bed of steamed beet greens is fantastic. Salmon is loaded with vitamins B and D, which aid the body in the absorption of the magical mineral magnesium.

BERRIES

Eating all types of organic berries (strawberries, blueberries, blackberries, raspberries, and cranberries) helps to build one of your bodies most powerful antioxidants–superoxide dismutase (SOD). SOD is important in disarming the most harmful of free radicals–specifically those that like to break down the synovial fluid that lubricates our joints, leading to arthritis. Berries are also rich in flavanoids that reduce inflammation and repair cellular damage.
Blackberries have the unique ability to reduce the amount of adrenaline that is released from your adrenal glands during periods of stress. Prolonged elevation of stress hormones will surely lead to weight gain around the middle, as they inhibit the burning of fat and increase the burning of lean muscle.
Strawberries are high in the antioxidant anthrocyanin, which protects us from the damaging effects of our environment, especially the sun.
Blueberries and raspberries contain polyphenols that have been shown to fight adipogenesis, which is the development of fat cells.
Concentrated cranberry juice has been shown to kill the harmful, inflammation-causing *H. pylori* bacteria in the stomach and urinary tract.

Sidekick: Dandelion and berries are a perfect pairing in salads. Try Dandelion Greens with Blueberries and Pine Nuts on page 217. Dandelion is rich in lutein, which benefits your eyesight. It may also protect skin from UV damage and reduce cardiovascular disease.

BROCCOLI

Broccoli is part of the large family of cruciferous vegetables. Other superheroes in this family include bok choy, radishes, cauliflower, rapini, kale, and cabbage. All provide indol-3-carbinol (I3C). I3C reduces inflammatory intermediates in the blood that signal increased blood flow to an injured area, causing inflammatory symptoms. Broccoli is also loaded with fiber. Foods high in fiber and nutrients can improve your efforts at weight loss by increasing your feeling of being full—actually helping you to eat less. Fiber is also necessary to "soak up" the toxins dumped into the intestines by the liver. Broccoli also possesses an ability to enhance detoxification in the body in both phases of the liver detoxification process. A dynamic trio of nutrients—glucoraphanin, gluconasturtiin, and glucobrassicin—assist in the first step of liver detoxification (Phase I). Broccoli contains a compound called sulforaphane, which increases the amount of active Phase II enzymes responsible for neutralizing toxins. Once we eliminate these unwanted contaminants, we feel lighter and more able to cope.

As a good source of many of the B vitamins, broccoli is excellent for women who are currently on or have previously used oral contraceptives (the birth control pill). Oral contraceptives are proven to dramatically reduce levels of circulating B vitamins in the body. The B-complex vitamins are required for a number of metabolic reactions in the body, including fat and carbohydrate metabolism for proper energy production.

Note: If you suffer from low thyroid function, it is important to cook cruciferous vegetables to reduce goitrogenic compounds that reduce thyroid hormone function.

BURDOCK ROOT

Burdock root has been shown to actually prevent allergic reactions and inflammation. Used both topically and internally, burdock inhibits the enzymatic reactions that occur to produce tissue inflammation. You can use burdock in your favorite recipe or as a first-aid compress! Burdock is an extremely effective blood cleanser. It is known as a diaphoretic—a class of herbs that increases perspiration and eliminates impurities from the blood as well as supports the clearance of toxins from the liver. Keeping the liver in good health prevents stagnation that could lead to ailments such as gallstones.

Sidekick: Carrots and burdock are traditionally served together in Asia.

CHERRIES

When it comes to reducing inflammation, cherries are superstars! They can actually reduce joint pain and gout. The red pigment in cherries is created by anthocyanins. Anthocyanins have been shown to reduce the inflammatory markers in the blood. This means that there is a reduction in inflammation of your joints, and, ultimately, a reduction in pain. Cherries are also showing great promise in the fight against obesity. They are an excellent source of vitamin C and contain plant sterols. These two important nutrients work synergistically to reduce the accumulation of fat in the body. Cherries also provide a good dose of fiber, which helps to eliminate unwanted toxins.

Sidekick: Chocolate and cherries are a natural combination.

CHIA AND FLAXSEEDS

Research has shown that adding both flax and chia to your diet can have a big impact on your health. Both seeds offer a high content of alpha-linolenic acid (ALA), which the body can convert to anti-inflammatory EPA and DHA as long as you have enough of the nutritional co-factors—vitamin B, magnesium, and zinc. The slippery texture of these seeds comes from the large quantities of soluble fiber that not only encourage smooth digestive movements but can also help to lower cholesterol. Flaxseeds are a rich source of lignans, plant compounds that can modulate the metabolism and use of estrogen in a positive way. Lignans can reduce menopausal symptoms, including hot flashes, sweating, and vaginal dryness. Alongside lignans, ALA works to decrease inflammation and promote healthy functioning of the immune system. Flax and chia seeds may be useful to manage autoimmune and inflammatory disorders such as rheumatoid arthritis, psoriasis, and lupus.

Sidekick: Applesauce
Grinding the flax or chia seed and adding it to the applesauce makes an excellent breakfast. See the Alpha-Omega Breakfast Pudding on page 161.

CHOCOLATE

Why is chocolate the hands-down, number-one food women crave? Is it the high levels of magnesium that calm us down and help to curb PMS? Or is it the caffeine that perks us up? Maybe it is the phen-ylethylamine (PEA) that releases endorphins, causing feelings of passion and love! Consuming dark chocolate—in moderation, of course—can help in the prevention and improvement of diabetes. Flavanols found in dark chocolate can also increase insulin sensitivity and the activity of pancreatic beta-cells, the cells responsible for secreting insulin in response to high blood glucose levels. Eaten regularly and in small amounts (20 grams every three days), chocolate can reduce inflammation associated with conditions ending in "itis" as well as allergies, skin disorders, asthma, and heart disease.

FENNEL

Fennel has been used for centuries as a digestive remedy. It is known in herbal medicine as a carminative, which coats the esophagus and gastrointestinal lining to soothe heartburn, relieve indigestion, and prevent flatulence. Like many other herbs, fennel has very potent diuretic properties, though it does not deplete your body of potassium, a much-needed electrolyte that is instrumental in cardiac health. Fennel can also relieve PMS symptoms such as bloating, cramping, and general edema without any side effects. Fennel contains a compound called anethol, which has been shown in studies to have strong anti-inflammatory and analgesic properties, especially in situations where inflammation is acute and persistent. At only 28 calories per cup, and with good amounts of vitamins A, B, and C, fennel may become your new best friend for fighting inflammation and weight gain.

GARLIC

Garlic is the ultimate slimming food and a key player in healing inflammation. It adds flavor to your food without the calories. Garlic gets a gold star in the prevention category, as it contains more than 100 biologically powerful antioxidant compounds that do everything from lower cholesterol to fight off viruses. Garlic has been shown to protect against the common cold, regulate blood sugar, reduce free-radical damage to the arteries, and lower levels of homocysteine in the blood. Homocysteine is a marker that indicates inflammation and cardiovascular disease.

Sidekick: Horseradish assists in the digestion of fats. Check out the Buffalo Strip Loin on page 257.

HEMP HEARTS

Hemp hearts (aka shelled seeds) contain both essential fatty acids necessary for muscle and joint repair. They also have all the essential amino acids in an easily digestible form. Two tablespoons of hemp hearts contains 7 grams of protein–equivalent to the same amount found in a large boiled egg. What's more, 65 percent of the total protein content of hemp seed comes from an easily digestible protein called edestin, which is readily absorbed and utilized by the human body. Edestin has the unique ability to stimulate the manufacture of antibodies against foreign invaders, boosting the immune system. Hemp hearts fight inflammation because they contain omega-3 and an especially beneficial type of omega-6 fat called gamma linolenic acid (GLA). GLA is a direct building block of PGE1, a type of prostaglandin that works in the body as an anti-inflammatory messenger. GLA can decrease inflammation, and supports healthy hair, nails, and skin.

Many women use hemp hearts to help with menopausal symptoms, including hot flashes and depression. They are also helpful for PMS symptoms due to their high levels of GLA and magnesium.

Hemp's high protein content makes it a perfect addition to meal replacement bars, cereal, porridge, salads, pesto, pasta, dressings, sauces, smoothies, desserts, and side dishes.

HERBS AND SPICES

Adding herbs to all your dishes is a surefire way to slim down; they add flavor without adding calories. Parsley may help to modulate the immune system by suppressing an over-stimulated immune response. This makes it a key player in the fight against allergies and autoimmune and chronic inflammatory disorders. It also contains a volatile oil called eugenol that has been shown to reduce the pain and swelling associated with arthritis. Rosemary, sage, oregano, basil, marjoram, thyme, and mint contain a compound called rosmarinic acid that has been shown in clinical trials to reduce inflammation.

For spices, top anti-inflammatory honors go to ginger and turmeric. Ginger has the ability to beat painful inflammation by inhibiting the effects of arachidonic acid, a necessary fat responsible for triggering the inflammation involved in the immune response and that ultimately leads to pain. In Ayurvedic medicine, the 5,000-year-old natural healing system of India, turmeric is used as a cleansing herb for the whole body and as a remedy for minor wounds, poor digestion, arthritis, inflammation, and pain.

Herbs and spices play sidekick to all healthy foods, but they are real heroes!

KALE

Kale is considered by most experts to be one of the healthiest foods on the planet. There is a new rating system called the ANDI scale, developed by Dr. Joel Fuhrman, that rates the density of nutrients per calorie. The scale is ranked 0 to 1,000, and kale takes the top spot because it delivers the most nutrients for only 36 calories a cup! To balance our weight and reach ultimate vitality, we need to eat foods that offer us the biggest vitamin and mineral "bang for our buck." The consumption of a variety of phytochemicals, such as indole-3-carbinol, found in kale, enables and enhances the body's detoxification and cellular repair mechanisms that protect us from chronic diseases. Kale will detoxify you, protect you, slim you down, and, most important, reduce pain and inflammation in your body.

Kale is high in vitamin K, which is needed to obtain optimal bone mineral density and prevent osteoporosis. A lack of vitamin K in the diet can contribute to excessive inflammation in the body, leading to joint pain and symptoms of arthritis.

Because of its high levels of vitamin C, kale can also help to prevent the development of gout and kidney stones. Vitamin C stops the buildup of uric acid in our systems. This buildup can deposit in our kidneys and joints and lead to the development of these painful stones.

Note: If you suffer from low thyroid function, it is important to cook cruciferous vegetables to reduce goitrogenic compounds that reduce thyroid hormone function.

OLIVES AND OLIVE OIL

Olives and olive oil are fantastic anti-inflammatory tools, and by adding them to your diet you can naturally reduce the pain of chronic inflammatory diseases such as arthritis. Olives contain the phenolic compound oleocanthal, which has been shown to have strong anti-inflammatory properties, mimicking the action of ibuprofen. Other polyphenols found in olives help to combat the *H. pylori* bacteria that is responsible for causing stomach ulcers. Studies have shown these compounds to have strong antibacterial activity against eight strains of *H. pylori,* three of them resistant to some antibiotics.

Eating olives will also help build your blood, as they possess a substantial amount of iron. Iron is a key factor in the formation of hemoglobin, the protein that carries oxygen throughout the body via the bloodstream. Iron also helps to build the enzymes responsible for regulating immune function and cognitive development.

It is well known that following the traditional Mediterranean diet has been proven to reduce the risk of heart disease. This is due in large part to the use of olive oil. Studies show that this diet is also associated with a reduced risk of overall and cardiovascular mortality, a reduced incidence of cancer and cancer mortality, and a reduced incidence of Parkinson's and Alzheimer's diseases.

POMEGRANATES

In ancient times, pomegranate seeds were known as the seeds of fertility. As it turns out, they do so much more. Joint pain begins with a cascade of enzyme reactions that result in the body triggering inflammation. Recent studies show that pomegranates halt this enzyme reaction before the inflammation is able to occur, leaving you pain free!

Sidekick: Green Tea is high in pain-relieving antioxidants and delicious with a splash of pomegranate juice.

PUMPKIN AND SQUASH

Not only does the flesh of pumpkin and squash have a subtle sweetness, which helps to curb cravings, it is super nutrient-dense. Squash and pumpkin are both high in antioxidants. The fiber in these vegetables makes them slow-burning carbohydrates, helping to balance blood sugar, which is essential if you are trying to slim down.

Sidekick: Pumpkin and Squash Seeds
Phytonutrients in pumpkin seeds called lignans help to balance out the body's sex hormones. Pumpkin seeds are high in magnesium and are also a rich source of plant sterols, which have the power to stimulate an underactive immune system or relax an overactive one. Pumpkin seeds are a good vegetarian source of zinc, another critical nutrient for the immune system, as it helps our T cells protect the body from infection. A quarter-cup serving will provide close to 20 percent of your daily zinc needs.

QUINOA

Quinoa has become the nutritional superstar of the decade. It is genetically related to Swiss chard, spinach, and beets. Like other seeds, it is high in protein and fiber. Quinoa's high fiber content helps regulate blood sugar by slowing down the conversion of complex carbohydrates into sugar. It helps you feel full and reduces cravings, making it the perfect weight-loss tool. One cup of quinoa has about 15 percent protein by weight, or as much protein as two deli slices of chicken breast. As an alternative to grains, quinoa offers the benefit of fiber and B vitamins without the exposure to gluten and the allergic reactions that can result. Quinoa is a good source of tryptophan, which promotes the production of our happy hormone serotonin, reducing the tendency toward depression.

Sidekick: Pumpkin seeds are another excellent source of vegetarian protein. Sprinkle onto quinoa salad.

SEAWEED

Seaweed (e.g., nori, wakame, dulse) is the perfect food for cleansing and for reducing the waistline. It is made up of about one-third protein and one-third dietary fiber. Both help to balance blood sugar and help you feel satisfied. It also contains high proportions of iodine, a critical nutrient for your thyroid gland, which controls how fast you burn calories. Iodine has also been shown to decrease insulin resistance and allow glucose into your cells to be burned for energy. This keeps your blood sugar levels manageable so your pancreas doesn't have to work overtime. Seaweed has good amounts of iron and B vitamins that improve mood and energy, along with magnesium, which reduces pain.

SESAME SEEDS

Sesame seeds contain sesamin and sesamolin, substances that are part of a group of fibers called lignans, believed to prevent high blood pressure and protect the liver against damage. Half a cup of sesame seeds contains three times more calcium (600 mg) than half a cup of whole milk. One of the greatest health benefits of sesame seeds is that they are high in phytosterols. These compounds can lower LDL, or "bad" cholesterol, improve heart health, and balance the immune system. Sesame seeds have one of the highest phytosterol contents of common foods (400–413 mg/100 grams).

SHIITAKE MUSHROOMS

Shiitake mushrooms are very high in polyphenols—nutrients that are effective in protecting liver cells from damage. Supporting the liver is critical to fighting inflammation. Studies show that shiitake mushrooms may prevent fat storage and lower triglyceride levels that may be a risk factor in cardiovascular inflammation. High levels of a compound called lentinan makes the shiitake mushroom a powerful cancer-fighting food. Lentinan also confers antibacterial properties, helping to protect against food-borne pathogens and other bacterial contamination.

Sidekick: Job's Tears are an extraordinary gluten-free grain from Asia with strong anti-inflammatory benefit. The meaty texture of shiitake mushrooms works well with Anti-inflammatory Fish Chowder found on page 272.

SPINACH

Spinach is the perfect superfood to add to your diet when you want to minimize weight gain; it is packed with minerals and vitamins and is low in calories. Not only that, it is a great source of protein. In fact, spinach is a vegetarian source of protein that contains a complete amino acid profile. Complete proteins contain all of the amino acids necessary for rebuilding muscle tissue and supporting collagen growth, which is crucial in the maintenance of healthy skin and joints.
Eating spinach is one way to get your calcium, which you need to support healthy bone growth and prevent the onset of osteoporosis. This makes spinach the perfect, allergy-free alternative to dairy. Balancing out the calcium in spinach is high levels of magnesium, which is necessary for muscle relaxation, reducing pain, and hormone development in our adrenal glands (to cope with high stress levels).

Sidekick: Olive Oil
It is no surprise that Popeye loved Olive Oyl because together they make a perfect marriage. The spinach gives us energy, and the olive oil helps the body absorb more phytonutrients.

SPIRULINA

Spirulina is a simple, one-celled organism that is so nutrient dense you could almost survive on it and water alone. This blue-green algae is 60 to 70 percent protein by weight. It is high in most vitamins, especially beta-carotene and iron. It is a powerful antioxidant that is loaded with chlorophyll, which oxygenates our cells, alkalizes tissues, and binds to toxins in the intestine and prevents them from being absorbed into the bloodstream. It has a strong stimulating effect on the immune system and not only improves the body's ability to fight bacterial infections but helps to clear cellular debris from the blood following an immune response to an infection or inflammation.
Note: Spirulina is not a viable source of B12.

SUSTAINABLE FISH

Sustainable fish (i.e., anchovies, herring, mackerel, and sardines) contain the omega-3 fatty acids eicosapentaenoic acid (EPA) and docosahexaenoic acid (DHA), both powerful anti-inflammatory fats that are crucial to the health of the heart, brain, and nervous system.
Hormones benefit greatly from the high levels of zinc and omega-3 fatty acids found in fish. These nutrients will boost the antioxidant capacity of the body as well as improve each cell's membrane strength and permeability. These fish are high in vitamin D, which is also essential to maintaining your immune health. Vitamin D deficiency is linked to an increased risk of cancer, cardiovascular disease, multiple sclerosis, and rheumatoid and osteoarthritis as well as type 1 diabetes. Adding sustainable fish to your diet will help you to build muscle; reduce inflammation and pain; and combat depression, obesity, and autoimmune disorders. Other fish sources that are healthy but not as sustainable include wild salmon, rainbow trout, black cod, and Arctic char.

Sidekick: Ginger is the perfect accompaniment to fish. It has anti-inflammatory properties that amplify pain relief. Enjoy the Slimming Spring Roll-Ups on page 250.

THREE STRESS-BUSTING ROOTS

ASHWAGANDHA

Ashwagandha (pronounced ah-shwa-GAN-dah), also known as Indian ginseng, is a powerful root regarded as an adaptogen, an herb that helps you adapt to stress while enhancing your energy. The root of ashwagandha contains flavonoids that are anti-inflammatory, anti-tumor, anti-stress, antioxidant, mind-boosting, and immune-enhancing. No wonder it has been used for centuries to promote healthy libido! A 2008 study showed that when combined with glucosamine sulphate (GLS), ashwagandha could protect against inflammation and cartilage damage associated with osteoarthritis.

ASTRAGALUS

Astragalus is known in the world of herbal medicine as a deep regenerative and restorative immune tonic. Studies show it helps to lower and regulate blood sugar levels, enhancing the effects of anti-diabetic drugs. Astragalus is an excellent source of selenium, which is essential for fighting cancer, boosting immune function, healing wounds, and supporting antioxidant enzyme function, which slows down the effects of aging. This amazing root tastes so sweet you can chew on slices of it as a snack. You can also add it to soups or smoothies, or use it to make a delicious tea.

THREE STRESS-BUSTING ROOTS (CONT'D.)
MACA
Maca is a wonderful root that grows in the mountainous and rugged terrain of the Peruvian highlands. Its actions focus mainly in the hypothalamus and pituitary glands, assisting the body in balancing hormones, providing more energy and better moods, enhancing libido, and more. It even has the power to reduce the stress hormone cortisol. This superfood is loaded with vitamins such as A, B, C, D, and E. As well, maca naturally contains zinc, glucosinolates, and plant sterols, which are potent immune enhancers to help keep you healthy and energized during cold and flu season. Maca is also loaded with energy-producing, protein-building amino acids that fuel the body and assist with recovery after a strenuous workout. With its incredible nutrient profile, supplement-savvy athletes use maca to improve their energy level without over-stimulating their body. Maca boosts immunity and increases mental acuity, supercharging your body to give you a more energized life!

What links many of the superfoods listed above is their high micronutrient content. Micronutrients are vitamins, minerals, and phytochemicals that make a major anti-inflammatory contribution. Let's have a look at the need to balance our intake of macronutrients—carbohydrates, proteins, and fats—in order to have the greatest and fastest weight-loss response.

ARE CARBS MAKING ME FAT? THE GLYCEMIC INDEX

One way to evaluate the relative healthfulness of a carbohydrate food is to examine its impact on your blood sugar levels. The concept of low–glycemic index (GI) foods was developed in 1981 by Dr. David Jenkins and his team at the University of Toronto to assess the effects of different foods on blood sugar levels. Low-GI foods are, by definition, carbohydrate-based foods that, once digested and absorbed, result in a small, gradual increase in blood sugar levels. On the other hand, high-GI foods cause a large, rapid rise in blood sugar levels and a correspondingly high insulin release. High insulin levels increase fat storage, so the more you balance the release of insulin, the greater chance you have of staying slim.

While high-GI foods leave you feeling hungry, low-GI foods are satiating. The likely reason is that low-GI foods stimulate the production of the appetite-suppressing hormone glucagon-like peptide 1 (GLP-1). In a study published in the March 1999 issue of *Pediatrics,* David Ludwig, founder of

Optimal Weight for Life at Children's Hospital Boston, and his colleagues found that low-GI foods reduced hunger in obese teenage boys. Also, a study published in the *British Journal of Nutrition* in 2007 found that overweight adults were less hungry following a low-GI meal than those who had consumed a high-GI meal. Those who had consumed the low-GI meal also had lower levels of total cholesterol and LDL than the other group.

As researchers further explored the glycemic index of foods and learned about how the macronutrients in foods influence the body, they began to understand how much more there is to know about the influence of nutrition on overall metabolic rate and health. With this deeper understanding, a measure of glycemic load (GL) emerged.

Glycemic Load

Glycemic load expands on the concepts of the glycemic index. The glycemic index compared all foods to a single food and serving size; glycemic load measurements take a much more practical approach by evaluating the way a standardized serving size for a particular food may affect your blood sugar. Although the glycemic load does a better job of describing the impact of a standardized serving size on your blood sugar, it's still up to you to learn what the standardized serving sizes are of the foods you like to eat. Take watermelon, for while watermelon has the potential to spike blood sugar (ranking 76 on the GI), if the serving is reasonable (a 10-oz slice), then the impact to your blood sugar is low (only 4 on the GL).

Because blood sugar levels have such an enormous influence on how your body regulates inflammation, knowing the glycemic index and glycemic load scores of a food will help you distinguish between foods and serving sizes that have the potential to promote inflammation and foods that tend to discourage inflammation.

Although you should choose mostly foods with a GI of less than 55, you can eat foods with a GI of 56 to 69 as long as you slow down the absorption of carbohydrates they contain. Eat small portions of high-GI foods; avoid eating them on an empty stomach; and combine them with foods high in fiber, protein, or good fats. Refined foods with a GI of 70 or more should be avoided because they increase your blood sugar too rapidly and are common inflammation triggers. Low-GI foods are recommended, as they help reduce inflammation. Medium-GI foods can be reintroduced one at a time once you're sure that you're not allergic to them.

CONDENSED GLYCEMIC INDEX CHART

(for a five-page version, please see *Meals That Heal Inflammation*)

FOOD/FOOD CATEGORY	GLYCEMIC INDEX	GLYCEMIC LOAD	HIGH/MED/LOW
BEANS AND LEGUMES			
Beans and lentils, boiled	28–30	3–5	Low
Peas, frozen, boiled	48	4	Low
BEVERAGES			
Fruit juice (apple, orange, pineapple, prune juice), no sugar added	40–50	13	Low
Tomato juice	33	4	Low
Carrot juice	43	10	Low
Orange soda	68	23	Med
Gatorade	78	12	High
Smoothie, mango	32	9	Low
BREAD			
3-grain, sprouted	55	5	Low
Wonder Bread, white	80	37	High
Country Life, gluten-free, multigrain	79	10	High
BREAKFAST CEREALS			
All Bran, Kellogg's	49	12	Low
Cheerios/Corn Flakes	74–86	19	High
Gluten-free muesli	39	5	Low

FOOD/FOOD CATEGORY	GLYCEMIC INDEX	GLYCEMIC LOAD	HIGH/MED/ LOW
CAKES AND MUFFINS			
Cupcake, donut	73–76	26	High
Bran muffin, commercially made	60	14	Med
Macaroon, coconut	32	6	Low
CEREAL GRAINS			
Quinoa, raw	53	18	Low
Calrose rice, white, medium grain, boiled	83	36	High
SunRice, medium grain, brown	59	30	Med
Rice pasta, enriched	51	24	Low
Puffed rice cake, white	82	17	High
FRUIT AND SWEETENERS			
Apple, pear	38	5–6	Low
Banana	52	11	Low
Berries	25–53	1–5	Low
Cherries, raw, sour	22	9	Low
Dates, pitted	45	22	Low
Fruit-and-nut mix	15	4	Low
Glucose syrup	100	10	High
Grapefruit	25	7	Low
Grapes	53	11	Low
Honey	52	11	Low
Maple syrup, pure, Canadian	54	10	Low
Mango	51	8	Low
Orange	42	4	Low
Peach, nectarine	42–43	3–4	Low
Pineapple	59	6	Med
Sugar, white	68	8	Med
Watermelon	76	4	High

FOOD/FOOD CATEGORY	GLYCEMIC INDEX	GLYCEMIC LOAD	HIGH/MED/LOW
MEAT AND DAIRY			
Beef, chicken, eggs, fish, cheese	***		Low
Milk, 3.6% fat	30	4	Low
NUTS, SEEDS, AND DRESSINGS			
Tree nuts, tropical nuts, seeds	***		Low
Cashew nuts, raw	22	3	Low
Salad dressing, homemade oil, and vinegar	***		Low
CONVENTIONAL SNACKS			
Chocolate, dark, plain	41	15	Low
Gummy confectionary, based on glucose syrup	94	16	High
VEGETABLES			
Asparagus, green beans	***		Low
Beets, canned	64	5	Med
Broccoli, cabbage, kale	***		Low
Carrots, peeled, boiled	41	2	Low
Celery, lettuce, peppers, zucchini	***		Low
Potato, peeled, boiled	101	21	High
Potato, Ontario, white, baked in skin	60	21	Med
Squash, butternut, boiled	51	8	Low
*** Contains little or no carbohydrates			

Source: The Glycemic Index has been reprinted with permission from *The New Glucose Revolution Shopper's Guide to GI Values 2008* by Dr. Jennie Brand-Miller and Kaye Foster-Powell (Da Capo Press).

You may notice in the chart that fruit ranks quite low on the glycemic index. That is because a fruit sugar known as fructose needs to be converted in the liver to glucose before it is used for fuel. This conversion reduces the insulin response, so for many years it was seen as a solution for those needing to watch their blood sugar. The trouble comes when fructose is refined and consumed in quantities that overwhelm the liver.

Vinegar and Carbohydrates

The fastest trick to reduce blood sugar is to enjoy sour foods. Pairing carbohydrates (for instance, a bowl of rice) with apple cider vinegar has at least a fourfold effect on weight-loss promotion. First, vinegar may induce satiety and help you eat less. Second, vinegar may actually prevent the metabolism of some carbohydrates. According to researchers, vinegar affects the activity of carbohydrate-digestive enzymes located on the surface of the small intestine. Digesting enzymes act like a pair of scissors that cut big macronutrients like proteins, carbohydrates, and fats into smaller pieces that can then be absorbed. Because the vinegar affects the activity of the carbohydrate-digesting enzymes, the carbohydrates are not properly digested and are instead eliminated. Third, vinegar may even make you more responsive to insulin and diminish the release of this fat-promoting hormone. And fourth, preliminary studies in laboratory mice suggest that vinegar may turn on specific genes that burn fat in the liver.

ARE FATS MAKING ME FAT?

Fats were demonized for decades as being the cause of weight gain, but not all fats are created equal, and there are essential fats that can assist in weight loss.

Omega-3

Without a doubt, the omega-3 polyunsaturated fatty acids (PUFAs) are the most heroic anti-inflammatory compounds that you can obtain from your diet. Plant-derived omega-3s include alpha-linolenic acid (ALA) and stearidonic acid (SDA). Fish and algae containing omega-3s include eicosapentaenoic acid (EPA) and docosahexaenoic acid (DHA). Fish oil from sustainable sources is a great way to get these essentials into your diet.

Based on a vast number of human studies, it appears that more than 2 grams of EPA + DHA are required daily to reduce chronic inflammation in the body. Subjects who suffer from rheumatoid arthritis, a long-term disease that leads to inflammation in the joints and surrounding tissues, require daily intakes of 1.5 to 7 grams of EPA + DHA (an average of about 3.5 grams/day). It is important that you don't give up on fish oil; studies show it can take three to 12 months to reap the full benefit.

In addition to their anti-inflammatory effects, omega-3 fatty acids can improve or prevent a variety of conditions, including asthma, diabetes, colitis, nervous and mental disorders, cancer, arthritis, hormonal imbalances, skin conditions, and even weight gain. According to researchers from the National Taiwan University, DHA suppresses the accumulation of fat in your fat tissue, thereby preventing the fat cells from expanding in size.

Omega-3 fatty acid supplementation can accelerate the weight-loss process. A two-month randomized, double-blind study of 27 women with type 2 diabetes showed interesting results. Women with type 2 diabetes who consumed 1.8 grams daily of omega-3 fatty acids (1.08 g EPA + 0.72 g DHA) experienced a significant (3.9 percent) decrease in fat mass percentage over the group consuming a placebo.

Combining omega-3 fatty acid supplementation with a healthy diet and exercise provides even greater results. In a three-week, randomized controlled study that examined the effects of combining 2.8 grams daily of omega-3 supplementation (2:1 ratio of EPA to DHA) with both caloric restriction and regular exercise in twenty severely obese women, the group that added a fish oil supplement experienced 33 percent greater weight loss compared with those consuming the placebo while undertaking the exercise program and consuming the very low-calorie diet.

How does fish oil help us lose weight? Omega-3 researcher Marc St. Onge explains, "Omega-3 fatty acids inhibit key enzymes that are responsible for fat synthesis, enhance fat breakdown, and rev up our fat-burning engine known as thermogenesis, while preventing fatty acids from entering fat storage.

Omega-3 fatty acids also promotes recovery from exercise-induced inflammation. Another benefit is it increases insulin sensitivity, preventing diabetes!"

Another potential omega-3 fatty acid mechanism of action is appetite suppression and subsequent reduction in energy intake. Omega-3 fatty acids may exert their effect on appetite and energy intake by stimulating the release of gastrointestinal hormones such as cholecystokinin (CCK).

Finally, omega-3 fatty acids found in fish oils have the ability to decrease the amount of cortisol secretion in times of stress. Cortisol has the ability to force your body to store fat in the abdomen.

Eating fatty fish regularly also reduces the risk of depression. When your moods are brighter, you are more likely to avoid the foods that cause weight gain.

Omega-6

While the scientific evidence indicates that omega-3 fatty acids have an anti-inflammatory effect, the omega-6 linoleic acid and its potentially sinister derivative, arachidonic acid, can *increase* inflammation. When omega-6 fats break down into arachidonic acid, it initiates the production of pain-inducing inflammatory prostaglandins and leukotrienes (e.g., PG2). Omega-6 fatty acids not only lead to the formation of these pro-inflammatory and pain-causing compounds, they also inhibit the formation of anti-inflammatory compounds from EPA and DHA.

The harmful effects of arachidonic acid are so pronounced that some scientists now believe that an increased insulin resistance coupled with an increased consumption of omega-6 fatty acids (that is, linoleic acid and arachidonic acid) is responsible, at least in part, for a number of the health problems we now face.

Unfortunately, the typical Western diet contains a massive excess of omega-6 fatty acids compared to omega-3 PUFAs. The ratio of omega-6 to omega-3 fatty acids has been reported to be as high as 20:1 instead of the ideal 1:1 to 4:1. It has been suggested that this imbalance could potentially promote many chronic conditions, including cardiovascular diseases, atherosclerosis, inflammatory bowel disease, and depression. Therefore, it is important to increase the ratio of the omega-3 to omega-6 fatty acids in the diet by consuming foods rich in omega-3 PUFAs.

WILL PROTEIN REALLY HELP ME SLIM DOWN?

In general, proteins, especially lean cuts of poultry, certain fish, seeds, and organic meats, are an important part of a weight-loss or weight maintenance diet. Proteins promote satiety, and the benefits of high-protein diets seem, in part, to be due to the satiety-enhancing effects of a protein-rich diet rather than to a restriction in the amounts of carbohydrates. One way that protein-rich diets may encourage you to eat fewer calories is by stimulating the release of GLP-1 (glucagon-like peptide-1). Like leptin, GLP-1 is a hormone that induces satiety, causing you to feel full on fewer calories. By choosing protein sources that are anti-inflammatory, you are not only healing your body, you are also quenching the cravings that may be causing you to devour the rest of the caramel-swirl cheesecake sitting on the kitchen counter.

Hemp hearts (aka shelled hemp seed) are one of the richest sources of anti-inflammatory vegan proteins and have been used for millennia. In the *Anatomy of Melancholy* published in the year 1621, hemp was recommended as a treatment for depression, and in the 1800s, Great Britain's Queen Victoria consumed them as a remedy for menstrual cramps.

Important non-inflammatory organic meat sources of protein include bison/buffalo, lamb, emu, quail, rabbit, and wild game. When selecting fish, choose fresh or frozen anchovies, sardines, mackerel, trout, and wild Pacific salmon. Proceed with caution when it comes to crab, lobster, mussels, oysters, and shrimp; if you have a shellfish allergy, these could lead to inflammation. Avoid tuna and other large fish, which tend to contain higher levels of mercury.

Salmon has proven to be beneficial in the treatment of osteoarthritis and other inflammatory joint conditions. Salmon contains small proteins called bioactive peptides. One in particular, called calcitonin, is similar to the human form made by the thyroid gland. Calcitonin from salmon has been shown to increase, as well as regulate and stabilize, collagen synthesis in human osteo-arthritic cartilage. When you shed debilitating joint pain, you are far more likely to embrace regular physical exercise and shed pounds!

Now that you understand the nutrition facts, you are armed with the proof you need to mentally commit to the SMTH plan. The next step is to get in touch with the emotions that may be sabotaging your weight-loss efforts. When you get your mind, body, and spirit aligned, you will have the breakthrough combination for success!

"Breath by breath, let go of fear, expectation, anger, regret, cravings, frustration, fatigue. Let go of the need for approval. Let go of old judgments and opinions. Die to all that, and fly free."

—LAMA SURYA DA

CHAPTER 5

THE LIVE-IT TOOL KIT: STRATEGIES TO COMBAT EMOTIONAL EATING

Emotional eating is eating in response to feelings rather than hunger, usually as a way to suppress or relieve negative emotions. Stress, anxiety, sadness, boredom, anger, loneliness, relationship problems, and poor self-esteem can all trigger emotional eating. We have a conflicted itch toward self-destruction—we know that what we are about to do is self-destructive when we eat an entire row of cookies or pint of ice cream, but that we're doing it for the instant gratification it brings. Sigmund Freud called this harmful compulsion the "death drive." We consciously engage in behavior that is not good for us because it brings a thrill, and the closer we are to danger, the more alive we feel. Self-destructive behavior is often cathartic, providing an emotional release. By causing harm with food, our emotional upset can be translated into something physical. Since many of us find physical pain easier to deal with than emotional pain, we rationalize that it is the lesser of two evils. Many people would debate that emotional eating is based on the fact that we aren't thinking about repercussions at all, at least not in the moment. Or if we are, we're thinking, "I don't care. I just want to feel good." It is important to look beyond the momentary feelings and start to journal how you feel the day after a binge. When you start to register the deeper pain as the cause of your food choice, you will have made the first major step in recovery from overeating.

When I was first in recovery for emotional eating, my therapist, Kate Kent, guided me to create my own list of techniques, called "The Tool Kit," to help me address and let go of my food addictions in a healthy way. If you find yourself regularly eating in response to emotions, try to break the habit with some of the strategies below. By being conscious of these simple changes, you can empower yourself to take control of your cravings and turn them into intuition! Once you can tell the difference between real hunger and cravings, you will be well on your way to feeling healthy, relaxed, connected, energetic—and free.

THE TOOL KIT

Eat Enough

Calorie-restricted diets are proven to fail. Eat breakfast, lunch, and dinner. Plan to have healthy snacks throughout the day. This is important, as skipping nutritious foods may make you feel uncontrollably hungry!

Here are some words of wisdom from my friend Kris Carr: "If eating healthy feels like deprivation, lean into it. Do it because you want to feel good. Do it because you love your life. Do it because you want more energy. If smoking and drinking and eating fast food is what you do for fun, know that it is not real fun, it is covering up sadness." I promise that if you embrace healthy eating for more than 60 days, your taste buds will change and you will start to fall in love with real food.

Eat Protein with Every Main Meal

Protein has the ability to release satiety hormones faster than fat or carbohydrates and causes you to feel fuller while eating less. A study published in *Nutrition & Metabolism* indicates that increasing your protein intake to 30 percent can reduce total caloric daily intake by up to 450 calories. Michael F.

Roizen, M.D., writes, "Drinking 2 glasses of water and eating 1 oz of nuts or seeds [equivalent to 2 tbsp hemp seeds or 12 almonds] when you're hungry between meals can extinguish cravings by changing your body chemistry and controlling hunger hormones."

Learn to Recognize Your Hunger

Before you automatically pop something into your mouth, rate your hunger on a scale of one to five, with one being ravenous and five being full. Make an effort to avoid going long enough without food to become ravenous. Also, avoid eating when you're at four or five.

Pray for Consciousness

Thich Nhat Hanh, one of the best-known and most respected Zen masters in the world, often talks about a craving being like a crying baby who is trying to draw our attention. When the baby cries, the mother cradles the baby to try to calm it right away. By acknowledging and embracing our cravings through a few breaths, we can stop ourselves from going on autopilot and reaching out for the cookie or the bag of chips.

Without talking, smell your food for one minute before eating. Look at it closely. Notice the color and texture of the food or how the steam rises from it. Look at your food as though you are seeing it for the very first time. Try saying a version of this conscious prayer: "I offer up my heartfelt gratitude for this meal and this day. Thanks to the farmers who created it and the cook who prepared it. I ask that any pain or negativity be removed this food. I ask that this food be filled with love and healing energy. Let me absorb what I need and easily let go of the rest."

Now take a mouthful of food, put your fork down, and *chew patiently*. It's not easy, but try to slow down. Taste and savor each bite, aiming for 25 to 30 chews per mouthful. If you master the art of eating slowly, you will eat less food and absorb more nutrients, and your body will thank you.

Hypnosis for Stubborn Cravings

I have found incredible results with hypnosis. My hypnotherapist, Josie Driver, explains: "Hypnotherapy can help with food cravings and attaining health goals. It can effectively assist with helping to change old patterns of how we view food, lifestyle habits, and ourselves. Sometimes, we have blocks to our conscious desires because somewhere in our subconscious mind is a very old program from childhood, we have a belief system about our bodies and what we are capable of physically doing, how and when we 'use' food, et cetera. The core of motivation, success, or self-sabotage is our subconscious beliefs. Hypnotherapy allows us to place suggestions in the subconscious mind that can allow more healthy patterns to develop, replacing old, unhealthy patterns and beliefs that stop us from having the health and life that we want."

Tap Your Troubles Away

Sometimes it's hard to get over our anxiety or upset and stay conscious about what we are eating. In those situations, the Emotional Freedom Technique (EFT), also known as "Tapping," is an incredible tool.

We become so dependent on food to help us feel relaxed and comforted that even the thought of letting go of that dependency can make us panic. How can we feel comforted and relieve stress without using food? When you find yourself with a strong impulse to overeat, it's time to take a deep breath and take a close look at the stress that's triggering your cravings. EFT is a great stress-relief technique that helps lower anxiety and the craving itself.

When you focus on what is bothering you while stimulating certain acupressure points, you send a calming signal to the amygdala part of your brain that is firing that "fight or flight" response. You are literally communicating with your brain, letting it know that it is safe to relax.

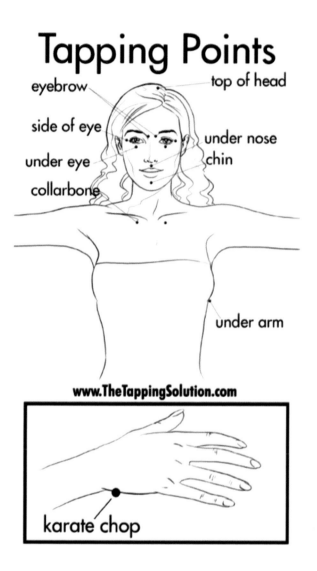

Tapping Points

eyebrow — top of head

side of eye — under nose

under eye — chin

collarbone

www.TheTappingSolution.com

under arm

karate chop

Here's how a basic Meridian Tapping sequence works:

1. Identify the problem you want to focus on. It can be general anxiety, or a specific situation or issue that causes you to feel anxious.

2. Consider the problem or situation. How do you feel about it right now? Rate the intensity level of your anxiety, with zero being the lowest level of anxiety and 10 being the highest.

3. Compose your set-up statement. Your set-up statement should acknowledge the problem you want to deal with. Follow it with an unconditional
   affirmation of yourself as a person—for example:

   "Even though I'm anxious and need this food, I deeply and completely accept myself and these feelings." This statement helps neutralize
   any judgment you have around the problem and sets you up for the
   tapping process.

   Next, perform the set-up. With four fingers, tap the Karate Chop point
   on your other hand. The Karate Chop point is on the outer edge of the
   hand, on the opposite side from the thumb. Repeat the set-up statement
   three times aloud while simultaneously tapping the Karate Chop point.
   Now, take a deep breath!

4. Using the tips of the index and middle fingers, begin tapping on the
   points while focusing on and talking about your anxiety. It isn't about
   having the perfect words; rather, it's about simply bringing up the feeling
   you want to clear. By bringing up the thought and tapping the points,
   you're letting your brain know that this thought does not cause any
   danger and you can now relax.

5. Now, tap five to seven times on each meridian point shown in the
   diagram above.

6. Tap a few rounds until you feel a release. Take a deep breath and check
   in with how you feel.

To download a free tapping meditation to relieve cravings and anxious eating, by Jessica Ortner, please visit www.JulieDaniluk.com/tappingmeditation.

Drink Up Between Meals

Try a non-caffeinated herbal tea, fruit-flavored water, or cup of broth. There
are several drinks on the market with no caffeine or sugar—buy a lot of all
different kinds—and keep it on hand. Before you have a snack, drink 8 ounces
of your favorite drink, then decide if you're really still hungry.

Find Alternatives to Eating

Prepare a list of activities that are appealing and accessible to you. Go for a walk, listen to nostalgic music (anything that brings you back to a happy time), take a hot shower or bath, clean your house, surf the Internet, schedule outstanding appointments, clean your purse, organize your closet, or look through a photo album. One of the most relaxing and detoxifying activities you can add to your program is infrared sauna therapy. Studies show it reduces heavy metals while combating stress. Look for a reputable company that uses sustainable wood, ceramic plates, nontoxic finishes, and stainless steel.

The simple act of watching TV encourages mindless snacking. You're sitting there watching your favorite show, and every 10 minutes, pictures of unhealthy comfort foods flash in front of your eyes. It's no wonder we snack while we watch! Find something you can do with your hands when enjoying your favorite show: paint your toenails (with nontoxic nail polish), take up knitting, do a puzzle, sew, or perform a light stretching workout. I find that recording a show and fast-forwarding the commercials while stretching or doing light exercise reduces nighttime eating.

Keep a Food Journal

Logging your food intake will help to identify your toughest time frames. Consider sharing your food journal with a friend via e-mail or text. It will make you accountable, and you'll be less apt to reach for unnecessary food.

Get Enough Sleep

Research shows that sleep deprivation can increase hunger by decreasing levels of leptin, the appetite-regulating hormone that signals fullness. Most snacking happens late at night. If you go to bed early, you automatically stop eating earlier. With those extra hours of sleep, you'll have more energy and more resolve to fight off the urge to grab foods for comfort. If you struggle to fall asleep, consider yogic meditation you can download from www.shambunata.com.

Call in the Troops

I used to hide cookies in my clothes hamper until the day I decided to start being honest with my food choices. If you have a temptation to binge-eat, find three friends to call when you are about to binge and keep their numbers handy. Before you open the cupboards, call for help and address what is really going on underneath your cravings.

Three-Food Interference

Make the commitment to first eat three specific healthy foods before starting on comfort foods (e.g., an apple, one ounce of hemp seeds, and a cup of soup).

Fiber, essential fats, and protein are good for curbing cravings.

If, after eating your three foods, you still want to continue with a comfort food, you will find it easier to eat less of it. You will find that, most of the time, those three nutritious foods are enough to stop you from moving on.

Brush Up to Win

When you're finished with a meal or a planned snack, brush and floss your teeth. Not only will this boost your oral health, it will also help you stay away from food for about an hour.

Increase Your B Vitamins

When it comes to crushing your cravings, B6 is particularly important, but all B vitamins have a synergistic effect, so make sure you get a B-complex. B vitamins are responsible for converting carbohydrates into energy, and for the metabolism of proteins and fats. B vitamins are found mostly in green veggies and fruit like avocado. There are vitamin brands that make supplements that provide all of the B vitamins with a little extra B6 for therapeutic uses. Vitamin B6 is necessary for the production of serotonin in the brain, which has a direct relationship to emotional food cravings. When our serotonin is low, we crave more food. Choose foods that are high in B6—such as avocados, chicken, walnuts, and green peas—or try supplemental B6 totaling 100 mg/day for beneficial effects on cravings. Vitamin B6 also assists in relieving PMS symptoms by aiding in the metabolism of estrogens in the liver to reduce PMS cravings, and can minimize water retention through its diuretic action.

Increase Your Omegas

If you're craving fatty foods, try taking 2 teaspoons of sustainable fish oil (from anchovies, sardines, mackerel, or herring) or algae oil and wait 15 minutes. It will satisfy your cravings for fat while supporting a healthy metabolism and regulating hormones. This hormone regulation will help to control your cravings over time, especially those related to PMS.

Move to Heal

A Chinese proverb says, "Walk five hundred steps after every meal." It's good advice! By moving, you will start to burn some of the calories as fuel and take the pressure off the digestive tract. Daily exercise relieves stress and puts you in a positive mindset, which provides greater strength to pass on unhealthy fare. In the post-workout window of time, carbohydrates are stored as glycogen, so even if you do cave to temptation, it will have far less impact.

My personal trainer, Brent Bishop, is an incredible inspiration. He has countless free workouts on his website, www.iambishop.com.

For gentle stress-busting yoga tips, my yoga instructor, Shambunata, has wonderful techniques outlined on his blog, www.shambunata.com.

Dance Your Way to Fit

Personally, my favorite way to keep fit is to dance. Your lymph system does not have a pump, so the only way to get it moving to help reduce inflammation and balance your weight is to move! Dancing is sometimes referred to as Recovery Aerobics, which means that you get your heart rate up quickly during a song that moves you, and then, when you hit a mellow song, you allow yourself to rest and recover. What is your favorite happy dance song?

I have created a series of playlists on my website (www.juliedaniluk.com). From '60s classics to the latest hip-hop numbers, I've got you covered for tunes that will get you to your feet!

Let Go of Guilt

Next time you find yourself eating something that does not line up with your health goals, take one step back and two steps forward and, before you know it, you're dancing!

The most important thing you can do is to stop beating yourself up and let go of the guilt about your food choices or lack of motivation to get moving. When we replace negative self-talk with an empowering context, we have the strength and self-love to shift the "death drive" into a "life drive" and cultivate juicy vitality! I am sending you off with confidence, energy, and determination to begin this awesome journey.

PART TWO

THE SMTH PROGRAM

"If you want to go fast, go alone. If you want to go far, go together."

—AFRICAN PROVERB

CHAPTER 6

THE ANTI-INFLAMMATORY 5-STEP LIVE-IT PLAN

The best way to understand the SMTH plan is to travel back two hundred years to a time when a lot of food was fresh, natural, and whole. There was no frozen food, junk food, or preservative-filled processed food. Unlike fad diets, especially those that eliminate entire food groups (such as carbohydrates or fats), the SMTH program simply asks you to eat as your ancestors did. Instead of restricting or counting calories, the focus is on going back to fresh, wholesome, natural food that will satisfy your hunger as well as nurture and heal your body.

Research shows that results from slow change are often more permanent than those from quick and radical change. This is an organic program featuring five steps. I encourage you to take on the next step only when you are ready to do so. These steps will overlap and, in some cases, you may need a month, say, instead of two weeks to set yourself up powerfully before you continue.

We all know that it can be hard to resist bread, pasta, and cookies, so be sure to have the creative substitutions provided in this book close by as you embark on your journey of transformation. If you set yourself up for success by having delicious healing treats, you will crave the old, inflammatory options far less. The five steps set out in the SMTH plan are designed to gently ease you into a lifestyle that will become a new way of living for you.

As you look through steps one to five, you'll notice that this program is safe to follow for the rest of your life. Unlike a diet, which is totally unsustainable, the SMTH plan is a "live-it" that will continue to nourish you long after you have reached your goal weight. The great news is that the longer you stay on the "live-it," the more your palate will adapt. One day, you might find that a fruit-sweetened treat will satisfy an occasional craving even more than an inflammatory cookie. This is because you will begin to connect long-term happiness with reduced pain.

Note: I recommend that you get dietary clearance from a holistic medical doctor (M.D.) or a naturopathic doctor (N.D.) before you start the program. For faster results, you could consider having allergy and intolerance testing with a holistically minded allergist or naturopathic doctor at the beginning of the process. You may receive a false-negative test result if you do an IgG or IgE antibody test after being off the offending foods for the length of the test period because the antibodies go down substantially when avoiding your allergen. The information in the SMTH plan is groundbreaking, and may be outside the knowledge base of some practitioners. If you don't feel comfortable discussing this program with your practitioner, it truly is worth finding someone you'll feel more at ease with.

I also ask that you seek professional advice to get a proper diagnosis for whatever is causing your pain. Getting to the root cause of your pain is a crucial first step toward healing. It is very easy to go to the Internet and self-diagnose, but it is important to get a full medical examination, along with blood work, and to have your serious health questions answered.

STEP ONE—SETTING UP FOR SUCCESS

Duration: 2 to 4 weeks

Taking the time to prepare for a lifestyle shift will prevent you from being overwhelmed by new food choices as you go through the SMTH program. The worst things you can do are to stop eating or give up and go back to old habits because you're at a loss as to what you should or shouldn't eat.

I encourage you to keep a food journal, as it will help you see the progress and changes you have made over time. MyFitnessPal.com is an application available on your smartphone, your tablet, or online that makes keeping track of food choices a snap. As mentioned in chapter 5, sharing your food journal via e-mail with a willing friend will provide an extra bit of accountability and can make you think twice before reaching for poor food choices.

Many people find it difficult to go from eating fast food one day to cleansing with green juice the next. Our systems are designed to maintain a state of equilibrium, and some find that their bodies fight the rapid change. However you choose to start, the key is to psych yourself up. The first step is to remove the harmful foods from your kitchen cupboards. Refer to the charts on pages 91 to 94 to see which foods to keep, which to eliminate, and what you should replace these items with. An easy rule of thumb is to get rid of any items with ingredients that you can't pronounce or don't understand. Chances are, these ingredients were not found in the kitchens of your ancestors. Start by eliminating the foods that you don't mind giving up so that you don't feel like you're making unbearable sacrifices in the first days of the SMTH plan. You can take up to two weeks to cut these foods out of your diet.

Keep in mind that you don't necessarily have to get rid of everything. You may have many healthy foods that you can reintroduce after the eight-week plan. Put these foods out of sight on a top shelf for now. If it is a packaged, processed, or refined food that's included on the red list, then it's time to get rid of it to make room for healing choices.

If you feel uncomfortable throwing away food, consider donating unopened items to a food bank. While I don't expect you to give away your wine collection or toss the contents of your pantry, I encourage you to do what you need to do to avoid consuming these items in the first eight weeks of the plan. The "out of sight, out of mind" rule works for most people. Don't worry: we'll fill up the cupboard with tasty, nutritious alternatives—I promise! Everywhere you look there will be healthy, healing options!

WHAT TO TOSS

ITEM	WHY TOSS IT?
ARTIFICIAL ADDITIVES	Get rid of any boxed or processed food that contains additives and preservatives such as MSG, autolyzed yeast, hydrolyzed vegetable protein, BHA, BHT, food coloring (e.g., tartrazine, aka FD&C Yellow No. 5), glutamate, glutamic acid, sodium caseinate, and mineral oil. Many of these additives cause reactions, including headaches and skin rashes.
SUGAR AND ARTIFICIAL SWEETENERS	These include aspartame (also an ingredient in Canderel, Equal, EqualSweet, and NutraSweet), acesulfame-K, glucose, high-fructose corn syrup, lactose, maltose, mannitol, raw sugar, sorbitol, sucrose, and turbinado sugar. These can all dampen immune system function and feed candida and other unfavorable yeasts in your digestive system.
MOLDY OR OLD FRUIT	Grapes, melons, and berries harbor the highest amount of mold, so always keep them in the fridge. Candied fruit and prepared fruit juice are too concentrated with sugar, so it's best to eliminate them.
ALCOHOLIC BEVERAGES	Beer, spirits, and wine are laden with yeast and are hard on the liver, which is a key detoxifying organ in the body.
SOFT DRINKS AND CARBONATED BEVERAGES	Soft drinks can leach calcium out of bones. They are also full of refined sugar and synthetic additives such as color, preservatives, and artificial sweeteners.
COMMERCIALLY SMOKED AND CURED MEATS	Bacon, corned beef, hotdogs, and luncheon meat contain nitrates, which are carcinogenic. Processed meats are also very high in salt, which dehydrates the body and causes a mineral imbalance. Most processed meats are also sweetened with sugar.
WHITE VINEGAR AND VINEGAR-CONTAINING FOODS	Most refined vinegars are made from grains and can promote growth of candida yeast in the intestines or directly damage the intestines.

ITEM	WHY TOSS IT?
PROCESSED OIL PRODUCTS	Highly processed oils are often chemically extracted, exposed to high temperatures, bleached, and stripped of all valuable nutrients, such as vitamin E. Commercial mayonnaise, fractionated vegetable oils, hydrogenated or partially hydrogenated vegetable oils, margarine, modified vegetable oils, vegetable shortening, and salad dressings made with sugar and refined oils should be avoided. The processing that turns liquid oils into semi-solid fats creates trans fats, which increase inflammation.
CONVENTIONAL COFFEE AND REGULAR BLACK TEA	The caffeine in tea and coffee stresses the adrenal glands, leaving many people with anxiety, increased sensitivity to stress, and insomnia. Stress is the greatest enemy of the immune system.
YEAST	Avoid baker's yeast, brewer's yeast, or other foods prepared with active yeast (i.e., bread and pastries). If you have a candida infection or yeast sensitivity, you may need to avoid nutritional yeast as well.
DAIRY	Eliminate butter, cheese (the worst kinds are moldy cheeses, such as blue cheese, and soft varieties, such as Brie), ice cream, milk, and yogurt. If you're lactose intolerant or allergic to casein, dairy can cause inflammation.
GLUTEN GRAINS	Avoid all barley, kamut, oats, rye, spelt, and wheat, as well as the flour made from these grains. This includes prepared foods such as bread, cereals, candy, malt, and pasta. Gluten is one of the proteins found in some grass grains that can be very difficult to digest and can cause many sensitivity symptoms, such as back and joint pain, dark circles under the eyes, weight gain, IBS, and skin disorders. Oats must be tested to ensure they're tolerated, as they may contain gluten.
PEANUTS AND RANCID NUTS OR SEEDS	Peanuts grow underground and are often high in mold. They can be potential allergens because mold aflatoxins are harmful to the liver and immune system. Rancid nuts and seeds contain damaged oils that promote inflammation.
CORN	Corn is often genetically modified and a potential allergen. Avoid cereal, corn bread, corn chips, crackers, and other snack foods made from corn; dextrose-sweetened foods; and sweetened drinks made with high-fructose corn syrup.

ITEM	WHY TOSS IT?
NIGHTSHADE-FAMILY VEGETABLES	Eggplants, green peppers (including jalapeño), potatoes, and tobacco may trigger inflammation because they contain alkaloids that can affect nerve-muscle function, digestion, and joint flexibility. Cayenne has pain-reducing qualities but can trigger irritable bowel and irritate the stomach, so it is best avoided. Alkaloids are especially high in the nightshade leaves, unripe fruit such as green peppers and green tomatoes, and older potatoes. Red peppers (including paprika), tomatillos, and tomatoes contain less of the irritating alkaloids if they are fully ripened. To ensure your pain is not caused by nightshades, avoid them for one month. Then, enjoy ripe red peppers and vine-ripened tomatoes as a test, and chart if you have increased inflammation. Tobacco is also a nightshade plant, so smokers may be more susceptible to a sensitivity. Goji berries are part of the nightshade family and may irritate people who are sensitive to alkaloids.
PROCESSED SOY PRODUCTS	Processed soy foods, such as soy milk and meat substitutes (including soy burgers, cheese, ice cream, mayonnaise, and yogurt) and textured vegetable protein (TVP), promote inflammation in people who are sensitive or allergic to soy.

WHAT TO KEEP OR BUY

ITEM	WHY KEEP OR BUY IT?
NATURAL SWEETENERS	Coconut syrup, honey (raw varieties for raw dishes and unpasteurized liquid forms for cooked dishes), tree sap syrups (e.g., birch, maple, etc.), and stevia (liquid extract or whole leaf powder) are some suitable sweeteners to help you transition into a sugar-free lifestyle.
VARIETY OF HEALTHY OILS	Buy unrefined, cold-pressed oils in glass jars. For low-moderate temperature cooking, use avocado, coconut, extra-virgin olive, camelina, or sesame seed oils. For raw dressings and cool dishes, use omega-3-rich oils cold-pressed from algae, fish, seeds (chia, flax, hemp, perilla, pumpkin, and sacha inchi), and walnuts.
FRESH VEGETABLES	Focus 50 percent of your diet on bright colors and dark green vegetables (aim for 7 to 10 servings a day). Eat as many low-starch greens as possible, such as broccoli, cabbage, celery, celery root, chard, dandelion, fresh herbs, kale, radish, snap pea, and zucchini. Choose one to two servings of beetroot, carrot, Jerusalem artichoke (also called sunchoke), sweet potato, winter squashes, and yam as substitutes for white potatoes on workout days when you can utilize the higher levels of carbohydrates as fuel. If you have IBS or IBD, it's best to cook vegetables until they're tender.

ITEM	WHY KEEP OR BUY IT?
DAIRY ALTERNATIVES	Use unsweetened nut (almond, cashew) milk, coconut beverage (same fat as 2% milk), seed milk (hemp, sesame), and small amounts of coconut milk (same fat percentage as table cream).
GLUTEN-FREE GRAINS	Amaranth, buckwheat, Job's tears, millet, quinoa, sorghum, teff, whole rice (black, brown, red, etc.), and wild rice are safe gluten-free seeds and grains. Due to their high carbohydrate content, you may wish to minimize your grain portion a few days a week in order to speed up results of the SMTH program. Rotate a different grain each workout day to avoid developing an allergy. Note: Some people are sensitive to all grains, so keep track of how you feel during testing.
MEAT AND FISH	Consume free-range or organic chicken, eco-friendly fish (anchovy, Arctic char, sardine, spring trout, and wild line-caught Pacific salmon), emu, lamb, turkey, and wild game (venison, bison, elk).
NUTS AND SEEDS	Eat fresh almonds, Brazil nuts, hazelnuts, macadamias, sancha inchi, and walnuts, as well as chia, flax, hemp, pumpkin, sesame, and sunflower seeds. Nut and seed butters (raw is healthier than toasted) are also great choices.
BEANS AND LEGUMES	Adzuki, black, lima, mung, navy, and turtle beans, as well as lentils and peas, are good sources of protein and fiber. Organic soy can be eaten safely as edamame (young soybeans) or as a fermented food (e.g., miso, natto, wheat-free tamari sauce, and tempeh). People with digestive issues may find garbanzo (chickpea) and red and white kidney beans difficult to digest. Some people with IBS and IBD must avoid all beans and legumes because they are not able to digest them.
SALAD DRESSING ALTERNATIVES	Lemon and lime juices make good substitutes for white vinegar. Unpasteurized apple cider vinegar and coconut vinegar sold in glass bottles have health-promoting qualities and can be used if yeast isn't a serious concern. Unrefined organic brown rice, fruit, red wine, and umeboshi plum vinegars contain antioxidants. Avoid conventional balsamic vinegar because it often contains added sugar. Enjoy lots of fresh garlic for its antifungal qualities. Experiment with herbs and spices for adding flavor.
ORGANIC COFFEE AND GREEN OR HERBAL TEA	Freshly roasted and ground organic coffee may be helpful around workouts to increase insulin sensitivity and improve performance. Check out www.risecafe.ca for more details. Avoid overuse that may cause nervousness and stop drinking by 2 p.m. to assure a good night's sleep. Green tea and herbal tea (e.g., honey-bush) have beneficial qualities for weight loss. Avoid green tea if you have a thyroid imbalance or osteoporosis, due to high fluoride content. An extract of green tea called EGCG (epigallocatechin gallate) may be helpful for people who cannot tolerate whole leaf tea (the fluoride is removed).

Now that you've taken the time to master Step One—replacing some of your former unhealthy food choices with better alternatives—it's ready to move on to Step Two.

STEP TWO—ELIMINATING PAIN TRIGGERS AND CRUSHING CRAVINGS

Duration: 2 weeks

Step Two provides you with a schedule for eliminating the foods that trigger pain, inflammation, and cravings. You will be cutting out all refined food (white sugar, white flour, deep-fried food, and harmful fats). This step is crucial to the success of the program; once you have completed it, your cravings for harmful, processed foods will be a thing of the past, and your blood sugar will be in balance. Ideally, this phase should be completed over a two-week period, but feel free to give yourself more time if necessary.

Most refined foods make up for their lack of fiber and nutrients with extra sugar. Did you know that the average person in North America eats his or her weight in sugar a year? The US Department of Agriculture states that this is equivalent to consuming 156 pounds of high-fructose corn syrup and white sugar in the form of breakfast cereals, ketchup, soft drinks, and cookies.

Note: If you have already stocked your pantry and fridge with healthy substitutions and would like to speed up your weight-loss efforts, feel free to eliminate the entire list of foods below on Day 1. But remember to avoid the "diet mentality" and maintain a "live-it" attitude. Be wary of harsh caloric restriction and deprivation because this tends to backfire as your mind rebels. Listen to your body and let it guide you. There is no failure with a "live-it." We all have rough days; consider them just a step back in the dance. Tomorrow you can take two steps forward, and soon enough you will be dancing yourself toward a youthful, revitalized body.

ELIMINATION SCHEDULE

DAYS 1–5	DAYS 6–9	DAYS 10–14
Cut out fried foods, margarine, vegetable shortening, and hydrogenated or partially hydrogenated vegetable oils. Avoid processed foods that contain food coloring and preservatives. Cut out refined sugar and other sweeteners, including aspartame and related sweeteners, brown sugar, cane juice, cane sugar, fructose, glucose, lactose, malt, maltose, mannitol, raw sugar, sorbitol, Sucanat, sucrose, Sweet'N Low, turbinado sugar, yellow sugar, and candy.	Cut out corn and corn products such as breads, cereals, chips, crackers, muffins, nachos, tacos, tortillas, and other snack foods; avoid corn-based ingredients such as foods and drinks sweetened with dextrose or high-fructose corn syrup, or soups and sauces containing cornstarch. Cut out wheat products such as couscous, wheat bread, pasta, and prepared cereals. Eliminate butter, cheese, ice cream, milk, and yogurt. Eliminate alcoholic beverages, including beer, all hard liquors, and wine.	Temporarily avoid foods that are healthy but potential allergy/inflammation triggers to figure out whether or not you're sensitive to them. First, eliminate the nightshade-family plants (eggplant, peppers, potato, and conventional tomatoes), then peanuts, and then the rest of the gluten grains. If you suffer from chronic pain, you may also need to cut out red peppers and organic tomatoes until after 4–8 weeks to test if you suffer from a nightshade sensitivity. You'll also have to avoid bananas and oranges because they're common allergens.

To begin making substitutes for refined products, eat the foods you added to your cupboard in Step One and increase your daily servings of fruits and vegetables.

Aim for one to two fruits and 7 to 10 vegetable servings a day. If that sounds like a lot, keep this in mind: one large carrot is equal to one serving of vegetables. If you have one carrot, ½ cup of sugar snap peas, and a 2-cup bowl of baby spinach, you are already up to four servings.

As you continue with this process of saying good-bye to unhealthy foods, it is helpful to assess and acknowledge the emotional attachment you may have with particular foods you crave. Keep in mind that changing your eating habits can be harder than quitting smoking. With harmful addictions like smoking, you can abstain completely and do it for life. Addiction to food is a little more complicated because you still have to eat! Temptation is always there, and it is much harder to stay on track. Food is a comfort, and it can be a close friend if nothing else is working. I remember when I had to say good-bye to my favorite chocolate bar because it was full of sugar and dairy that was causing me pain. I wrote down a resolution that I was going to stop eating it for an entire year. I shared the promise with my husband and talked about how painful it was to let go of an old friend that nursed me through breakups and stressful exams. By the time I reached the one-year mark, I had stopped looking back. I had found a new raw cocoa bar sweetened with coconut nectar that made me happy in the moment (aka little fun) and pain-free long term (aka big fun)!

Use the recipes in this book to experiment with alternatives and become creative with your food. To support your substitutions, check out the health swap section on page 127. Before you know it, these healthier slimming recipes will become your new family favorites.

Note: It is crucial to eliminate all dairy in the first phase of the SMTH plan. This allows you to determine whether or not you are allergic to or intolerant of it. Fresh leafy greens, fish, sea vegetables, nuts, and seeds are all excellent sources of calcium, so don't be concerned about the lack of dietary calcium from dairy sources during these eight weeks.

Step Two is all about staying committed to the plan physically and emotionally each and every day. For the next eight weeks, use the recipes in this book to eat five times a day: three meals and two snacks. Take one day of the week and prepare your meals and snacks in advance and throw them in the freezer. Having something ready for you when you need it can really help to keep you on track and free up time for friends and family. Make sure your grocery list is always consistent with the SMTH plan. Check out the Slimming Anti-inflammatory "Live-It" Food Chart on page 105. Print a copy and post it on your fridge for quick reference.

Another tip to save time and help keep you on track is to designate a shelf in your cupboards to healing snacks so you know where to look for a quick bite. Always carry a snack with you and create a secret stash in your desk at work or the glove box of your car. This simple practice will help keep your blood sugar level stable and keep you from resorting to fast food, coffee shops, and/or vending machines.

STEP THREE—TURBO-CHARGE YOUR PROGRAM WITH SUPERFOODS

Duration: 8 weeks

Once you have adjusted to your new eating habits and the fog of food allergies and sensitivities has lifted, adding more superfoods to your "live-it" will boost your weight-loss efforts.

You will find a rainbow of nutrients in fruits and vegetables. Beyond being a feast for the eyes, each color brings with it its own anti-inflammatory power.

- Foods high in vitamin A, like carrots, squash, and yams, are most often yellow or orange. They help to repair the skin and digestive lining.
- Foods high in vitamin B tend to be green: think asparagus, chard, spinach, and green beans. These foods work to nourish the nervous system.
- Red foods like berries and red cabbage are high in vitamin C and are critical for the production of collagen, the protein we use to make skin, joints, tendons, and ligaments.
- The foods that have the highest number of antioxidants are blue and purple, such as blackberries, blueberries, concord grapes, purple cabbage, and figs.

Superfoods are vibrant, nutritionally dense foods that offer tremendous healing potential. They are packed with protein, vitamins, minerals, enzymes, antioxidants, healthy fats and oils, essential fatty and amino acids, and phyto-nutrients. See chapter 4 for a list of their benefits and try to include several superfoods in your meal plan every day.

STEP FOUR—FOOD REINTRODUCTION CHALLENGE

Duration: 12 weeks

Step Four is an important part of the program. This is where we uncover any food allergies, sensitivities, and intolerances you might have. We do this by reintroducing the key allergenic foods you have been avoiding for the past three months into your diet one at a time. This will allow you to figure out which foods, if any, make you feel unwell. This can be a difficult step for some people because it is so easy to fall back into old habits.

Note: Be cautious when reintroducing foods into your diet. As you learned in chapter 2, exposing your body to allergens can be very destructive, resulting in cell and tissue damage. It is important to gradually remove these allergens and chemical-laden processed foods from your diet so that you give your body time to detoxify and repair tissues. Reintroducing foods that may be a problem for you quickly and in large quantities will arrest the healing process and overburden the detoxifying organs.

Always start by reintroducing the healthiest foods. If you suffer from chronic pain and have cut out peppers and tomatoes, this is the best time to reintroduce them to find out if you are sensitive to nightshade alkaloids. If you find that you can tolerate cooked tomatoes, your food selection will expand widely, as many world cuisines use tomatoes in their dishes. Next, introduce bananas; a week later, try oranges. Both of these fruits are full of nutrients and add great variety to your diet if you tolerate them. Bananas are very versatile and can be used to thicken and sweeten shakes and baked dishes.

It's important for you to stay committed to Step Four for the full 12 weeks. It can take up to 72 hours for an intolerance reaction to show up, and you will need at least three days between separate food tests to give your immune system a rest. Be patient and remember that you are getting to know your body better so that you can keep it in good working order for the rest of your life. The following schedule is the classic guide recommended by health practitioners for reintroducing foods. What you notice is that there is a "tapering down" of the time between tests. After the first test, wait 3 full days. If there is a noticeable reaction, stop eating the food for at least 8 weeks, then test again. If no reaction is noticed, do a second test, wait 2 full days. As before, if there is a reaction, wait at least 8 weeks to test again. If no reaction, do a third test. At this point, if no reaction is noticed, the food can be added into your healing menu, and you can move on to the next test food.

FOOD TESTING GUIDE

TYPE OF FOOD	WHEN TO REINTRODUCE	SYMPTOMS TO WATCH OUT FOR
Tomatoes (cooked, then raw)	After 8 weeks (you may test after 4 weeks if you do not suffer from chronic pain or IBS/IBD)	Rashes, joint and stomach pain
Peppers	After 9.5 weeks (you may test after 5.5 weeks if you do not suffer from chronic pain or IBS/IBD)	Hives, rashes, stomach pain
Tangerine/orange/grapefruit	After 11 weeks	Rashes, joint and stomach pain
Banana (ripe)	After 12.5 weeks	Hives, bowel problems
Shellfish (eco-harvested)	After 14 weeks	Sinus problems, dark circles under eyes
Goat yogurt and cheese	After 15.5 weeks	Sinus problems, dark circles under eyes
Ghee (clarified cow butter)	After 17 weeks	Blackheads
Sheep yogurt and cheese	After 18.5 weeks	Throat itchiness, rashes
Oats and other gluten grains (barley and rye)	After 20 weeks	Joint pain, fatigue, brain fog, bloating, weight gain, depression, mental illness, anxiety
White potatoes	After 21.5 weeks	Joint pain, fatigue, brain fog, bloating, weight gain

FOOD REINTRODUCTION TESTING SCHEDULE

DAY 1	DAY 2	DAY 3	DAY 4	DAY 5	DAY 6	DAY 7	DAY 8	DAY 9
Eat three portions* of 1 test food.	Avoid test food.	Avoid test food.	Avoid test food.	Eat three portions* of 1 test food.	Avoid test food.	Avoid test food.	Eat three portions* of 1 test food.	If no negative reaction, test next food.

* For portion sizes, see Food-Serving Guide on page 126.

Important Note: After 14 weeks, you may want to jump back to your old favorites. Wheat, dairy, and potatoes are among the most inflammatory food choices and are best avoided for long-term health. Studies have shown that milk and dairy foods from small animals such as sheep or goats are easier to digest than cow's milk and can be healing to the digestive tract. People with European or East Indian heritage may tolerate small amounts of cultured dairy products and ghee. High-fat cheese and milk from cows are less ideal because they are difficult to digest and contain certain fats that can trigger inflammation.

An anti-inflammatory diet is free of all wheat gluten. If you feel you must reintroduce gluten grains, I suggest you begin with oats, as they are technically free of wheat gluten as long as they are processed in a separate gluten-free facility. Next, introduce barley and then rye, as they're also relatively low in gluten. Spelt and kamut are close relatives to wheat and contain high amounts of gluten. To keep your joints mobile and your inflammation down, I recommend that you completely eliminate gluten for life.

With the reintroduction of certain foods, you might notice some physical changes, such as congestion, itchiness, swollen tongue, irritability, bloating, dark circles under your eyes, fatigue, hives, or an infection in your ears, nose, or throat. These are typical signs of an allergic reaction to food. These are the answers you have been looking for! Keep in mind that it's possible to experience almost any symptom with any allergen. The reaction you experience will depend on your body, the food you're allergic to and how strongly your body reacts to the allergen. Use a food journal to keep track of what you eat, and record any symptoms that are out of the ordinary. Stop eating a food once you've confirmed that you're sensitive or allergic to it and keep it on your list of foods to avoid for three to six months; then test it again.

When testing these foods be careful not to confuse euphoria and adrenaline with food tolerance. Your desire to have these foods back in your diet can cloud your judgment, and so can your body's physiological reaction to them. We often crave the foods that we are unable to tolerate; these foods can mask our symptoms and make us feel better in the short term. There are many theories on this, but some researchers have found that we can become addicted to certain chemical messengers, like histamine and cortisol, that the immune cells produce when we are exposed to allergens. It is well known that allergens can cause symptoms such as a rash or itchy eyes. Not many people realize that the chemical messengers that are secreted in an allergic reaction can also have a calming, sedative effect on the body. These feelings of bliss increase our desire to reach for that food again.

STEP FIVE—THE LIVE-IT . . . BODY, MIND, AND SPIRIT
A lifetime

Welcome to the first day of the rest of your life. In Step Five you're "living it" and making the SMTH plan a natural part of each and every day. I encourage you to continue with your food journaling, as it will help you see the progress and changes you have made over time. Small changes like substituting kale chips for potato chips can add up and have a profound impact on your overall health. If you ever feel temptation, remember this mantra, "My will is greater than my will not." Share your story with the people in your life. Let them know why you are doing the SMTH plan and how it has helped you. Encouraging the people you love to be a part of your journey to health and healing will strengthen your commitment to this new lifestyle and benefit everyone, including you!

CHAPTER 7

A FOCUS ON FOODS: BUILDING A SLIMMING KITCHEN

As I stated right at the start, the way we obtain our "vitality weight" is to get clear on what foods are driving or healing the inflammatory conditions that make our bodies lose or gain weight. In this chapter, I'm going to give you powerful guidelines that will assist you in achieving your natural weight balance.

First up is the SMTH food pyramid, which provides a concise one-page reference of healing foods. Next is the "green light, yellow light, red light" table, followed by a sample seven-day menu plan to get you started on using the healing recipes in this book. Finally, there's a list of healthy food swaps to give you loads of ideas for slimming anti-inflammatory eating day to day.

THE ANTI-INFLAMMATORY FOOD PYRAMID

HEALTHY TREATS
Servings: Occasional

SUPPLEMENTS
Servings: Daily

PROTEIN
Total Servings: 3–4 per day;
eat the following sources to meet
your protein dietary needs:

MEAT & EGGS
Servings: 0–2 per day

FISH
Servings: 2–6 per week

NUTS & SEEDS
(both are sources of protein and fat)
Servings: 1–3 per day

BEANS & LEGUMES
(both are sources of carbohydrate and protein)
Servings: 0–3 per day

**GREEN OR
HERBAL TEA**
Servings: 2–4 cups per day

**HEALTHY
FATS & OILS**
Servings: 3–5 per day

**NON-GLUTEN
GRAINS**
Servings: 0–2 per day

FRUITS
Servings: 0–3 per day

VEGETABLES
(includes sea vegetables)
Servings: 7–10 per day

**HEALTHY
HERBS & SPICES**
Servings: Use generously

WATER
Servings: 6–12 per day

For a six-page explanation of the slimming anti-inflammatory food pyramid, check out www.juliedaniluk.com.

THE ANTI-INFLAMMATORY "LIVE-IT" FOOD CHART

The best way to make the "live-it" food plan easy for everyone to adopt and tailor to individual needs and preferences is to classify foods into three categories.

- Green light: These foods are generally healing and, unless you have an allergy or sensitivity to them, they can be eaten freely.
- Yellow light: These foods are more likely than green-light foods to cause allergic reactions, especially in people who tend to suffer from multiple sensitivities or inflammatory conditions. One of the easiest ways to determine whether these foods are healing or hurting you is to eliminate them completely from your diet for eight weeks. Then, slowly reintroduce them one at a time to assess how your body reacts.
- Red light: This category includes refined and processed foods or additives that are highly inflammatory and should be eliminated from your diet completely and permanently. Other red-light foods include common allergens that can worsen inflammatory or sensitive conditions. These foods should be avoided for as long as possible to allow the body to heal from chronic inflammation.

Note: Follow the green light (healing) food "what to do" guidelines to replace red light "hurting" foods.

VEGETABLES

GREEN LIGHT (HEALING)

Most vegetables reduce inflammation and minimize fat storage. Artichokes, celery, cucumber, cruciferous vegetables (e.g., arugula, bok choy, broccoli, cabbage, collard, dandelion, kale, and rapini), leafy greens, root vegetables, and squashes are excellent options.

Sea vegetables (e.g., dulse, nori, and wakame) increase thyroid function and improve metabolism, and are one of the richest sources of minerals, vitamins, essential fats, and phytonutrients.

WHAT TO DO

Enjoy ripe, organic vegetables as fresh and whole as possible: raw, steamed, boiled, broiled, baked, or sautéed.

Eat different-colored vegetables at every meal. Colors represent various nutrients and antioxidants (e.g., beta-carotene in orange yams).

People who suffer from IBD may be sensitive to the high-fiber content of sea vegetables. Eat dried (flaked or powdered) sea vegetables in moderation to avoid intestinal inflammation.

FRUITS

GREEN LIGHT (HEALING)

Most fruits are healing because they're high in minerals, vitamins, enzymes, antioxidants, and fiber. Fruit grown in the northern hemisphere is lower in sugar than tropical fruit and best for people who want to reduce an insulin response and lose weight.

WHAT TO DO

Eat organic, fresh, cooked, and raw fruit. Choose fruits low in sugar (e.g., apple, apricot, avocado, berries, cherry, fig, passion fruit, peach, pear, plum, pomegranate, and prune).

Pineapple and papaya are high in the anti-inflammatory enzymes bromelain and papain, respectively.

Lemon and lime support digestion, boost liver detoxification, and are natural antihistamines.

YELLOW LIGHT (CAUTION)

Nightshade vegetables (eggplant, hot and sweet peppers, white potato, and tomato) can be inflammatory because they contain certain alkaloids that can affect nerve-muscle function, digestion, and joint flexibility in animals and humans.

Nightshade alkaloids are especially high in green tomatoes and older potatoes.

Corn is a common allergen and is best avoided until you know that you don't react to it.

WHAT TO DO

Avoid nightshade vegetables for eight weeks if you suffer from pain. Reintroduce them one at a time to see if you're sensitive to them.

Substitute celery root, sweet potato, taro, or sunchokes for white potato. These substitutes aren't members of the nightshade family and contain more fiber than white potatoes. Substitute whole grains like Job's tears for corn.

Avoid popcorn if you have digestive issues. Popped amaranth and quinoa are good substitutes.

RED LIGHT (HURTING)

Steer clear of all processed and fried vegetables, such as corn chips, corn nuts, French fries, fried eggplant, potato chips, and tempura.

Avoid green, old, raw, or sprouted potatoes, as these are especially high in the inflammatory alkaloid solanine.

Avoid all genetically modified (GM) vegetables (e.g., corn, potato, sugar beet, and zucchini).

Avoid tomato ketchup that contains high amounts of sugar and/or corn syrup.

YELLOW LIGHT (CAUTION)

Bananas and oranges are commonly over-consumed and may cause irritation for people who are sensitive to them.

Goji berries are part of the nightshade family. IBD patients should use caution when eating fruits that contain many small seeds, such as berries and figs.

If you're prone to food-induced hives, some fruits (e.g., avocado, banana, fig, and red plum) can trigger a reaction.

WHAT TO DO

Rotate (do not eat the same choice every day) the use of banana and oranges to minimize potential allergies.

If you are sensitive to nightshades, avoid goji berries.

If you have IBD, cook fruit to soften the fiber and strain out small seeds that may irritate inflamed intestines.

Some fruits contain biogenic amines that can trigger hives. If you suffer from hives, journal your reactions and avoid all offending fruits.

RED LIGHT (HURTING)

Avoid all GM fruits, such as papaya from China and Hawaii.

Avoid canned fruit, especially those preserved in syrup, as well as fruit chutneys, jams, jellies, and sauces made with refined sugar.

Eat dried tropical fruits such as mangos and bananas in moderation, as they contain concentrated sugar.

GRAINS AND BEANS

GREEN LIGHT (HEALING)	WHAT TO DO
Choose gluten-free grains and pseudo-grains[1] such as amaranth, buckwheat, kasha, Job's tears, millet, quinoa, whole rice, sorghum, teff, and wild rice. Organic beans/legumes are healthy choices unless you have an allergy or sensitivity.	Eat whole, well-cooked grains. Substitute other grains for wheat. Try teff or quinoa porridge and wild rice pilaf. Whole-grain gluten-free crackers and pasta made from these grains are also suitable but should be eaten in moderation. Try lentil soup, mung bean curry, adzuki bean salad, and bean dips. Eat legumes well cooked, moist, and warm to increase digestibility and minimize bloating and gas.

FISH AND SHELLFISH

GREEN LIGHT (HEALING)	WHAT TO DO
Select sustainably caught fresh or frozen fish (check the www.seachoice.org fish list to help you make an informed choice).	Eat small fish (which are shorter-lived and lower on the food chain than large species) to minimize exposure to heavy metals. Choose anchovies, butterfish, herring, mackerel, sablefish, sardine, trout, or wild Pacific salmon as sources of anti-inflammatory omega-3 fats. Edible jellyfish are an excellent and ecologically sustainable source of protein.

1. A pseudo-grain or pseudo-cereal is a seed that's derived from a plant that isn't a true cereal grass. Pseudo-grains and pseudo-cereals are gluten free. Unlike other seeds, pseudo-grains require cooking.

YELLOW LIGHT (CAUTION)	WHAT TO DO	RED LIGHT (HURTING)
Gluten grains (barley, kamut, oats, rye, and spelt) may cause inflammation, even in people who may not be aware of their sensitivity to gluten.[2]	Avoid eating all gluten grains. After 12 weeks, test them one at a time and watch for signs of allergy or intolerance.	Wheat is a common allergen. Avoid this grain as much as possible.
Grains and legumes may be unsuitable for some IBD patients.	Avoid all grains and legumes if you have grain- or legume-sensitive IBD.	Avoid all processed and refined grains, flour, and commercially baked foods.
It's best to rotate soybeans in your diet to avoid having an allergic reaction or developing a soy allergy.	Eat only organic (non-GM) soy if you have no sensitivity or allergy to it. Choose steamed young soybeans (edamame) or fermented soy foods such as miso, natto, tempeh, and wheat-free tamari sauce.	Soybeans are so widely used in foods, beverages, and supplements that many people have developed soy allergies. Eating processed soy products will increase your risk of an allergic reaction.
		Avoid GM soy and processed soy products such as soy cheese, soy burgers, and texturized vegetable protein (TVP).

109

YELLOW LIGHT (CAUTION)	WHAT TO DO	RED LIGHT (HURTING)
Canned fish is heated at extremely high temperatures for sterilization and may contain plastic toxins that leach out of the can.	When fresh or frozen fish isn't available, consider sustainable varieties that are water-packed in a BPA-free can.	Large fish such as shark, tuna, and orange roughy are unsustainable and contain higher levels of contaminants such as mercury.
Clams, crab, lobster, mussels, oysters, and shrimp are common allergens and may contribute to inflammation.	Crustaceans (shrimp, lobster, crab) cause the greatest number of allergic reactions. Many shellfish-sensitive people can tolerate mollusks (scallops, oysters, clams, and mussels). Consider avoiding for 8 to 12 weeks and then test one species at a time.	Mercury and other toxins can affect your nervous and immune systems and increase inflammation.
Some farmed fish, such as catfish and tilapia, contain high levels of the pro-inflammatory fat arachidonic acid.		

2. In the United States, 1 in every 133 people has celiac disease, which causes a powerful allergic reaction to gluten.

MEAT AND POULTRY

GREEN LIGHT (HEALING)	WHAT TO DO
Turkey, bison, rabbit, emu, deer, elk, duck, quail, goat, moose, and sheep.	Ensure meat is from free-range or organically raised and ethically treated animals. Choose lean cuts to reduce inflammatory fats.

DAIRY AND EGGS

GREEN LIGHT (HEALING)	WHAT TO DO
Most plant-based milks make suitable dairy substitutes. These are most often fortified with vitamins and minerals and can be nutritious additions to a vegan diet. Organic eggs are an excellent source of lecithin, protein, B vitamins, and minerals such as the antioxidant selenium.	Try drinking almond, coconut, hemp seed, or sesame seed milk. Choose unsweetened varieties whenever possible or make your own. For a cream substitute, use diluted coconut milk in moderation. Poultry fed on omega-3–rich seeds will produce eggs high in these anti-inflammatory fats. To avoid developing an allergy to chicken eggs, rotate the type of egg you eat. Try eggs from organically fed and hormone-free duck, emu, ostrich, pheasant, and quail.

YELLOW LIGHT (CAUTION)	WHAT TO DO	RED LIGHT (HURTING)
Eat grass-fed beef, grass-fed pork, and naturally raised chicken in rotation to avoid overexposure.	Reduce beef, chicken, and pork because these are over-consumed potential allergens and because many cuts are high in inflammatory arachidonic acid.	Avoid conventional beef, chicken and pork (especially bacon) because they contain antibiotics and hormone residues. Avoid processed, smoked and deli meats as they usually contain carcinogenic nitrate preservatives.

YELLOW LIGHT (CAUTION)	WHAT TO DO	RED LIGHT (HURTING)
Dairy is a common allergen. Milk fermented with probiotics can be very nutritious and can reduce your chances of experiencing a reaction. Goat and sheep milks are easier to digest than cow's milk. Conventional eggs are a common allergen.	After avoiding dairy for 8 to 12 weeks, reintroduce organic goat or sheep yogurts to see if you can tolerate them. Then try organic cow yogurt in moderation. When reintroducing cheese, choose varieties that are low in lactose (old cheddar, Parmigiano-Reggiano, and frugal) and are mold free (cottage cheese and quark). Limit portion size, as even these varieties are potentially inflammatory. Stick with organic eggs. Eat them only a few times a week and monitor your reactions.	Conventional dairy can be a source of xenoestrogens, antibiotics, and synthetic growth hormones.[3] Avoid processed dairy, such as ice cream that's high in saturated or trans fats and loaded with refined sugar, artificial flavors, and artificial colors.[4] Moldy cheeses (blue, Brie, camembert, and Gorgonzola) may contain high amounts of mold toxins that could elicit inflammatory reactions. Steer clear of these cheeses, especially if you have sensitivity to yeasts and molds.

3. Recombinant bovine growth hormone (rBGH) isn't legally approved for use in the Canadian dairy industry. However, it's commonly injected into conventional dairy cows in the United States. Antibiotics are administered to conventionally raised cows in both Canada and the United States.

4. Cow's milk naturally contains small amounts of trans fats. However, many dairy products, such as ice cream, may contain additional processed oils such as hydrogenated fats, which increase the amount of trans fats present in the final product.

SEASONINGS

GREEN LIGHT (HEALING)

Almost all fresh herbs and spices are safe and anti-inflammatory, provided you don't have an allergy to them.

WHAT TO DO

Use anti-inflammatory seasonings generously, including anise, basil, bay leaf, caraway, cardamom, celery seed, cilantro, cinnamon, clove, coriander, cumin seed, dill, fennel, fenugreek, garlic, ginger, marjoram, mustard seed, oregano, nutmeg, parsley, rosemary, sage, savory, star anise, thyme, and turmeric.

SEEDS AND NUTS

GREEN LIGHT (HEALING)

Chia, flax, hemp, and perilla seeds are rich sources of omega-3 fats. Other anti-inflammatory seeds include pumpkin, sesame, and sunflower.

Almond, Brazil nut, chestnut, filbert/hazelnut, macadamia nut, pecan, pine nut, and walnut are nutritious sources of protein and healthy fats, such as essential fats and vitamin E. All tree nuts are potential allergens, so be mindful to rotate all nuts to avoid overexposure.

WHAT TO DO

Freshly grind chia, flax, or perilla seeds in a small grinder or food processor to maximize the freshness of the polyunsaturated fats and other vitamins. If you must store seeds, keep them in glass jars in the freezer. Eat seeds and nuts raw and as fresh as possible to protect unsaturated oils and nutrients.

Soak nuts in water overnight to make them more digestible.

YELLOW LIGHT (CAUTION)

Spicy and pungent peppers such as cayenne, chili, jalapeño, paprika, and scotch bonnets are nightshade plants and therefore contain alkaloids that may cause intestinal inflammation or exacerbate arthritis and heartburn/acid reflux.

Black and white peppercorns may irritate the intestinal lining.

WHAT TO DO

Season your food with cayenne-free curry spice blends for a flavor kick. Pungent spices such as clove, garlic, ginger, mustard, and turmeric are anti-inflammatory.

Substitute black pepper with an anti-inflammatory blend of finely ground papaya and onion seeds.

RED LIGHT (HURTING)

Monosodium glutamate (MSG) is an excitatory neurotoxin that can cause the death of nerve cells, including brain cells. People may experience side effects such as headaches and irritability from exposure to MSG.[5] Artificial preservatives, sweeteners, colors, and flavoring may cause sensitivity reactions and are toxic to the body. Avoid all artificial flavoring and other additives (including preservatives).

113

YELLOW LIGHT (CAUTION)

Some whole seeds may irritate inflamed or sensitive intestines.

Cashews and pistachios are healthy nuts when consumed fresh. However, they're easily contaminated with mold, especially when stored for long periods.

WHAT TO DO

Soak and chew seeds thoroughly before swallowing. Smooth seed butters, pastes, and milks are less likely to cause intestinal discomfort.

Minimize your intake of cashews and pistachios if sensitive to mold.

Buy nuts as fresh as possible and store them in the fridge or freezer.

RED LIGHT (HURTING)

If you have IBD and/or diverticulitis, whole seeds may irritate inflamed intestines.

Avoid nuts that are pre-chopped, over-roasted, fried, and/or seasoned with sugary glazes or commercial oil and salt. Seeds and nuts that are rancid and/or heated at high temperatures contain damaged (peroxidized) oils.

Peanuts are often contaminated with mold and should be avoided. Peanut butter made with hydrogenated oil is highly inflammatory.[6]

5. Avoid isolated and concentrated sources of MSG such as autolyzed yeast extract, glutamate, glutamic acid, sodium caseinate, and hydrolyzed vegetable protein. Sources include conventional bouillon cubes and powder, buffet and fast foods, flavoring (in chips, crackers, popcorn, and snack foods), packaged foods, prepared sauces and soups, restaurant food, and seasonings. Carefully check ingredient labels.
6. Peanuts are technically legumes. They're a type of groundnut and are rich in nutrients, including the powerful antioxidant resveratrol. Unfortunately, an increasing number of people have profound allergies to peanuts and/or to the toxic mold that commonly contaminates this food.

OILS AND FATS

GREEN LIGHT (HEALING)	WHAT TO DO
Mechanically cold-pressed chia seed, flaxseed, hemp seed, perilla seed, hemp, algae, fish, krill, and walnut oils are rich sources of omega-3 polyunsaturated fats.	All oils rich in essential fats should be enjoyed raw and never cooked. Once you open the bottle, consume quickly to avoid rancidity. Store these oils in opaque glass jars in the fridge or freezer to avoid damage from heat, light, and moisture.
Mechanically cold-pressed almond, black currant seed, borage seed, evening primrose seed, pine nut, pumpkin seed, safflower seed, sesame seed, and sunflower seed oils are good sources of omega-6 polyunsaturated fats.	Oils high in monounsaturated or saturated fats may be used for cooking at low temperatures (with a water or broth spritz) but are best consumed raw.
Mechanically cold-pressed avocado, extra-virgin olive, and almond oils are rich in heart-healthy monounsaturated fats, and raw whole coconut oil has antimicrobial properties.	Store all oils in a cool, dark place to maintain freshness.

YELLOW LIGHT (CAUTION)	WHAT TO DO	RED LIGHT (HURTING)
Organic butter and ghee (clarified butter) are healthy choices when eaten in moderation by people who are not sensitive or allergic to dairy. Olive oil that isn't labeled as extra-virgin may have been blended with other cheaper oils such as chemically extracted canola, safflower, and sunflower.[7] Oils labeled "high oleic" contain fewer polyunsaturated fats such as omega-6 fats.	Avoid dairy fats for 8 to 12 weeks. Use coconut oil/butter or cacao butter when a recipe calls for saturated fat. Then slowly reintroduce organic goat and sheep ghee to determine if you can tolerate them. Introduce organic cow ghee and then cow butter after you're sure you tolerate goat and sheep dairy. Use extra-virgin olive oil as often as possible. The term "extra-virgin" is regulated by the European Union but isn't recognized in other olive-producing countries.	Refined, processed, chemically extracted, bleached, damaged, and hydrogenated oils are toxic to every cell in your body. Almost all canola (also called rapeseed), corn, and soybean crops are genetically modified or contaminated by GM crops and should be avoided whenever possible. Contaminants in plastic bottles can leach out of plastic oil containers and are best avoided. Commercial dressings and sauces usually contain high amounts of sugar, white vinegar, and processed bleached oils, all of which contribute to inflammation.[8]

115

7. For more information, read my blog post on olive oil at www.juliedaniluk.com, where I talk about the large amounts of fraudulent olive oil on the market.

8. Avoid all refined and modified fats, chemically extracted and bleached oils, fried foods, hydrogenated and partially hydrogenated oils, fractionated and partially fractionated oils, margarine, and trans fats. Read product labels carefully, as it is becoming law to list trans fat content. Make up a fast, healthy dressing and store it in the fridge instead of using prepared products.

SWEETENERS

GREEN LIGHT (HEALING)	WHAT TO DO
Moderate amounts of sweeteners such as birch syrup, carob powder, coconut syrup, coconut nectar, coconut sugar, unrefined date sugar, raw and dry fruit, honey (raw is best), licorice root powder or syrup, lo han kuo, lucuma fruit powder, maple syrup, mesquite flour, stevia, sweet cicely leaf, tiger nut powder, vanilla, and yacón syrup are suitable choices. Note: Most sweeteners are contraindicated for IBD.	Use sweeteners sparingly to avoid spikes in blood levels of insulin that can cause inflammation.[8] Consume sweet foods with high-fiber foods to balance blood sugar. Be careful to watch portion sizes of dried fruit, as it's very concentrated in sugar. Water down fruit juice to avoid excess sugar and look for fruit-sweetened sauces and jams.

8. Low to moderate sugar consumption impairs glucose and lipid metabolism and promotes inflammation. A recent study suggests that men consuming only 155 calories of sugar per day increased inflammation markers significantly.

YELLOW LIGHT (CAUTION)	WHAT TO DO	RED LIGHT (HURTING)
Blackstrap molasses can be a nutritious sweetener. However, because it's derived from sugarcane, which has been over-consumed, some people may have developed sensitivity to it. Jaggery and Sucanat are unrefined dehydrated cane juice and contain more minerals and vitamins than white sugar. Commercial agave syrup is high in fructose and can be inflammatory.[9] Raw cacao is high in nutrients, but it can be inflammatory for people who are sensitive to its stimulating alkaloids.	Avoid all sugarcane products for eight weeks in Step Three of the plan to determine if you're sensitive to them. Then slowly reintroduce unrefined jaggery, Sucanat, or molasses. Avoid or minimize use of agave syrup. If possible, choose organic products that are pure, don't contain high-fructose corn syrup, and aren't processed with black mold (Aspergillus). Eliminate all cacao products for eight weeks. Then slowly reintroduce raw, unsweetened cacao seeds to gauge your body's reaction. People who are sensitive to caffeine should avoid cacao.	Refined cane sugar and sugar beet products suppress immune system function and promote inflammation.[10] Avoid all artificial sweeteners such as Aspartame, saccharin, and sucralose (Splenda), which may cause tissue irritation or an inflammatory reaction. Avoid commercial chocolate that contains refined sugar or artificial sweeteners, dairy, hydrogenated oils, and artificial flavors.

9. Commercial agave syrup can be inflammatory in people who suffer from liver disorders, fructose sensitivity, insulin resistance, or mold sensitivity. As well, there is reason to believe that many agave syrup producers are not ecologically sustainable.

10. Avoid all refined beet and cane sugars, including white sugar, berry (extra fine), brown, confectioners, golden, icing, turbinado, and raw sugar. Avoid confectioner's syrup, dextrose (glucose), glucose-fructose, high-fructose corn syrup, and levulose (fructose). Don't consume artificial sweeteners.

BEVERAGES

GREEN LIGHT (HEALING)	WHAT TO DO
Water is the most important liquid for health, and you must drink adequate amounts every day. Herbal teas, fresh seed milks, and fresh fruit and vegetable juices can also be healing.	Drink 6 to 12 cups of fluids (filtered or spring source) per day, depending on your body size. Add a squeeze of lemon or lime to water for extra zing and detox support. Drink diluted coconut water, seed milks (e.g., hemp, sesame), fresh fruit and vegetable juices, herbal teas, and sugar-free lemonade or limeade. Sweeten herbal teas and lemonade with stevia or raw honey. Brew herbal teas overnight and store in the fridge to make a refreshing home-made iced tea. Good tea choices include honeybush, ginger, nettle, roasted dandelion, and tulsi. For more herbal tea choices, refer to my first book, *Meals That Heal Inflammation*. Read all ingredient labels to avoid sugar and artificial sweeteners in juices or iced teas. Drink mineral water and honey-sweetened herbal teas instead of soft drinks.

YELLOW LIGHT (CAUTION)

Freshly roasted and freshly ground coffee beans retain their potent antioxidant activity and health-promoting properties.

Black and oolong teas, green tea, guarana, kola nut, and yerba maté contain caffeine, but they can also be healthy choices for people who don't suffer from adrenal exhaustion or liver congestion. These drinks are rich in antioxidants and beneficial phytonutrients.

Low-thyroid patients may have to avoid green and black tea due to their high fluoride content.

Some studies suggest that in small doses red wine and sake may support cardiovascular health.

WHAT TO DO

If you drink coffee, moderate your consumption and drink freshly roasted and freshly ground coffee. Lightly roast a one-week supply and store it in a glass jar in the freezer. Mix it with powdered reishi mushroom, ground chicory, or dandelion root to minimize caffeine intake and to support detoxification.

People sensitive to caffeine should completely avoid caffeinated beverages such as coffee, tea (black, green, oolong, and white), guarana, kola nut, and yerba maté. Generally, people with strong nerves and robust adrenal health can tolerate moderate amounts of caffeine.

Avoid all alcohol for eight weeks and reintroduce red wine or sake to see if you're sensitive to its sulfite and histamine content. If you're tolerant, keep consumption to three glasses or less per week.

RED LIGHT (HURTING)

Juices and soft drinks sweetened with sugar or artificial sweeteners like aspartame and Sweet'N Low can cause adverse effects such as spikes in blood levels of insulin, headaches, or allergic reactions.

Pre-ground packaged coffee is oxidized and has lost most of its health-boosting properties.

Substitute roasted chicory or dandelion root tea for coffee. They taste similar to coffee yet are cleansing and not stimulating.

Alcohol, especially when consumed in excess, impairs liver function, may cause fatty liver or liver cirrhosis, may increase bowel permeability (aka leaky gut), and can lead to metabolic disorders such as insulin resistance and diabetes.

Minimize intake of alcohol to minimize liver stress. Choose red wine or unfiltered sake over premixed drinks, which tend to be high in sweeteners, artificial flavors, and artificial colors.

THE MENU PLAN

It's important to understand that the menu plan in this book is only one way you might approach meal planning. Planning a menu that is free of all known allergens would be next to impossible, so I have removed the most common allergens and hope that you will use the information you gathered from the testing phase to fine-tune your diet even further. The exceptions I have made are small amounts of eggs, pepper, tomatoes, fermented soy, and tree nuts. All of these foods are healthy and will only cause inflammation in the body if you happen to have an allergy or sensitivity to them.

While it can be challenging when the body tags certain foods as allergens, there are always solutions. Those who have a tree nut allergy can often handle seeds that are processed in a separate facility. Try to substitute seeds when a recipe calls for nuts. I also have a few recipes that contain eggs; if you can't tolerate eggs, just move on to another recipe. Alternatively, if eggs are called for in a baking recipe, feel free to try a vegan egg substitute such as ground flaxseeds (page 286) to act as the binding agent. The most important thing to do is to start experimenting to find out what works for you.

Most recipes in this book yield two to four servings. If you have a large family, you can easily double them. If you are cooking for yourself or for you and your partner, you will always have leftovers to freeze and enjoy later, when there is no time to cook. I am always encouraging my clients to start eating dinner for breakfast, so plan to use leftovers in the morning as well. Protein-rich, savory dishes in the morning will balance blood sugar better than the typical sweet, carbohydrate-laden, rich breakfasts to which we have become accustomed. I have included some sweet-tasting breakfasts in the SMTH menu plan. These recipes are specially designed with protein and healthy fats to help you stay balanced and avoid an early morning spike in insulin.

Modifications to the SMTH Plan

If you suffer from ileocecal valve syndrome or any inflammatory bowel disease such as ulcerative colitis, diverticulitis, ankylosing spondylitis, or Crohn's disease, you will have to make food modifications to the SMTH plan. I suggest you reduce or completely eliminate (depending on the severity of your condition) foods high in roughage, such as raw foods, whole nuts and seeds, and whole grains. You also may need to reduce starch found in beans, so consult a naturopathic doctor for guidance and specific protocols. Eat fruits and vegetables fully cooked to soften them, and avoid swallowing indigestible seeds such as those in berries, tomatoes, peppers, eggplants, cucumbers, and grapes. Blend nuts and seeds into butters to ease digestion. You may need to completely avoid strawberries, raspberries, blueberries, and related fruits. Eat soupy dal (split beans and peas with the outer skins removed) instead of whole legumes. Eliminate spicy foods and avoid stimulants such as alcohol, cocoa, and caffeine. Blending your food into a hearty soup may help improve your digestion, soothe your intestines, and help calm inflamed areas.

Suggested Seven-Day Omnivore or Vegetarian Menu Plan

In this plan, the days are interchangeable. If you are short on time, simplify a meal by eating steamed greens, squash, and a protein of your choice. It is very important that you rotate your food choices to avoid allergies and improve your nutrient diversity. Be brave and experiment with new foods and your taste buds will adapt quickly. Consider making meals on the weekend and freezing them into portions for fast weekday/night meal choices. Wash produce and chop produce when you get home from shopping so vegetables become an instant snack item. There are traditional breakfast items suggested, but for faster healing, eat lunch or dinner suggestions as the first meal to ensure your blood sugar will be more balanced throughout the day. Time treats to follow a workout for maximum results.

121

DAY	CLEANSING BEVERAGE	BREAKFAST	MORNING SNACK
1	Ultimate Green Juice	Superfood Quinoa Porridge	Anti-inflammatory Trail Mix
2	Lemon & Water	Leftover Artichoke-Leek Baked Frittata or Monster Superfood Breakfast	Superfood Shake
3	Spicy Anti-inflammatory Carrot Juice	Alpha-Omega Breakfast Pudding	Celery sticks with Mock Sour Cream and Chive Dip
4	Limeade	Eggs in the Bunny Hole or Coconut Granola	Sugar Snap Peas or Jicama with Dopamine-Boosting Dip
5	Nettle Tea (store-bought)	Breakfast Pudding (Mock Tapioca)	Raspberry Breakfast Sorbet
6	Honeybush Chai Tea (store-bought)	Life-Changing Loaf with nut or seed butter	Painted Fruit
7	Ginger Tea (store-bought)	Kasha Crepes and/or Painted Fruit	Jule Bar

LUNCH	AFTERNOON SNACK	DINNER
Happy Wraps with Healing Ginger Green Soup	Salad Bars	Artichoke-Leek Baked Frittata and/or Kelp Noodles with Raw Tomato Sauce Side dish: Ezra's Gazpacho
Curried Sloppy Joes and Hempy Purple Coleslaw	Coco Kale Chips	Cashew-Crusted Chicken or Stewed Maple Beans with Dandelion Side dish: Jicama Fries
Grain-Free Tabouli Salad and Blender Broccoli Soup	Key Lime Shake	Grilled Rainbow Trout with Tomato-Fennel Ragout or Buffalo Strip Loin Side dish: Garlic Bok Choy Stir-Fry
Bust the Blues Hemp Salad with leftover trout or chicken and Fastest Spinach Soup EVER	Peppermint Patty	Low-Cal Turkey Chili or Sea Scallops with Harvest Vegetables Side dish: Lemon-Roasted Green Beans with Chopped Hazelnuts
Life-Changing Loaf with Julie's Super Iron-Rich Pâté or Life-Changing Loaf with Mexican Black Bean Garlic Dip	Zucchini sticks with Popeye Hummus	Turkey Burgers on Portobello "Buns" or Spiced Black Cod Side dish: Lemonade-Marinated Fennel
Vietnamese Beef Salad or Lovely Lentil Salad	Spicy Anti-inflammatory Carrot Juice	Butter Me Chicken or Anti-inflammatory Fish Chowder Side dish: Far East Broccoli
Grain-Free Sushi with Sesame Salad Optional Protein Boost: Japanese Deviled Eggs	Sliced apple with pumpkin seed butter	Chicken Stew à la Julie or Warm White Beans with Summer Vegetables Side dish: Festive Pomegranate Tabouli

MEAL-PLANNING GUIDELINES

Good Eating Habits to Establish

- Eat your first meal within two hours of waking. Eat low-GI food.
- Eat dinner items for breakfast to establish balanced blood sugar.
- Eat three meals and two snacks spaced over the day to keep energy levels up. Finish your last meal by 7 p.m.
- Instead of a sugary treat, enjoy a serving of fruit for dessert or as a snack.
- Make sure half of your plate is filled with vegetables. (Vegetables must be cooked if you suffer from any inflammatory bowel conditions.)
- Include two to three vegetables in every meal for a minimum of seven servings a day. The minerals in vegetables alkalize your body, helping to reduce inflammation.
- Try to eat 35 grams of fiber a day. You can achieve this by increasing your consumption of fruit, vegetables, whole grains, legumes, and seeds.
- Drink plenty of fluids.

Why We Don't Count Calories

A large section of the dieting industry was founded on the concept that if you count calories and reduce the amount you consume, you will lose weight regardless of the type of food you eat. So why is it not working?

Today's common method of counting calories is not a fine science; it is a blunt tool that can only be used to monitor the general trend of caloric intake. A calorie is the amount of heat energy needed to raise the temperature of 1 gram of water 1 degree Celsius. American chemist Wilbur Atwater developed the method of "measuring" a calorie more than a hundred years ago. He generalized that for every gram of carbohydrate or protein, four calories are counted. For every gram of fat, nine calories are counted.

The food industry's interpretation of the Atwater System relies on the idea that a carrot is a carrot is a carrot—but in reality, the amount of calories and nutrients present will change depending on how that carrot was grown, how ripe it is at the time of harvesting, the length of time it has been stored, how it is processed, and how it is cooked or prepared. The same is true for all foods. In addition, it turns out that a vegetable fat has a different calorie value than an animal fat. The generalization of the value of fat has led to the over-valuing or undervaluing of the caloric content of many foods. A July 2012 study found that almonds had about 20 percent fewer calories than originally thought.

Another study, released in June 2012, determined that not all calories are created equal. Subjects ate the same amount of calories but focused on either a high-glycemic diet (high in refined carbohydrates) or a low-glycemic diet (low in refined carbohydrates and high in fats and protein). Those who ate the low-GI diet burned more calories and lost more weight.

Though you may want to jump on the dramatically low-carbohydrate-diet bandwagon to lose weight quickly, it is important to know there are drawbacks. Consuming too few carbohydrates forces the body into a state of ketosis, which can stress the kidneys and start to waste muscle if prolonged. The body and brain require an adequate amount of carbohydrates in order to properly function. A "live-it" that has a healthy balance of carbs, fat, and protein will give you the long-term results you are looking for.

Once you have determined which healthy "live-it" plan is right for you, counting calories will no longer be an issue. A balanced plan filled with vegetation and a healthy dose of organic protein, fats, and carbs will have you on your way. It is also important to remember that you cannot use a "good" diet and pills as a substitute for daily exercise. Our bodies were meant to move, lift, and stretch . . . *every day*!

The distribution of the macronutrients you consume should be as follows: 40 to 50 percent from carbohydrates, 20 to 30 percent from fat, and 20 to 30 percent from protein.

Each of us has a built-in protein-portion meter—the size of the palm of your hand! The smaller your hand, the less protein you need per serving. It's really that simple. Use your palm as a guideline to determine how much protein you should be eating at each meal.

Here are a few general rules for portion sizes:

FOOD-SERVING GUIDE		
FOOD TO MEASURE	**EXAMPLE OF A SERVING**	**WHAT IT LOOKS LIKE**
A serving of vegetables	½ cup broccoli	Your fist
All leafy greens	1 cup salad	Coffee mug
Meat, poultry, fish, or vegetarian protein	3 oz salmon	Deck of cards
Legumes	¾ cup lentils	A heaping handful
Nuts and seeds	12 almonds	Golf ball
Pasta, rice, and cereal	¼ cup dry pasta	Lightbulb
Fruit	½ cup berries or one medium piece of fruit	Baseball
Oils and fats	1 tbsp	Thumb tip (tip to first knuckle)

How to Eat on the Run in a Healthy Way

Eating well is especially challenging when life gets busy because it takes a little planning. Here are a few tips to help you make sure you stick to the plan:

- Make a date to shop once a week at a store that carries fresh, organic food. Compared to the cost of eating out, the price of tasty, healthy food at home is a bargain.
- Prep once a week and freeze batches of food.
- Cut veggies when you get them home and store them in water in the fridge. This way, they are at your fingertips and ready to help you to make better choices when you are hungry.

- Make up a big batch of dressing for the month and keep it in the fridge at work so your salad is always crisp. (Also, see my Healing Salad in a Jar recipe on page 192).
- Stock your drawers at work and home with snacks that keep you fueled. Nuts, fruit, bars, shakes, crackers, and canned sustainable fish are all good choices.
- Make work lunches into a weekly potluck. With everyone bringing a different healthful contribution, you're sure to have a blast connecting over food and flavors.

THE HEALTHY SWAP LIST

Consider these scenarios: You have just been told you are intolerant to dairy and gluten and have no idea what to eat. Maybe your doctor has just informed you that your blood sugar is dangerously high and you need to cut back on sugar and carbohydrates. Maybe your favorite comfort food is the culprit behind your weight gain. What do you do when you realize that in order to heal, you have to give up your favorite foods?

Walking into a health food store or down the health food aisle of a grocery store can be a bit confusing at first, but with a little trial and error and some experimentation, you will find that you can satisfy even the deepest cravings with foods that are truly healing.

I was diagnosed with ADHD about 30 years ago. The health food options available have come a long way since then, and a huge multi-billion-dollar health food industry has a dizzying number of choices on offer. It's important to keep looking for new options so you can avoid developing intolerances and boredom. The following suggestions for healthy swaps of inflammatory foods should spur you on as you seek a happy palate and strong immune system.

Dairy Products

Problem:

Milk—Conventional dairy is very inflammatory and a known allergen. If you are using a dairy product from the US, you are most likely consuming rBHT, a genetically modified growth hormone that's use has been linked to cancer.

Solution: Today there are many products on the market to choose from: hemp milk, almond milk, rice milk, soy milk . . . the list goes on. Many of these alternatives are sweetened with sugar, so you need to read the label before buying. I do not recommend drinking soy milk; it is a common allergen, and there are better alternatives to a "milk" beverage than a high-carbohydrate rice product. Unsweetened hemp beverage is higher in protein than other milk substitutes, and unsweetened coconut beverage includes a healthy fat that can help you lose weight. I find it tastes the closest to cow's milk. (If you can't find coconut beverage, you can thin down canned coconut milk by mixing four parts water to one part coconut milk in the blender.)

Problem:

Cheese—Like all dairy products, cheese is inflammatory and a known allergen.

Solution: There are two great "faux cheese" recipes in SMTH on pages 186 and 187. Store-bought cheese is not an easy ingredient to substitute, but there are a few tapioca-based "cheese" products that are very convincing and melt well. This type of product is available in the refrigerator section of many health food stores (see Resources for suggestions).

Problem:

Butter—As a dairy product, butter is inflammatory and a known allergen.

Solution:

Organic Coconut Oil—Try using coconut oil in the same way you would use butter. It's a great substitute, and the health benefits are endless!

Problem:

Premade Breakfast Shakes—The most dangerous thing about these shakes is that they are marketed as healthy alternatives when they are, in fact, the opposite. I am averse to counting calories as a rule, but for the sake of comparison I would like you to consider these numbers: an 8-ounce serving of a typical breakfast shake contains 250 calories, 22 grams of sugar, 1 gram of fiber, and 9 grams of protein.

These beverages typically contain genetically modified corn, soy, and canola ingredients that slow down metabolism and spike insulin levels, causing you to gain more weight.

Be on the lookout for harmful ingredients such as corn maltodextrin, milk protein concentrate, soy oil, soy protein isolate, canola oil, corn oil, artificial flavor, salt, monoglycerides, and carrageenan.

Solution:

Organic hemp protein shake powder—Delicious and nutritious, Certified Organic 70% Hemp Protein Powder can be blended into beverages, stirred into breakfast foods, or added to baked goods. You can find flavored versions sweetened with organic palm sugar, which has the lowest glycemic index of all sugars and a slow sugar release. Hemp protein powder is a natural source of omega-3. It also contains GLA, a type of omega-6 that can be anti-inflammatory. It also contains all 10 essential amino acids and is made with fair-trade ingredients. An 8-ounce serving is 120 calories and contains 6 grams of sugar, 9 grams of fiber, and 8 grams of protein (see Resources for suggestions).

Grain Products

Problem:

Glutinous and Non-Glutinous Bread—Standard glutinous bread contributes to digestive problems and creates an unhealthy spike in blood sugar, which stimulates the release of the fat-storing hormone insulin. Unfortunately, many of the non-glutinous breads on the market are just as unhealthy, as they contain flour substitutes such as corn, potato, and white rice, which have the same effect on blood sugar.

Solution: There are specialized "breads" on the market that are organic and grain-free. Most of these creations come from the raw food community and can be found in health food stores or at raw restaurant outlets. It is important to note that the term "bread" is being used very loosely here. If you are expecting a light, fluffy loaf of white bread, you may be surprised by the texture of these products. These delicious creations tend to be more like a flatbread and are often made with seeds such as sunflower and flax.

Nut Flour Bread—Look for bread created from almond or another type of nut flour, sweetened with natural ingredients. See Life-Changing Loaf, page 178.

Raw Bread—Made from various vegetables and seeds, this raw food phenomenon has become very popular with people searching for a bread substitute that will hold up under the pressure of open-faced sandwich fixings such as avocado, roast chicken, and pesto. See Kale Flat Bread recipe on page 240.

Problem:

Cookies, Granola Bars, Baked Goods—Most commercially baked goods are filled with sugar; refined flours; bad oils and trans fats; and artificial flavors, colors, and preservatives.

Solution: There are now dozens of brands of baked goods on the market that are much better for you than the conventional cookie or cake. The raw food community is thriving, and if you ask me, their ingenious raw desserts taste better than their standard counterparts. Look for products with organic ingredients that are sweetened with honey, maple syrup, dates, coconut sugar, and/or stevia.

Problem:

Crackers—Many crackers have gluten, trans fats, sugar, genetically modified organisms (GMOs), and other refined toxic ingredients.

Solution: Look for crackers that are made with organic whole seeds and non-glutinous grains or nut/seed flours. Like bread, many "gluten-free" products contain highly refined, genetically modified ingredients to substitute for the glutinous flour. To make your own delicious crackers, check out Salad Bars on page 308.

Problem:

Wheat (Gluten) Pasta—Gluten is the protein found in wheat, spelt, kamut, rye, and barley. Wheat pasta also goes under the name of semolina or durum flour, so read labels carefully.

Solutions:

Kelp Noodles—A low-calorie alternative to regular pasta that can be used with a variety of sauces, kelp noodles are available in many health food stores.

Zucchini "Noodles"—There is an excellent gadget on the market called a spiralizer that can be used to create noodles from vegetables such as zucchini. A medium-sized zucchini is placed in the device and hand cranked into long spaghetti-like noodles, which can then be topped with hot or cold pasta sauces. Look online if you're interested in adding this tool to your kitchen.

Spaghetti Squash—Another substitute for pasta is the humble spaghetti squash. Slice in half, scoop out the seeds, and bake facedown on a baking sheet. Once cooked, the spaghetti squash easily pulls away from its skin with a fork in strands that resemble spaghetti. Serve hot with a pasta sauce.

Problem:

Cereal—Cereal has become such a big part of the morning ritual in North America that most people can't imagine living without it. The reality is that conventional cereal is junk food. The nutritional content of most cereals is no better than the average cookie, yet they are marketed to adults and children alike as a healthy way to start the day. Many cereals will spike your blood sugar and provide you with an unhealthy dose of trans fats, artificial dyes and flavors, and preservatives. Many are also made with GMO corn and soy, and sweetened with high-fructose corn syrup.

Solutions:

Make Your Own—If you are married to the idea of eating cereal for breakfast, I would suggest making your own. Check out my Coconut Granola recipe on page 168 or Quinoa Berry Granola, page 180.

Premade Cereals—Look for an organic/GMO-free product at your local health food or grocery store that is gluten and dairy free. Be sure it is naturally sweetened with honey, maple syrup, coconut sugar, and/or stevia. Also available now are completely grain-free products based on nuts, seeds, and fruit.

Snacks

Problem:

Potato Chips and Popcorn—Everyone loves a crunchy, salty snack when they are at the movies, but few people realize that conventional popcorn and potato chips are loaded with trans fats, artificial dyes, artificial flavors, and tons of sodium. You already know that these fat-filled "bad carbs" are hard on your waistline. What you may not know is that potato chips (along with French fries) contain acrylamide, a known carcinogen that is formed when foods are baked or fried at high temperatures.

Many butter substitutes and flavorings used in theaters and on microwave popcorn products contain diacetyl-based chemicals, which may harm brain cells.

Solutions:

Kale Chips—High in nutrients and low in calories, kale chips are all the rage in the health food industry. Read the label to be sure they are made with organic, gluten-free ingredients. Try creamy ranch, faux cheddar, and the Coco Kale Chip recipe on page 294. They all have their own unique taste, and you can hardly believe you are eating kale!

Organic Popcorn—I highly recommend removing corn from your diet for eight weeks to make sure that you can tolerate it. If you are safe and want to integrate this treat back into your diet, make sure you buy organic kernels and pop them in an air popper. Top with melted coconut oil, sea salt, spices, a touch of apple cider vinegar, and/or a sprinkle of buttery-tasting nutritional yeast (if you tolerate yeast).

Problem:

Conventional Chocolate Products—Chocolate creates a multitude of issues for someone trying to deal with inflammation and excess weight. It's unfortunate, because the raw cocoa bean is full of health-giving properties. Regular chocolate is often made with large amounts of sugar, milk, GMO soy, and non-organic cocoa that is often grown and harvested by severely under-paid labor.

Solution:

100% Organic Fair-Trade Chocolate—I buy 100 percent cocoa butter chocolate that is sugar free and then add my own sweetness from dates, figs, or honey. Raw organic cocoa powder makes a fantastic pre-workout drink. Check page 299 for the recipe. For those sensitive to chocolate, consider carob powder as a tasty substitute.

Sweeteners

Problem:

Refined Sugar/High-Fructose Corn Syrup/Maltodextrin/Sucralose— The list of refined sweeteners is lengthy. All of them can raise blood sugar to a dangerous level and reduce immune function.

Solutions: There are a number of ways to sweeten your life without the harmful side effects of sugar. Here are a few suggestions:

Local Unpasteurized Honey—Unrefined honey contains vitamins, minerals, and phytonutrients that bees collect from plants during their forage. It's a source of vitamins B2 and B6, iron, manganese, amino acids, and enzymes. For thousands of years, honey has been used medicinally, but only recently has scientific research revealed how it helps heal and soothe inflammation.

Organic Unrefined Coconut Sugar—Coconut trees and other palms have flower buds that can be tapped for their sweet sap and dried into a granular form. Unrefined coconut sugar is rich in antioxidants and phyto-nutrients that can help protect against diabetes and hypertension. Some of

133

these phytonutrients inhibit the activity of some carbohydrate-digesting enzymes (namely, alpha-glucuronidase and alpha-amylase) and therefore help to decrease the amount of glucose that is absorbed into the bloodstream from the intestines.

Organic Maple Syrup—Maple syrup contains 54 antioxidant compounds, which act as anti-inflammatory agents. It contains essential minerals such as manganese, zinc, magnesium, calcium, and potassium. Due to its high sucrose content, limit portion size to 1 tbsp.

Problem:

Artificial Sweeteners—Aspartame, Splenda, Sweet'N Low, etc., should be avoided at all cost.

Solution:

Stevia Liquid or Powder Extract—This is a natural, calorie-free sweetener derived from a South American plant that is related to the chrysanthemum. It is two hundred times sweeter than sugar, so you only need a few drops to sweeten drinks. Unlike aspartame, stevia is very healthy. It is antifungal and antibiotic, making it useful for people trying to balance levels of candida or other microorganisms in the body. It's also anti-inflammatory and safe for diabetics.

Problem:

Candy—Harvard School of Public Health reports that candy interferes with weight loss, contributes to weight gain, and can even lead to serious inflammatory conditions such as heart disease and diabetes. The blood sugar fluctuations that candy causes can lead to increased cravings for refined carbohydrates, creating a vicious circle. Just as an example, a small package of fruit chews has 240 calories, 5 grams of toxic fat, and 33 grams of sugar.

Solution: When craving candy, slice an apple thinly, sprinkle a splash of lemon juice onto the slices, then dip into sesame or hemp seeds.

Condiments and Seasonings

Problem:

Mayonnaise—Conventional mayonnaise is one of the most unhealthy substances you can eat. Full of trans fats, sugar, and artificial ingredients, it is a toxic powerhouse that should be avoided at all cost.

Solution: There are now mayonnaise substitutes on the market made with healthy oils such as olive and grapeseed, sweeteners such as rice syrup, and flavors such as apple cider vinegar. Look for an organic and/or GMO-free product. Soy and canola oil have their drawbacks and should be avoided. Look for a product that is stored in the refrigerator at your local health food or grocery store. As well, guacamole is an excellent swap for mayonnaise. It provides amazing omega-9 fat and vitamin B6 for inflammation reduction and hormone balance.

Problem:

Mustard—It is not uncommon for Dijon mustards to contain gluten and sugar.

Solution: Organic mustard made with apple cider vinegar and lots of turmeric contains only 5 calories a tablespoon and is free of sugar or gluten. The classic bright yellow prepared mustard is often free of chemicals, gluten, and sugar, so have a look at the label.

Problem:

Ketchup—The candy of the condiment world, ketchup is mostly high-fructose corn syrup and contains 5 grams of sugar per tablespoon.

Solution:

Organic, Sugar-Free Salsa—If you have gone through the Anti-inflammatory 5-Step Live-It Plan and have determined that you are able to tolerate tomatoes, salsa can be a great addition to many foods. It has only 5 calories a tablespoon and zero sugar, and the lemon juice content can reduce blood sugar. Make your own or choose a refrigerated store-bought version rather than one sold at room temperature; by doing so, you will avoid added sweeteners, preservatives, and extra sodium.

Problem:

Relish and Pickles—Pickle relish is often sweetened with high-fructose corn syrup or refined sugar. Many brands use an artificial color called tartrazine that is terrible for your brain, causing poor moods and reduced attention span. Watch out for sodium benzoate as well. Many people have allergic reactions to this chemical.

Solutions:

Make Your Own Happy Relish!—You can whip up a batch of pickle relish (using store-bought sugar-free pickles or ones you've canned yourself) in no time by chopping up the pickles and adding seasoning.

Sauerkraut—This pungent pickled cabbage provides a bit of fiber and a little bit of vitamin C for just 2.5 calories per tablespoon; its sodium content, at 90 mg per tablespoon, is comparable to that of relish. Because it is a fermented food, it also has healing probiotic powers that help to balance the gut flora.

Tapenade—Crushed olive paste satisfies those cravings for salt while providing iron-rich, inflammation-reducing olive polyphenols.

Problem:

Conventional Dairy Pesto—It is not unusual for conventional pesto to include ingredients such as dairy, poor-quality oil, and preservatives.

Solution: I would suggest making your own (see my Mint Kale Pesto that I use in my Pesto Pasta Salad recipe on page 210), but when you are on the run you can find delicious dairy-free pestos with high-quality oils at your local health food store.

Problem:

Table Salt—Regular processed table salt is refined sodium chloride (NaCl) with a little bit of dextrose (sugar) and iodine added. Sodium chloride is harmful in large quantities.

Solution:

Unprocessed Salt (gray sea salt or pink rock salt)—Not only does unprocessed salt enhance the flavor of food, it can also provide many trace minerals that help to balance the body's electrolytes. Unrefined salts can be found at all health food stores and in the health food aisle of many conventional grocery stores.

If your health practitioner has recommended a sodium-reduced diet, try a high-potassium, lower-sodium substitute. This type of product has the benefit of blood pressure–reducing potassium yet tastes just like salt. *Warning*: This product should not be used by anyone with reduced or non-existent kidney function. Dialysis patients should never use a high-potassium product without the consent of their nephrologist.

Problem:

Soy Sauce—Contains gluten and high amounts of glutamic acid that may cause a sensitivity in those who react to MSG.

Solution:

Tamari—Look for naturally fermented, gluten-free tamari (a type of naturally produced soy sauce) or use coconut aminos, a sauce made by fermenting coconut.

Now that you are armed with dozens of tasty flavor enhancers, you are ready to create delicious slimming recipes that will leave you satisfied, energized, and vitalized.

LEGEND FOR THE RECIPES IN THIS BOOK

 The recipe is free of eggs and egg products.

The recipe is free of soy and its derivatives.

The recipe is free of dairy and its derivatives. Nut, seed, and rice milks are used as substitutes.

The recipe is free of tree nuts. If you do not see this symbol and would like the recipe to be nut free, consider substituting a seed instead.

The recipe has a GI score of 55 or less on the glycemic index. The glycemic index (GI) is a system of measuring how fast a carbohydrate triggers a rise in circulating blood sugar. The higher the index number, the faster the blood sugar increases. A list of glycemic values for common foods is provided on page 69.

The recipe is gluten free. If you suffer from inflammatory bowel disease, ankylosing spondylitis, or irritable bowel syndrome, you may need to avoid certain forms of starch present in gluten-free grains. Be sure to keep a record of your progress and consult a health practitioner for a more individualized plan.

The recipe has more than 70 percent raw ingredients. Raw nuts, seeds, and produce are very nutritious, but must be minimized for patients with inflammatory bowel disease. If you suffer from a digestive disorder, you may want to steam produce and soak nuts or seeds to assist digestion.

This recipe may contain low-alkaloid nightshade ingredients (e.g., ripe tomatoes, red peppers, goji berries). High-alkaloid nightshades (e.g., white potatoes, green peppers, unripe tomatoes) are not recommended on the SMTH plan.

This recipe is slightly higher on the glycemic index and is best enjoyed after working out, when spiking insulin can recharge energy stores. If you eat high-GI foods at other times, it may slow results.

PART THREE

THE RECIPES

Liquid Healing

Meals to Begin the Day

Salads, Sauces, Dips, and Dressings

Starters, Soups, and Sides

Main Meals

Treats and Snacks

LIQUID HEALING

"You don't miss your water until your well runs dry." –WILLIAM BELL

APPLE PIE DETOX SHAKE

Apples contain calcium D-glucarate, a phytochemical that protects the body against cancer by increasing liver detoxification. Aloe has been shown to soothe the inflammation of joints, thereby reducing arthritis pain. Used internally, aloe can reduce inflammation throughout the body.

INGREDIENTS:

2 organic apples, unpeeled

¼–½ tsp ground ginger

½ tsp cinnamon

¼ cup hemp seeds

1 tbsp ground flaxseeds or chia seed powder

1 cup unsweetened coconut beverage (2% fat) or unsweetened non-dairy milk
(hemp, almond)

½ cup apple cider or juice

OPTIONAL ADDITIONS:

1 cup ice (only if you have strong digestion)

1 tbsp aloe vera gel (make sure it is recommended for internal use) or aloe vera juice
(use whole leaf filtered if you want a laxative effect)

DIRECTIONS:

1. Place all ingredients into a blender and blend until smooth.

Makes 2 small shakes.

BLUEBERRY THRILL

The blueberries, kale, and maca powder in this nourishing shake will provide you with an antioxidant boost, while the hemp seeds offer not only a dose of complete protein but also a rich source of plant-based omega-3s.

INGREDIENTS:

2 cups frozen organic blueberries

1 cup chopped kale or chopped fresh parsley, tightly packed

½ tsp cinnamon

1 tbsp virgin coconut oil

¼ cup hemp seeds

1 tbsp raw honey

2 cups unsweetened coconut beverage (2% fat) or unsweetened non-dairy milk
      (hemp, almond)

1 tbsp fresh lemon juice

1 tsp pure vanilla extract

OPTIONAL SUPERFOOD BOOST:

½ tsp maca powder

DIRECTIONS:

1. Place all ingredients into a blender and blend until smooth.

Makes 2 large shakes.

TRANSIT BREAKFAST

When you want a "stick to your ribs" breakfast but don't have a lot of time, try this hearty smoothie. The cinnamon and turmeric provide great anti-inflammatory benefits.

INGREDIENTS:

2 tbsp rolled quinoa flakes

1½ tbsp hazelnut butter or almond butter

1 tbsp hemp seeds

2 Medjool dates, pitted, or 1 banana

1 cup unsweetened coconut beverage (2% fat) or unsweetened non-dairy milk
(almond, hemp)

½ tsp cinnamon

⅛ tsp turmeric

DIRECTIONS:

1. Place all ingredients into a blender and blend until smooth.

Makes 1 shake.

ULTIMATE GREEN JUICE

This delicious and refreshing recipe can be made in a juicer or blender, although using a blender yields more nutritive benefit, as you retain all the beneficial fiber you would lose with juicing. The veggies in this ultimate juice provide vitamins A, B, C, and K; calcium; magnesium; and potassium!

INGREDIENTS:

2 cups cucumber

1 cup chopped kale, loosely packed

2 cups fresh parsley or cilantro, loosely packed

½–1 lemon, peeled (depending on how sour you like it)

1 green apple

¼ tsp ground ginger

2–3 cups water

DIRECTIONS:

1. Clean and chop produce and add to blender.

2. Add water and blend, at first pulsing mixture to assist in blending process. Thin as desired by adding more water.

Makes 2 thick shakes.

LIMEADE

This is a fantastic drink to make when you are entertaining and would like to have a party cocktail without the empty calories of sugar and alcohol. Lime juice alkalizes the body and aids digestion. You will wake up the next morning with the opposite of a hangover—feeling refreshed and hydrated.

INGREDIENTS:

2 cups sparkling water

1-gram packet stevia powder or 1 tbsp coconut nectar

2 tbsp fresh lime juice

OPTIONAL ADDITIONS:

1 cup ice (only if you have strong digestion)

DIRECTIONS:

1. Combine all ingredients in a pitcher and stir. Serve over ice if desired.

Makes 2 servings.

MINT JULIE-UP

Mint grows rampant in most parts of the world. It's a wonderful herb that soothes the digestive system and eases muscle cramps. Cucumber is a very energetically cooling plant, which is perfect for those blistering-hot summer days. Put these two together and you have an alkalizing energy drink to cool you down when the heat has you running through the sprinkler with the kids!

INGREDIENTS:

1 unpeeled English cucumber, diced

¼ cup fresh mint leaves, finely chopped

½ lemon, freshly squeezed (approx. 1½ tbsp lemon juice)

1 cup chopped apple

2 cups water

Whole mint leaves, for garnish

OPTIONAL ADDITION:

1 cup ice (only if you have strong digestion)

DIRECTIONS:

1. Place cucumber, mint, lemon juice, and water into a blender and blend until smooth.

2. Garnish with mint and serve.

Makes 2 servings.

Note: Cucumber is from the melon family, and even though it is very cleansing for the kidneys, it is important to enjoy this beverage separately from other food to assure proper digestion.

THE SUPERFOOD SHAKE

This shake features six of my favorite slimming superfoods. Combined, they offer all of the anti-inflammatory benefits your body needs. I guarantee that it will make you feel awesome. Consider this before or after a workout to provide great fuel. Due to the thickening power of chia, drink this immediately after making it.

INGREDIENTS:

1 cup blueberries, frozen

1–2 tsp raw cacao or carob powder

1 tbsp ground or whole chia seeds

2 tbsp hemp seeds

2 cups unsweetened coconut beverage (2% fat) or other unsweetened non-dairy milk
    (hemp, almond)

1 tbsp raw honey or coconut nectar

OPTIONAL SUPERFOOD BOOSTER:

2 tbsp goji berries

DIRECTIONS:

1. Place all ingredients into a blender and blend until smooth.

Makes 2 servings.

SPICY ANTI-INFLAMMATORY CARROT JUICE OR SOUP

This juice is rich in cancer-fighting phytonutrients and chelating agents that remove heavy metals from the body. Carrots also help to regulate the immune response, giving them great potential to be part of a new therapy for the treatment of autoimmune and allergic diseases. If you don't have a juicer, you can make this recipe into a delicious blender soup.

INGREDIENTS:

2 stalks celery, chopped

2 cups cilantro, loosely packed, or fresh parsley, chopped

1 tbsp lime or lemon juice

1-inch piece fresh ginger root

1 green apple, unpeeled and diced

5 carrots, unpeeled and sliced

Pinch turmeric

IF MAKING SOUP:

3 cups vegetable or chicken broth

DIRECTIONS:

IF YOU ARE USING A JUICER:

1. Add celery, cilantro, lime, ginger, apple, and carrots to juicer. (Finishing with the apple and carrots will clean the machine of the ginger and herbs.)

2. Pour into 2 large glasses and sprinkle with turmeric.

IF YOU ARE MAKING A SOUP:

1. In a large pot, add evenly sliced carrots, apples, parsley, celery, ginger and broth. Bring to boil, then reduce heat and simmer covered for 10 minutes.

2. Remove from heat and cool slightly before pouring into blender. Alternatively,

you can blend using an immersion blender. Add remaining ingredients and blend until smooth.

Makes 2 large glasses of juice or 4 servings of soup.

Note: If using organic produce, the skin contains high amounts of nutrients and does not need to be peeled.

THE G8

The G8, otherwise known as the Group of 8, normally refers to the world's eight wealthiest countries. Here, though, G8 stands for eight of the nutrition world's richest sources of anti-inflammatory goodness! Make this instead of buying a sodium-filled eight-vegetable concoction from the store.

INGREDIENTS:

1 cup chopped cucumber, unpeeled

1 tsp spirulina or chlorella powder (or other green powder)

1½ cups chopped celery

2 cups chopped apple, unpeeled

2 tbsp fresh lemon juice

1½ cups water

1 tsp ground ginger

¼ tsp turmeric

OPTIONAL SUPERFOOD BOOSTER:

1 tbsp sustainable fish oil

DIRECTIONS:

1. Place all ingredients into a blender and blend until smooth.

Makes 2 large drinks.

TIGER FERTILITY SHAKE

The hemp hearts, dates, and cinnamon in this shake are warming and soothing—especially welcome on cold winter mornings. Maca is a reproductive tonic, protecting against stress-induced imbalances in sex hormones that can have an impact on fertility. This shake gets its creaminess from sterol-rich tahini, a wonderful immune booster.

INGREDIENTS:

2 cups unsweetened coconut beverage (2% fat) or other unsweetened non-dairy milk
    (hemp, almond)

1 large apple, chopped

2 large Medjool dates, pitted

2 tbsp tahini

1 tsp maca powder or aswagandha powder

1 tsp cinnamon

3 tbsp hemp hearts

Pinch pink rock salt or gray sea salt

DIRECTIONS:

1. Place all ingredients into a blender and blend until smooth.

Makes 2 large shakes.

KEY LIME SHAKE

If you like key lime pie, you are going to love this shake. It will provide your body with electrolyte minerals like potassium and magnesium, which help to regulate many functions in the body—from the amount of water you retain to the acidity (pH) of your blood. Electrolyte minerals also help to keep your muscles working properly, making this a great shake to enjoy before or after a workout!

INGREDIENTS:

½ ripe avocado (about ⅓ cup)

3 cups roughly chopped baby spinach or 1½ cups loosely packed frozen, unthawed

¼ cup fresh lime juice (use lemon juice if unavailable)

2 cups unsweetened coconut beverage (2% fat) or other unsweetened non-dairy milk
      (hemp, almond)

2–3 tbsp raw honey (to taste)

OPTIONAL SUPERFOOD BOOSTERS:

1 tbsp hemp protein powder or hemp seeds

1 tsp sustainable fish oil

DIRECTIONS:

1. Place all ingredients into a blender and blend until smooth and creamy.

2. Adjust sweetness to taste.

Makes 2 shakes.

VANILLA HEMP MILK

Hemp seeds are rich in magnesium, zinc, and iron, making this a very healthy milk substitute. Hemp provides a special protein called edestin that is very easy to digest. Raw honey nourishes the nervous system and stimulates immune function. The milk will last in the refrigerator for three to five days.

INGREDIENTS:

½ cup hemp seeds

4 cups water

1 tbsp pure vanilla extract

1–2 tbsp raw honey or coconut nectar

OPTIONAL ADDITION

Pinch pink rock salt or gray sea salt

DIRECTIONS:

1. Place all ingredients into a blender and blend until smooth. Transfer to a mason jar and store in the fridge. Shake before serving.

Makes 4 cups.

AFTER EIGHT SHAKE

This shake really does taste like those famous After Eight chocolate mints of our childhood! Raw cacao powder possesses potent antioxidants and therefore has great potential for protecting us from a long list of chronic degenerative diseases—from heart disease and diabetes to stroke and cancer.

INGREDIENTS:

2 cups unsweetened coconut beverage (2% fat)

2 tbsp nut or seed butter

1 tbsp raw cacao powder

1½ tbsp raw honey

1½ tsp peppermint extract

1–2 tbsp hemp protein powder or hemp seeds

OPTIONAL ADDITIONS:

1 cup ice (only if you have strong digestion)

1 tsp spirulina powder

DIRECTIONS:

1. Place all ingredients into a blender and blend until smooth.

Makes 2 shakes.

Make sure you know the differences among coconut-based liquids available.

Coconut milk: Canned coconut milk is as thick as table cream, with 18 to 24% fat. Use it to add creaminess to soups or give gourmet flair to main dishes.

Coconut beverage: This delicious beverage goes great on cereal, in smoothies or in any recipe that calls for milk. If you can't find coconut beverage, you can thin down canned coconut milk by mixing 4 parts water to 1 part coconut milk in the blender.

Coconut water: Coconut water is the clear, low-fat, nutrient-rich liquid inside a green young coconut.

WHITE PINE NEEDLE TEA

This tea will make you want to plant a white pine tree in your backyard. Look at the end of the tree branch for new white pine needles that are light green in color. Did you know that pine needles have five times more vitamin C than a lemon? A well-known antioxidant and immune system booster, vitamin C improves cardiovascular system functions as well as skin and eye health. Pine needles also contain proanthocyanidins—antioxidants that protect the cardiovascular system, fight cancer, modulate the immune system, provide antibacterial and antiviral protection, and fight inflammation! The fresh tea's flavor is sweet and tangy. If your tea turns a bit bitter, you can sweeten with local raw honey or maple syrup. For more wonderful tea ideas, please have a look at my first book, *Meals That Heal Inflammation.*

INGREDIENTS:

¾ cup new white pine needles, loosely packed

3 cups water

DIRECTIONS:

IF USING AS A HEALING EXPECTORANT:

1. Chop new white pine needles into small pieces. Put needles into an enamel, glass, or stainless steel pan (do not use aluminum). Bring to a boil and simmer for 10 minutes.

2. Remove from heat and transfer tea and needles to a Thermos or mason jar. Let steep for 20 minutes to overnight. Strain to remove needles.

FOR A PLEASANT-TASTING TEA:

1. Bring water to a boil. Remove from heat and add white pine needles. Allow to steep for 10 minutes, then strain into a cup.

Makes 2 cups.

MEALS TO BEGIN THE DAY

"Do, or do not. There is no try." —Yoda

The first meal of the day doesn't have to be sweet. Breakfast for me often consists of dinner leftovers—steamed broccoli, chicken, or salmon. You may find time for eggs on the weekend. Try on the habit of "dinner for breakfast" and you will see the benefits of starting your day with alkalizing vegetables and healthy sources of protein. The combination will leave you with brainpower and energy to burn!

Note: All eggs indicated in recipes are large size and preferably organic. All vegetables used in the recipes are best organically grown and prepared without removing the skin to maximize nutrition. When a recipe calls for coconut beverage (which is very close to 2% cow's milk in fat and flavor), this is not to be confused with coconut milk, which is very rich and has a similar fat percentage to table cream. After one month of the elimination phase of SMTH, you may want to test nightshade ingredients such as tomatoes and red peppers. Make sure they are fully ripe, as green tomatoes and peppers are higher in inflammatory alkaloids.

ARTICHOKE-LEEK BAKED FRITTATA

Packed with veggies, this frittata makes a well-rounded meal for breakfast, lunch, or supper. Leeks contain the stress-reducing bioflavonoid quercetin, while oregano is deliciously antimicrobial and artichokes gently sustain liver function.

INGREDIENTS:

1 tsp extra-virgin olive oil

12 eggs

2 tsp dairy-free pesto

1 tsp dried thyme

1 tsp dried oregano (or 2 tsp fresh)

½ tsp pink rock salt or gray sea salt

2 cups leeks, trimmed and finely chopped (include greens)

14-oz can artichoke hearts (packed in water), drained

1 cup green beans, ends trimmed, cut into thirds

10 black olives, pitted and sliced

DIRECTIONS:

1. Preheat oven to 350°F. Grease a 10 x 14–inch casserole dish with olive oil and set aside.

2. Whisk eggs with pesto, thyme, oregano, and salt and pour into oiled casserole dish.

3. Sprinkle leeks, artichoke hearts, beans, and olives onto egg mixture.

4. Bake for 30 minutes or until eggs are set. Serve hot.

Makes 6 servings.

MONSTER SUPERFOOD BREAKFAST

While I like to encourage people to start their day with alkalizing vegetables and healthy sources of protein, occasionally we wake up in the mood for something sweet—it happens! When the sweet tooth strikes, pair carbohydrates with healthy protein and good fat. This slows down the absorption of sugar into the bloodstream and helps prevent the highs and lows of the blood sugar rollercoaster. This tasty mixture has extraordinary anti-inflammatory power.

INGREDIENTS:

1 cup unsweetened applesauce

1 tsp spirulina or chlorella powder

2 tbsp hemp seeds

½ tsp cinnamon

½ tsp ground ginger

1 tbsp pumpkin seeds

1 tbsp vegan protein powder (hemp, pea, flax, or pumpkin)

OPTIONAL SUPERFOOD BOOSTERS:

½ tsp maca powder

¼ tsp turmeric

2 tsp lemon–flavored fish oil

1 tbsp lecithin granules (make sure they are GMO free)

1 tsp bee pollen

¼ tsp acidophilus powder

DIRECTIONS:

1. Combine all ingredients and desired boosters in a bowl and mix well.

Makes 1 serving.

ALPHA-OMEGA BREAKFAST PUDDING

Apples are one of the most important items to buy organic because conventional apples are sprayed heavily with pesticides. Organic Ambrosia apples are rich in a phytonutrient called calcium D-glucarate, which enables the body to excrete hormones like estrogen so that they are not reabsorbed—so apples actually help us balance our hormones!

INGREDIENTS:

3 medium red apples, cored, cubed, skin on

½ cup water

2 tbsp ground chia seeds

2 tsp cinnamon

1 tbsp minced ginger root

OPTIONAL ADDITIONS:

1 tsp honey

1 tsp maca powder

2 tbsp hemp seeds

DIRECTIONS:

1. Bring apples and water to a boil in a medium saucepan, then cover and reduce heat to a simmer for 15 minutes. Mash in pot with a whisk or fork.

2. Remove from heat and stir in remaining ingredients.

Makes 2 large or 3 small servings.

162

BREAKFAST PUDDING (MOCK TAPIOCA)

Make this pudding before you go to bed, store it in the refrigerator, and you will wake up to a quick, omega-rich breakfast all ready to go on busy mornings. Two tablespoons of hemp hearts have 5 grams of complete protein, and 2 tablespoons of chia seeds have 5 grams of fiber. It is important to include protein and fiber in your breakfast routine if you want to slim down.

INGREDIENTS:

1½ cups unsweetened coconut beverage
    (2% fat) or other unsweetened
    non-dairy milk (hemp, almond),
    room temperature

⅓ cup white or black chia seeds

2 tbsp hemp hearts (hulled hemp seeds)

2 tbsp raw honey

1 tsp pure vanilla extract

1 tsp cinnamon

1 tsp ground ginger

½ tbsp fresh lemon juice

⅛ tsp pink rock salt or gray sea salt

GARNISH:

1 cup fresh raspberries or 2 tbsp dried
    cranberries, apple juice sweetened

OPTIONAL ADDITION:

2 tbsp unsweetened shredded coconut

DIRECTIONS:

1. Place coconut beverage in a medium bowl. Whisk in chia seeds until completely covered with liquid.

2. Add hemp hearts. Whisk in honey, vanilla, cinnamon, ginger, lemon juice, and salt until well combined. Cover and refrigerate until mixture thickens to a pudding texture, about 6 hours.

3. Scoop chia pudding into bowls. Top with berries and coconut (if using).

Makes 4 servings.

SUPERFOOD QUINOA PORRIDGE

Rolled quinoa is a wonderful, fast-cooking alternative to oatmeal. It's a nutty, gluten-free seed grain that provides 8 grams of protein and 5 grams of fiber in 1 cup, when cooked. Quinoa is also an excellent source of absorbable calcium and magnesium, plus a good source of iron, zinc, vitamin E, and selenium. Your adrenals will thank you for this high-protein, mineral-rich grain, which will help to balance your blood sugar, support insulin function, and nourish your nerves.

INGREDIENTS:

2 cups filtered water

¾ cup rolled quinoa flakes

¼ cup hemp hearts

½ tsp ground ginger

½ tsp cinnamon

1 cup chopped pear or whole raspberries

½ cup unsweetened non-dairy beverage (coconut, almond, hemp)

1 tsp coconut syrup or honey or mesquite powder

OPTIONAL SUPERFOOD BOOSTER:

¼ cup goji berries or mulberries

DIRECTIONS:

1. Bring water to a boil in a small saucepan. Add quinoa and stir for 2 to 3 minutes.

2. Remove from heat and let cool slightly. Mix in hemp hearts, ginger, and cinnamon.

3. Top with fruit, non-dairy beverage of your choice, and a splash of sweetener.

Makes 2 servings.

RASPBERRY BREAKFAST SORBET

The anti-inflammatory raspberries in this recipe make it tart yet sweet. Hemp is an excellent source of easily digestible protein, and having protein in the morning will help to balance your blood sugar, an essential factor for weight loss.

INGREDIENTS:

1 cup frozen organic raspberries

1½ cups ice

⅔ cup berry juice

¼ cup hemp seeds

1–2 grams stevia powder or 5–10 drops stevia liquid (depending on desired sweetness)

OPTIONAL SUPERFOOD BOOSTER:

1 tbsp lemon-flavored fish oil

1 tsp maca powder or ½ tsp liquid maca

DIRECTIONS:

1. Place all ingredients into a blender and blend until smooth. You may need to stir ingredients a few times for a more consistent texture.

Makes 3 servings.

COCONUT GLUTEN-FREE PANCAKES

I don't know about you, but regular pancakes made with refined white flour and sugar used to send my blood sugar soaring, causing me to crash and burn—hitting the wall before I even got to lunch! These delicious coconut pancakes are packed with protein and sweetened with applesauce and stevia so that you can feel energized all morning. Coconut flour is a terrific slimming substitute for wheat flour because it is gluten free, high in fiber, high in protein, and low in carbohydrates!

INGREDIENTS:

½ cup coconut flour

¼ cup hemp protein powder

½ tsp baking soda

1 tbsp coconut sugar (or 10–15 drops of stevia)

1 tsp cinnamon

½ tsp nutmeg

3 eggs

2 tbsp melted virgin coconut oil, divided

½ cup unsweetened coconut beverage (2% fat) or other unsweetened non-dairy milk
    (hemp, almond)

¼ cup unsweetened applesauce

OPTIONAL ADDITION:

1 cup blueberries (fresh or frozen)

DIRECTIONS:

1. Preheat pancake pan on medium-low heat.

2. In a large bowl, add coconut flour, hemp protein powder, baking soda, coconut sugar, and spices and whisk until combined.

3. In a separate bowl, whisk eggs. Add 1 tbsp oil, coconut beverage, and applesauce.

4. Carefully fold wet ingredients into dry ingredients until combined. By this time your pan should be ready to go.

5. Oil the pan with 1 tsp of oil per batch. Scoop 2 tbsp of batter into an oiled pan to create 3-inch pancakes, no more than ½-inch thick. Cook slowly for 5 minutes per side. If using, add blueberries to the formed pancake while batter is still soft to ensure proper cooking. Repeat process, oiling pan with another tsp of oil.

6. Top with coconut butter, maple syrup, raw honey, nut butter, sugar-free blueberry jam, or whatever you like.

Makes 12 pancakes.

COCONUT GRANOLA

This raw, gluten-free granola is high in protein due to its hemp and pumpkin seeds, making it a perfect way to start your day. Keep in mind that granola turns out best when it is dehydrated.

INGREDIENTS:

1 cup raw buckwheat groats

1 cup pumpkin seeds

1 cup sunflower seeds

1 cup coconut, shredded or flakes

1 tbsp pure vanilla extract

1 tbsp melted virgin coconut oil

⅓ cup coconut nectar or honey

1 tsp cardamom

1 tbsp cinnamon

½ tsp turmeric

1 tsp ground ginger

1 cup hemp seeds

1 cup goji berries (or cranberries if nightshade sensitive)

Pink rock salt or gray sea salt, to taste

QUICK-COOKING DIRECTIONS:

1. Preheat oven to 350°F.

2. Place buckwheat, pumpkin seeds, and sunflower seeds in a large mixing bowl and fill with soaking water. Let soak for 2 to 8 hours.

3. Drain water thoroughly. Add the rest of the ingredients except hemp seeds and goji berries and incorporate.

4. With clean hands, spread mixture onto parchment-lined cookie trays as thinly as possible, and bake for 30 minutes until dried out.

5. Allow to cool for 20 minutes. Add hemp seeds and goji berries and store in an airproof container.

DEHYDRATING DIRECTIONS:

1. Follow steps 1 to 3 above. With clean hands, spread wet granola onto parchment-lined sheets, as thinly as possible.

2. Set dehydrator at 115°F for about 6 to 8 hours.

3. Allow to cool for 20 minutes. Add hemp seeds and goji berries and store in an airproof container in fridge.

Makes 6 cups.

EGGS FLORENTINE

When was the last time you went out for brunch and ordered Eggs Florentine? Some popular restaurants' versions of this famous brunch use processed Hollandaise sauce with inflammatory ingredients and can have up to 54 grams of fat! Here's a great alternative to try at home. Serving poached eggs on a bed of Swiss chard or spinach is a great way to start incorporating vegetables into your breakfast!

INGREDIENTS:

2 tbsp virgin coconut oil

2 cups diced onion

1 clove garlic, chopped

4 cups spinach or Swiss chard, loosely packed

1 tsp white vinegar

1 tsp pink rock salt or gray sea salt

4 large chicken or duck eggs

DIRECTIONS:

1. Heat coconut oil in a medium frying pan on medium heat and sauté onion and garlic until tender (about 2 minutes). Add greens, stirring until they are wilted slightly (about 1 minute). Place greens mixture in the center of a plate and cover to keep warm.

2. In a wide saucepan, add enough water to fill to 2 inches deep. Bring to boil. Add vinegar and salt and reduce heat to a strong simmer. Working with one egg at a time, crack egg into a bowl, making sure not to break yolk. Take a fork and stir water, making a "vortex" in center of the saucepan. Carefully pour egg from bowl into vortex. It should wrap itself up into a bundle. Repeat with the other 3 eggs. Once all eggs are in the water, give water another swirl using a fork. This will ensure the eggs do not stick to bottom of the pan. Turn off the heat, cover, and let stand for 3 to 4 minutes until egg whites are completely cooked.

3. Top the plated greens with 2 eggs removed from water with a slotted spoon. Dry them quickly on a clean kitchen towel to absorb excess water that can make your plate wet.

4. Top with Vegan Hollandaise Sauce (below) if desired.

Makes 2 servings.

VEGAN HOLLANDAISE SAUCE

This is my version of one of the world's most decadent sauces. I have replaced the egg yolks and butter traditionally used with healthier ingredients to reduce the inflammatory response. This sauce is delicious on my Eggs Florentine recipe (page 170), or try serving it over steamed asparagus for a nice side dish. See Resources section for more on Vegenaise (Follow Your Heart).

INGREDIENTS:

½ cup Vegenaise (egg-free mayonnaise)

¼ cup yellow prepared mustard

1 tsp nutritional yeast

DIRECTIONS:

1. Mix ingredients in a small bowl until well combined.

Makes ¾ cup.

EGGS IN THE BUNNY HOLE

Just like Peter Rabbit, who loved digging holes in the vegetable patch, we are going to dig holes in this vegetable medley and gently poach our eggs to protect the lipid-rich yolk from oxidation. Shiitake mushrooms are a good source of all the B vitamins, and just 3 tablespoons pack more than 90 percent of your daily recommended intake of vitamin B5. Getting enough Bs in our diet helps us stay focused and happy and keeps our hands out of the cookie jar!

INGREDIENTS:

2 tsp extra-virgin olive oil

1 clove garlic, finely chopped

½ tsp chopped fresh basil

½ tsp chopped fresh oregano

1 cup diced onion

⅔ cup sliced shiitake mushrooms

1 cup diced zucchini

½ cup vegetable broth

4 eggs

Pink rock salt or gray sea salt, to taste

2 tbsp chopped fresh parsley

OPTIONAL ADDITION:

1 cup cherry tomatoes or ¼ cup sun-dried tomatoes, chopped

DIRECTIONS:

1. Heat a large cast-iron skillet over medium heat. Add olive oil, garlic, basil, and oregano and stir until well coated, about 15 seconds.

2. Add onion and shiitake mushrooms. Cook, stirring occasionally, for 3 to 5 minutes or until tender.

3. Add zucchini. Cook for about 2 minutes. Add tomatoes and warm gently for 1 minute.

4. Dig four holes into vegetable mixture. Fill holes with broth. Break eggs and pour them into holes. Cook until eggs reach desired consistency (about 3 more minutes).

5. Transfer to plates using a spatula, making sure to get both eggs and vegetables in each serving. Season to taste with salt and sprinkle chopped parsley over top. Serve immediately.

Makes 2 servings.

LOSE TWICE THE WEIGHT BY EATING A BIG BREAKFAST!

In 2012, researchers at Tel Aviv University conducted a three-month study with ninety-three overweight and obese women with metabolic syndrome (a cluster of health conditions associated with type 2 diabetes). The women were divided into two groups, each consuming 1,400 calories a day. The first group consumed 50 percent of the allotted calories at breakfast, 36 percent at lunch, and 14 percent at dinner. The other group ate 14 percent of their calories at breakfast, 36 percent at midday, and 50 percent at dinner. Participants were measured for various body and metabolic markers every two weeks.

The women who ate like queens at breakfast lost an average nineteen pounds and trimmed 3.3 inches from their waistlines over twelve weeks, while those who feasted at night shed only eight pounds and 1.5 inches.

JULE BARS

The Jule Bar is perfect for someone who is looking for a boost of energy without the excess sweetness of a standard post-workout bar. The rich, nutty flavor delivers important minerals like selenium, magnesium, zinc, and calcium. You don't have to dehydrate these bars, but if you do, they'll travel better and have the texture of a store-bought bar.

INGREDIENTS:

1 cup tahini

1½ cups chopped dried figs (stems removed)

2 tbsp ground chia seeds or flaxseeds

¼ cup honey or rice syrup

½ cup Brazil nuts, coarsely chopped

¾ cup walnuts

¼ cup hemp or pumpkin protein powder

½ tbsp pure vanilla extract

½ tbsp cinnamon

¾ cup pumpkin seeds

½ tsp pink rock salt or gray sea salt

1 tsp maca powder or ashwagandha powder

DIRECTIONS:

1. In food processor with the S-blade, blend tahini, figs, and chia until smooth but not a nut butter consistency. Add remaining ingredients, mixing well until blended, but with nuts and seeds still visible.

2. Evenly roll out mixture onto 2 parchment-lined dehydrator trays (or one 9 x 13–inch cookie tray if using an oven) to a thickness of ½ inch.

3. Freeze for 45 minutes, then cut into bars (with paper left underneath for support) with a sharp knife.

4. If you need bars to last a long time, dehydrate for 6 hours at 115°F. If using an oven, bake at 125°F for 2 hours. Be very careful not to overcook seeds, or the nutritional value of the essential fats will be lost.

5. Wrap bars individually or place in a cookie tin with parchment paper between layers so they don't stick together. Store and serve direct from freezer.

Makes 24 bars.

KASHA CREPES

In North America, buckwheat kernels or buckwheat groats are often called kasha. Despite the name, this is actually a wheat-free fruit seed that is related to rhubarb. It has many health benefits, one of which is its ability to balance blood sugar, thereby lowering the risk of developing type 2 diabetes. These crepes can be made as a sweet or savory dish—just make sure you omit the honey for a savory crepe. Double this recipe to pair it with Beef and Mushroom Stroganoff (page 258). Note: If you can't find buckwheat kernels in your local health food store, you can use quinoa. The texture of the crepe will be a bit chewy, but it still tastes good.

INGREDIENTS:

¾ cup unsweetened coconut beverage (2% fat) or other unsweetened non-dairy milk
    (hemp, almond)

2 tsp tahini

½ cup whole buckwheat kernels

1 egg

1–2 tsp honey

1 tbsp virgin coconut oil

OPTIONAL ADDITIONS:

2 cups berries (for filling for sweet crepes)

1 tsp dried basil (for savory crepes)

¼ tsp pink rock salt or gray sea salt (for savory crepes)

DIRECTIONS:

1. Combine coconut beverage, tahini, and buckwheat kernels in blender. Blend for about 3 minutes on high, occasionally scraping down sides of blender. Add egg and honey (if making savory crepes, omit honey and add basil and salt). Blend until well mixed.

2. When ready to make crepes, place 1 tsp of coconut oil in crepe pan for each crepe over medium-high heat. Pour batter into pan in small circles until you create a crepe that is 8 inches wide.

3. Cook until bubbles appears and crepe dries slightly. Loosen along edges with a thin spatula. Flip crepe and cook for another 30 seconds. Transfer to a plate and keep warm by covering with a light towel. Add another teaspoon of oil to pan and continue making crepes until batter is used up.

4. Fill each crepe lengthwise with desired filling.

Makes 3 crepes.

LIFE-CHANGING LOAF

My clients are always telling me that they miss their bread, so when I saw that Sarah Britton of My New Roots (www.mynewroots.org) had come up with this brilliant life-changing loaf, I had to try it. I have adapted it by replacing the rolled oats with rolled quinoa and swapping out the maple syrup with coconut nectar. It is delicious toasted, so you can store it sliced in the freezer and pop it into the toaster for a delicious snack.

INGREDIENTS:

1 cup sunflower seeds

½ cup whole flaxseeds

½ cup hazelnuts, almonds or pecans

1½ cups rolled quinoa

2 tbsp ground chia seeds

4 tbsp psyllium husks (3 tbsp if using powdered)

1 tsp pink rock salt or gray sea salt

1 tbsp coconut nectar or honey

3 tbsp melted virgin coconut oil

1½ cups water

DIRECTIONS:

1. In a large bowl, combine all dry ingredients, stirring well.

2. In a separate bowl, whisk together coconut nectar, coconut oil, and water.

3. Add to dry ingredients and mix until everything is combined and dough is very thick.

4. Transfer and press into a greased loaf pan. It is important to press dough very firmly into the pan to avoid loaf being crumbly.

5. Let pan sit out on counter for at least 2 hours. (You can also let it sit overnight.) You'll know that it's ready to bake when the dough is stiff and holds the bread–pan shape when you pull a bit of dough away from a corner of the pan.

6. When ready to bake, preheat oven to 350°F.

7. Place loaf pan in oven on middle rack and bake for 20 minutes. Remove loaf from pan and place upside down directly on rack and bake for another 30 to 40 minutes. You will know that bread is done when it sounds hollow when tapped.

8. Let cool completely before slicing. Store in a tightly sealed container for up to 5 days or slice and freeze. (I doubt that this bread will even make it to the freezer!)

Makes 12 slices.

QUINOA BERRY GRANOLA

I created this recipe so everyone can enjoy the goodness of quinoa, even when they're crazy busy in the morning. Overly sweet commercial granola is full of fat and sugar. Here, dried fruit is the main event. If you have a nut sensitivity, swap pumpkin seeds for the nuts. This granola tastes great on top of stewed apples.

INGREDIENTS:

1 large, ripe banana

2 tbsp tahini

½ tsp pure vanilla extract

2 tbsp honey

2 cups rolled quinoa flakes

¾ cup chopped almonds or hazelnuts

2 tsp cinnamon

½ tsp nutmeg

½ tsp cardamom

1 tbsp ground flaxseeds

½ cup dried cranberries, apple juice sweetened

½ cup goji berries

DIRECTIONS:

1. Preheat oven to 275°F.

2. Mash banana in a large bowl with a fork. Add tahini, vanilla, and honey, and stir to combine.

3. Add nuts and spices into wet mixture. Stir until combined and spread onto a parchment-lined baking sheet, breaking up large clumps with your fingers to ensure even cooking.

4. Bake for 45 minutes to 1 hour (or longer if you have a cool oven). Stir every 15 minutes to ensure even browning. The granola is done when it starts to crisp up and nuts are getting toasty.

5. Remove granola from oven and stir in flaxseeds and dried berries. Allow granola to cool completely on pan before transferring to an airtight container. It will get crunchy as it cools.

Makes 8 servings.

PAINTED FRUIT

This is a fun and delicious way to serve fruit for breakfast. Spirulina is one of nature's most powerful superfoods. It contains a highly digestible form of complete protein as well as various minerals that boost the immune system to fight off bacteria and viruses. When the fruit is added to the sauce and mixed with the salad, it looks like it has been painted rich green.

INGREDIENTS:

4 cups northern fruit (e.g., apples, pears, plums, peaches, or berries), cubed

1 tsp fresh lemon juice or lime juice

¼ cup nut or seed butter

1 tbsp raw honey or coconut nectar

2 tbsp apple juice

1 tsp spirulina powder

1 tbsp hemp seeds

½ tsp cinnamon

¼ tsp nutmeg

OPTIONAL SUPERFOOD BOOSTERS:

1 tsp bee pollen, coconut flakes, or maca powder

1 tsp lemon-flavored fish oil or hemp oil

DIRECTIONS:

1. Mix cubed fruit together in a bowl.

2. Squeeze lemon juice over fruit to protect it from oxidation.

3. In a separate bowl, blend together nut butter, honey, apple juice, spirulina, and hemp.

4. Add cinnamon and nutmeg and combine.

5. Pour over fruit and mix.

6. Top with a sprinkle of bee pollen, coconut, or maca powder, if desired.

Makes 4 servings.

SALADS, SAUCES, DIPS, AND DRESSINGS

"You are what you eat so don't be fast, cheap, easy, or fake." –Unknown

BLUEBERRY VINAIGRETTE

A confirmed salad lover's new addiction! I always have a bag of frozen wild blueberries in the freezer for my smoothies. One day I thought, "Why not throw some into my salad dressing?" This dressing is a fine complement to a salad with fresh apples and green onions.

INGREDIENTS:

½ cup frozen blueberries

2 tbsp apple cider vinegar

¼ cup hemp oil or olive oil

½ tbsp minced fresh ginger root

1 tsp raw honey

⅛ tsp pink rock salt or gray sea salt

DIRECTIONS:

1. In a large blender, blend together all ingredients. This will keep refrigerated for over a week.

Makes 1 cup of dressing.

VINEGAR AND CARBOHYDRATES

The fastest trick to reduce blood sugar is to enjoy sour foods. Pairing carbohydrates with apple cider vinegar has several weight-loss benefits. First, the vinegar may induce satiety and help you eat less. Second, vinegar may actually prevent the metabolism of some carbohydrates. Third, vinegar could make you more responsive to insulin and diminish the release of this fat-promoting hormone. Finally, preliminary studies in laboratory mice suggest that vinegar may turn on specific genes that burn fat in the liver.

CURRIED HONEY-LIME DRESSING

This creamy dressing will add zest to any salad. It's easy to just toss all the ingredients into a mason jar; give it a shake and it's ready to go. If you're sensitive to nightshades, then substitute turmeric powder for the curry and experience extra anti-inflammatory effect.

INGREDIENTS:

1 tbsp fresh lime juice

2 tsp lime zest

½ cup Vegenaise or homemade mayo or avocado

1 tbsp raw honey

1 tsp finely grated fresh ginger root

½ tsp curry or turmeric

¼ tsp pink rock salt or gray sea salt

½ tsp minced garlic

DIRECTIONS:

1. Mix all ingredients in a mason jar and shake well, then toss with your favorite salad greens. If using avocado, combine all ingredients in a blender to mix smoothly.

Makes ¾ cup.

FAUX PARMESAN CHEESE

Nutritional yeast is a wonderful flavor enhancer that adds a savory, cheesy, nutty taste to dishes. As you might guess from its name, it is packed with nutrients, specifically B vitamins, folic acid, selenium, zinc, and protein. This recipe can be used anywhere you might use Parmesan cheese. My husband loves it on his popcorn along with a sprinkle of apple cider vinegar.

INGREDIENTS:

2 tbsp cashews

2 tbsp pine nuts

2 tbsp nutritional yeast

½ tsp pink rock salt or gray sea salt

DIRECTIONS:

1. Place all ingredients in a food processor and blend until texture resembles finely grated Parmesan cheese. Store in refrigerator for freshness.

Makes ¼ cup.

FAUX RICOTTA CHEESE

This recipe is adapted from one I found in *Ani's Raw Food Kitchen*, by Ani Phyo. It makes the perfect substitute for regular ricotta cheese in the World's Healthiest Gluten-Free Lasagna (page 288). It is also simply delicious and will bust a dairy craving. If you are sensitive to soy, try it with tahini and increase the sea salt.

INGREDIENTS:

2 cloves garlic, peeled

1 cup pine nuts or cashews

1 cup walnuts

1½ tbsp light miso or tahini

1 tbsp nutritional yeast

2 tbsp fresh lemon juice

¼–⅓ cup water

½ cup fresh parsley

½ tsp–1 tsp pink rock salt or gray sea salt

DIRECTIONS:

1. Add garlic to food processor. Using the S-blade attachment, process into small pieces.

2. Add pine nuts and walnuts and process into powder.

3. Add miso, nutritional yeast, and lemon juice. Process, adding water just until mixture has the texture of ricotta cheese.

4. Add parsley and lightly process until combined. Add salt to taste. Will keep in fridge for up to 4 days or frozen for up to 3 months.

Makes 4 servings.

CREAMY FIG-CASHEW DIP

This dip is creamy and rich with a natural sweetness from both the figs and the cashews. Three small figs contain 5 grams of fiber! Studies show that eating figs helps to improve gut motility, thereby preventing and treating constipation. Figs can reduce inflammation and are being studied for their ability to prevent cancer. I like this dip best served with flax crackers (see Salad Bars recipe variation on page 309) or on the Life-Changing Loaf (page 178).

INGREDIENTS:

1 cup dried figs, stems trimmed

1 cup raw cashews

2 tbsp nutritional yeast

½ tsp pink rock salt or gray sea salt

1 tbsp fresh lemon juice

DIRECTIONS:

1. Place figs and cashews in a bowl. Cover and soak in water for 2 to 8 hours.

2. Drain figs and cashews and place in food processor.

3. Add nutritional yeast, salt, and lemon juice, and blend.

4. Halfway through blending, use a spatula to scrape down sides to ensure proper mixing. Resume blending to a smooth consistency.

Makes 2 cups.

DOPAMINE-BOOSTING DIP

I used fava beans in this recipe because they are rich in a chemical called dopamine. Research has shown that the human brain uses dopamine to tell the body when to stop eating. Low dopamine levels may also play a role in overeating, especially for people who have a genetic predisposition to low levels of this brain chemical. This dip is great for entertaining guests who may be allergic to nuts. By using the food processor on high for a few more minutes than usual, you create a smooth and creamy dip that is tangy to start and mellows over time. Serve with raw asparagus, celery sticks, and fresh snap peas.

INGREDIENTS:

19-oz can fava beans

¼ cup unsweetened coconut beverage (2% fat) or other non-dairy beverage or water

¼ cup extra-virgin olive oil

¾ cup hemp hearts

¼ cup apple cider vinegar

½ tsp pink rock salt or gray sea salt

1 tsp nutritional yeast (optional)

1 tsp dried basil

DIRECTIONS:

1. Rinse fava beans thoroughly (to reduce their gassiness).

2. Mix all ingredients in a food processor, using the S-blade, for 5 to 7 minutes or until extra creamy. For a thicker dip, cut back 2 tbsp of coconut beverage.

Makes 3 cups.

FESTIVE POMEGRANATE TABOULI

I remember when pomegrantes were precious imports brought over on ships once a year for a Christmas treat. Today they are available for several months of the year, but to me they still have an exotic quality. While their seeds have been used for fertility since ancient times, it turns out they offer so much more. Pomegranate seeds are high in dietary fiber, folate, vitamin C, and vitamin K, and are literally bursting with antioxidants that help to cool inflammatory fires in the body.

INGREDIENTS:

1 cup quinoa

1½ cups water

1 cup pomegranate seeds

1 cup fresh mint, chopped (if unavailable, add extra parsley or cilantro)

2 cups fresh parsley or cilantro

½ cup pecans, chopped

¼ cup extra-virgin olive oil

¼ cup fresh lemon juice

½ tsp pink rock salt or gray sea salt

OPTIONAL ADDITION:

1 cup cherry or grape tomatoes, halved

DIRECTIONS:

1. In a saucepan, bring quinoa and water to a boil. Lower heat and simmer for 20 minutes. Let cool.

2. Meanwhile, seed pomegranate and chop mint, parsley, pecans, and tomatoes (if using).

3. Once quinoa has cooled, combine all ingredients in a medium bowl and mix well. Serve immediately or cover and refrigerate for up to 3 days.

Makes 6 servings.

HEALING SALAD IN A JAR

If you like to take a salad for lunch but don't have time to prepare it in the morning, I have the solution for you. By using a Mason jar and putting the dressing in first, you can make salads ahead of time. When you are ready to eat, just give the salad a shake and enjoy. Feel free to change up the ingredients of the salad. Just remember to always place the greens at the top of the jar to keep them from coming into contact with the dressing.

INGREDIENTS:

4 tbsp Roasted Garlic Vinaigrette (page 193)

¼ cup diced red onion

1 cup cooked black beans, drained and rinsed if canned

1 cup chopped apples

1 cup shredded carrot

¼ cup walnuts

1 cup cooked red quinoa

2 cups spinach or arugula

DIRECTIONS:

1. Find 2 wide-mouth 32-oz Mason jars with tight-fitting lids.

2. Pour half the dressing into bottom of each jar, then add onion, beans, and apples so they can marinate.

3. Add carrot, walnuts, quinoa, and, at the very top, spinach or arugula.

4. Shake well just before serving to coat ingredients.

Makes 2 servings.

ROASTED GARLIC VINAIGRETTE

INGREDIENTS:

3 tbsp extra-virgin olive oil

3 tbsp apple cider vinegar

2 tbsp water

1 tsp dried basil

2 tbsp raw honey

¼ tsp pink rock salt or gray sea salt

2 cloves garlic, roasted, or 1 clove raw garlic, crushed

DIRECTIONS:

1. Place all ingredients into blender and blend for about 30 seconds. Use immediately or store in a jar for 1 to 2 weeks

JULIE'S SUPER IRON-RICH PÂTÉ

If you are feeling exhausted, run-down, and forgetful, you may not be getting enough iron. Many women suffer from anemia or iron deficiency, and this can be a major cause of fatigue and brain fog. Liver is one of the richest food sources of iron. The added vitamin C in this recipe helps the body to absorb the iron and supports adrenal function.

INGREDIENTS:

1 lb organic chicken liver or beef liver, sliced into 1-inch chunks

2 cups chopped onion

2 tbsp extra-virgin olive oil, divided

2 tbsp stone ground or yellow prepared mustard

1 tbsp sliced sun-dried tomatoes

⅓ cup green or black olives, pitted

¼¼ tsp vitamin C powder (1,000 mg ascorbic acid) or 1 tbsp fresh lemon juice

DIRECTIONS:

1. In a frying pan over medium heat, sauté liver and onions in 1 tbsp olive oil until liver is cooked through, approximately 7 to 10 minutes.

2. Transfer liver and onions to a food processor, add all remaining ingredients, and blend until smooth.

Makes 3 cups or 25 servings (1 serving = 2 tbsp).

GREAT GOMASIO

I suggest that you toss the salt shaker and make up some of this great-tasting seasoning instead. Of all the people on earth, the Japanese live the longest, and they grace their tables with gomasio rather than the white sodium chloride we sprinkle on our food every day. You can reduce sodium while adding calcium, magnesium, iron, protein, and fiber to your next meal! Gomasio is made by lightly grinding dry-roasted sesame seeds with sea salt. You can purchase it prepared from health food stores, but it's easy to make, and fresh-roasting your own sesame seeds ensures the healthy oils are preserved, providing you with the best nutrition.

INGREDIENTS:

½ cup raw, unhulled sesame seeds (black or white or mixed)

1 tsp pink rock salt or gray sea salt

DIRECTIONS:

1. Place seeds in a clean, dry frying pan and toast on low heat, stirring often, until warmed gently (10 to 12 minutes). The longer, lower-temperature toasting will result in a more even heat distribution, reducing damage to the oils in the seeds.

2. Allow seeds to cool for about 10 minutes, then place in a small electric grinder with salt and pulse a few times until most of the seeds are cracked open. Be careful not to grind to a flour consistency; you want some of the texture of the seed to remain. If you don't own a coffee/spice grinder, grinding seeds by hand with a Japanese mortar and pestle works well.

Makes ½ cup.

HEMPY PURPLE COLESLAW

The zip in this recipe is from the tangy sour flavor of the sauerkraut. Look for unpasteurized sauerkraut in your local health food store, as the natural process of fermentation creates beneficial probiotic bacteria. I love Ambrosia apples because they are slow to brown when cut and are ideal for salads. Nutty hemp hearts offer the healing benefits of magnesium and omega-3 fatty acids.

INGREDIENTS:
SALAD:

1 cup unpasteurized sauerkraut, drained

4 cups finely shredded purple cabbage

½ cup finely sliced red onion

2 organic apples, unpeeled, cored and thinly sliced

2 tbsp hemp hearts

DRESSING:

2 tbsp hemp oil

2 tbsp sauerkraut liquid

1 tsp dried dill weed

Raw honey, to taste

2 tsp pink rock salt or gray sea salt

DIRECTIONS:

1. Drain sauerkraut and reserve liquid. Mix together salad ingredients.

2. In a separate bowl, whisk dressing ingredients together.

3. Add dressing to salad and combine until salad is evenly coated.

Makes 6 servings.

IMMUNE-BOOSTING CAESAR SALAD

This salad is a great departure from the standard offering of Parmesan cheese, a dressing high in fat, and salty croutons. There's fiber from the celery, and the dates give the dressing a creamy texture without dairy, so it can be served to anyone with lactose intolerance. Raw garlic is a surefire way to boost your immune system and protect yourself from catching the latest virus going around.

INGREDIENTS:

SALAD:

1 head romaine lettuce or 2 romaine
    hearts

1 head purple endive, leaves separated

½ fresh pineapple, diced

1 tbsp capers

10 gluten-free flax crackers, broken into
    pieces as croutons

DRESSING:

½ cup extra-virgin olive oil or garlic flax oil

2–3 cloves garlic

1 celery stalk, chopped fine

¼ cup water

2 tbsp fresh lemon juice

1 tbsp wheat-free tamari or coconut aminos

3 anchovy fillets

1 Medjool date (or 1 tsp honey if dates
    are unavailable)

OPTIONAL ADDITION:

½ tsp nutritional yeast

DIRECTIONS:

1. Wash and dry romaine and endive leaves and place on a serving plate. Layer pineapple on top of greens, then sprinkle on capers and flax cracker croutons.

2. Using a blender, whip all dressing ingredients together. Pour over salad. (Leftovers can be stored in fridge for up to 2 weeks.)

Makes 2 full salads or 4 side salads.

LOCAVORE FENNEL-APPLE SALAD

One of the best things about this salad is that it can easily be made with locally grown ingredients that you can find in most North American farmers' markets. Fennel has very potent diuretic properties but does not deplete your body of the important electrolyte mineral potassium. The diuretic properties of fennel can relieve PMS symptoms such as bloating, cramping and general edema without any side effects.

INGREDIENTS:

DRESSING:

4 tbsp apple cider vinegar

1 clove garlic, minced

½ tsp cumin

1 tsp yellow prepared mustard

1 tsp raw honey

¼ tsp pink rock salt or gray sea salt

¼ cup extra-virgin olive oil or flax oil

SALAD:

2 medium apples, cored

1 fennel bulb, cored

8 cups baby spinach, packed

OPTIONAL ADDITIONS:

⅓ cup chopped fresh mint

¼ cup hemp seeds or walnuts

DIRECTIONS:

1. In a small bowl, whisk vinegar with garlic, cumin, mustard, honey, and salt. Gradually whisk in oil and set aside.

2. Slice apple and fennel as thinly as possible, preferably using a mandoline. A regular vegetable peeler will also produce thin but shorter slices of fennel.

3. In a separate bowl, toss baby spinach with half of the dressing. Assemble salads on individual plates. Layer apples on top of spinach and top with a pile of thinly sliced fennel. Drizzle more dressing on top. Garnish with mint and seeds or nuts if desired.

Makes 4 salads.

BUST THE BLUES HEMP SALAD

If you want a stress-busting meal, this salad is for you. Live sprouts provide B vitamins that nourish your nervous system. The red pepper is an excellent source of vitamin C, which is important for adrenal health. Blueberries have been shown in clinical trials to reduce the stress hormone cortisol. Tie all those superfoods together with the nutty flavor of omega 3–rich, mood-boosting hemp hearts and you have a truly happy salad!

INGREDIENTS:

4 cups sunflower or pea sprouts

½ cup sliced red pepper

⅔ cup blueberries

1 cup snow peas

¼ cup extra-virgin olive oil

2 tbsp dairy-free pesto or 1 tbsp basil, dried, plus 1 tbsp oil

2–3 tbsp fresh lemon juice

1 tsp raw honey

Pink rock salt or gray sea salt, to taste

¼ cup hemp hearts

DIRECTIONS:

1. Combine sprouts, red pepper, blueberries, and snow peas in a large bowl.

2. In a small mason jar, add oil, pesto, lemon juice, honey, and salt, and shake vigorously until well mixed.

3. Pour over salad and top with hemp hearts.

Makes 2 large salads.

LOVELY LENTIL SALAD

This hearty new spin on an old classic makes a great fast meal and packs well for lunch the next day. The steady, long-lasting energy you can expect from this vitamin- and mineral-charged dish will obliterate those mid-afternoon cravings. The fennel, artichoke, and fresh herbs have wonderful anti-inflammatory action.

INGREDIENTS:

DRESSING:

¼ cup fresh lemon juice

¼ cup extra-virgin olive oil

1 tbsp minced garlic

1 tsp stone-ground or yellow prepared
    mustard

2 tsp dried oregano

½ tsp pink rock salt or gray sea salt

SALAD:

1 cup thinly sliced fennel bulb

½ cup finely diced red onion

½ cup water-packed artichoke hearts,
    drained and chopped

½ cup olives, preferably black

19-oz can green lentils, rinsed and drained

1 cup chopped flat-leaf parsley or cilantro

8 cups baby spinach

OPTIONAL ADDITIONS:

1 cup julienned red pepper

¼ cup chopped sun-dried tomato (dried,
    not packed in oil)

DIRECTIONS:

1. Mix all dressing ingredients in small bowl.

2. In a large bowl, add all salad ingredients, except for spinach. Top with dressing, and mix well.

3. Serve on a bed of spinach, either on individual salad plates or on a platter. The flavor improves as salad marinates, so consider making it ahead. It can be refrigerated for up to 3 days.

Makes 4 side salads.

MEXICAN BLACK BEAN GARLIC DIP

Bean dips are great appetizers for dinner parties, especially when you are trying to slim down. They are filled with fiber, which will help to curb your hunger before a meal and stop you from overeating once the main course is served. The fiber in beans also helps to keep blood sugar nice and steady so you can avoid the highs and lows of dinner party indulgences!

INGREDIENTS:

¼ cup chopped purple onion

½–1 clove garlic, minced

¼ cup chopped cilantro (plus extra for garnish)

1 tbsp extra-virgin olive oil

2 tbsp fresh lime juice

1 tsp dried oregano

1½ tsp cumin

½ tsp pink rock salt or gray sea salt

19-oz can black beans, rinsed, well drained

DIRECTIONS:

1. Place onion, garlic, and cilantro in food processor, and process until roughly chopped.

2. Add olive oil, lime juice, oregano, cumin, salt, and beans, and purée until smooth. (If mixture is a bit thick for a dip, thin with a little water.)

3. Garnish with chopped cilantro.

Makes 2½ cups.

MARINATED CARROT-RIBBON SALAD

This is a beautiful salad, especially if you are able to use sweet and crunchy heirloom carrots. Studies show that while heirloom seeds produce smaller yields, they are higher in nutrients and may be more nutritious than the industrially grown vegetables you find in your supermarket. The pro-vitamin A found in carrots stimulates the production of special white blood cells that attack inflammation-causing bacteria, viruses, and yeast. Another good reason to shop at your local farmers' market!

INGREDIENTS:

3 cups heirloom carrots, sliced into
    ribbons

1 cup thinly sliced fennel bulb

¼ cup sunflower seeds (plus extra for
    garnish)

¼ cup chopped fresh dill (plus extra for
    garnish)

¼ cup chopped cilantro (plus extra for
    garnish)

DRESSING:

1 tbsp raw honey

¼ cup extra-virgin olive oil

1 tbsp apple cider vinegar

1 tsp wheat-free tamari or coconut aminos
    or ¼ tsp sea salt

½ tsp caraway seed

½ tsp cumin

1 clove garlic, crushed

DIRECTIONS:

1. Place carrot strips and fennel in a mixing bowl and add sunflower seeds, dill, and cilantro.

2. Combine all dressing ingredients in a small bowl and mix well.

3. Add dressing to salad and toss gently. Marinate for 2 to 8 hours.

4. Before serving, garnish with extra sunflower seeds, dill, and cilantro.

Makes 4 side salads.

MOCK MAYO TUNA SALAD

You probably won't be surprised to hear that when I travel, I tend to bring a lot of my own food. My kit always includes a few cans of sustainably caught fish. Here is a simple little salad that I came up with in a small hotel room in Paris while traveling in Europe with my sister for the Gourmand World Cookbook Awards. Tuna and mackerel are excellent sources of EPA and DHA—both critical for keeping inflammation in check. Be sure to avoid bluefin tuna, which is known to be high in mercury.

INGREDIENTS:

2 tbsp yellow prepared mustard

1 tbsp fresh basil, chopped

2 tsp Great Gomasio (page 195)

1 tbsp tahini or pumpkin seed butter

1 tsp raw honey

1 can sustainable tuna or mackerel

¾ cup finely chopped celery

OPTIONAL SUPERFOOD BOOSTER:

1 tbsp lemon-flavored fish oil

DIRECTIONS:

1. Mix mustard, basil, gomasio, fish oil (if using), tahini, and honey in a small dish until well blended.

2. Mix in tuna and celery and combine well. Serve on a bed of spinach or with whole-grain gluten-free crackers.

Makes 2 servings.

POPEYE HUMMUS

It's a great idea to stock your freezer with a few packages of frozen spinach. It has the same nutritional value as fresh cooked spinach, so feel free to use it whenever you are pressed for time or don't have any fresh spinach on hand. Spinach is an excellent plant-based source of iron. Making sure that you get enough iron in your diet is crucial for reaching optimal health, as it ensures that a good supply of oxygen is reaching all areas of the body.

INGREDIENTS:

2 cups chickpeas (well-cooked or canned) or cannellini beans (rinsed and drained)

⅓ cup fresh lemon juice

1 tbsp flax oil or walnut oil or ½ tbsp fish oil or olive oil

3 tbsp sesame meal or 2 tbsp tahini

3 cloves garlic, chopped

½ tsp pink rock salt or gray sea salt

1 tsp cumin or ground ginger

1½ cups frozen chopped spinach, partially thawed and loosened

DIRECTIONS:

1. Place all ingredients in food processor and process until very smooth.

2. Place in a serving bowl, cover, and refrigerate until serving time.

Makes 2 cups.

SESAME SALAD

This salad is inspired by the delicious dish served at Japanese restaurants just before the sushi arrives. It is simple to make at home. Serve it as a side salad or add some of your favorite protein for a light lunch. Ginger's pungency comes from a constituent called gingerol, which has strong anti-inflammatory and pain-relieving powers. Sesame contains a phytonutrient known as sesamin that inhibits the conversion of omega-6 fats to inflammatory messengers.

INGREDIENTS:

1 cup julienned heirloom carrots

1 cup julienned cucumber

2 tbsp sesame oil

2 tbsp vinegar (your choice)

2 tbsp sesame seeds

1 piece nori, roughly chopped

OPTIONAL ADDITION:

1 tbsp grated fresh ginger root

DIRECTIONS:

1. In a bowl, combine carrots and cucumber.

2. Add sesame oil, vinegar, and ginger to a small Mason jar, and shake vigorously. Pour over carrots and cucumber.

3. Garnish with sesame seeds and chopped nori.

Makes 2 servings.

PESTO PASTA SALAD

The pasta salads you buy at the deli counter are typically dripping with carbs and calories and usually have few or no vegetables. This recipe is my answer to the deli pasta salad—once you try it, you will never go back. Mint Kale Pesto is a staple around my house. I make a big batch every so often and freeze what I don't use in ice cube trays so it is easy to access when I need it. I like to add it to soups, sauces, and salads to kick the flavor and nutrition up a notch.

MINT KALE PESTO INGREDIENTS:

2 cups purple or green kale leaves, loosely packed

¼ cup raw pine nuts or hemp seeds

1 clove garlic, large

1 tbsp apple cider vinegar

1 cup fresh mint, loosely packed

¾ tsp pink rock salt or gray sea salt

¾ cup extra-virgin olive oil

DIRECTIONS:

1. In a blender or food processor, combine all ingredients and blend until smooth.

Makes 1½ cups.

NOODLE INGREDIENTS:

2 medium zucchini

1 large carrot

DIRECTIONS:

1. Using a spiralizer, vegetable peeler, or mandoline, create long strips of zucchini and carrots.

2. Toss half of the pesto with vegetables noodles and enjoy. Freeze the other pesto portion to enjoy another time.

Makes 2 salads.

PUMPKIN-CILANTRO PESTO

Pumpkin seeds are a good vegetarian source of zinc, a critical nutrient for the immune system. Zinc also protects the prostate and stimulates sex drive by ensuring healthy testosterone levels. Men lose 1.5 percent of their testosterone per year after the age of 30, so lots of pumpkin seeds can make a difference! This pesto is wonderful tossed with steamed greens.

INGREDIENTS:

1 cup roasted pumpkin seeds

1 cup raw pumpkin seeds

4 cups fresh cilantro leaves, well packed

2½ tbsp fresh lemon juice, divided

2 cloves garlic, chopped

1½ tsp cardamom

1 tsp pink rock salt or gray sea salt

1 cup extra-virgin olive oil

DIRECTIONS:

1. Place seeds and cilantro in a food processor and begin processing. Add lemon juice, garlic, cardamom, and salt, and then, with the machine running, slowly add oil to ensure even mixing.

2. Transfer to silicone ice cube trays or muffin trays and freeze to create perfect easy-to-thaw portions.

Makes 3 cups.

VIETNAMESE BEEF SALAD

One of the healthiest ways to enjoy beef is to pair it with lots of greens. Meat protein tends to increase acidity levels in the body, while vegetables will help to create a more alkaline environment. As you shift your body from an acidic to alkaline state, you will bring your pH levels into natural balance. With this new balance, you will begin to see positive changes in your health, such as increased energy levels, improvements in your ability to fight infections, and natural weight loss.

INGREDIENTS:

¾ lb lean round steak, about 1-inch thick

2 cups sugar snap peas

1 cup thinly sliced red or yellow pepper

2 green onions, thinly sliced

1 cup coarsely chopped mint leaves

1 cup grated carrot

3 tbsp rice wine vinegar or coconut vinegar

1 tbsp extra-virgin olive oil

1 tbsp dark sesame oil

2 tsp raw honey

2 cloves garlic, minced

1 tsp minced fresh ginger root

½ tsp pink rock salt or gray sea salt

6 cups baby greens

DIRECTIONS:

1. Oil grill pan and place steak under broiler with medium heat and cook for 3 to 4 minutes on each side (for medium-rare). Alternatively, on the stove top with a bit of oil, sear steak 3 to 4 minutes per side until desired doneness is achieved. Let steak cool and then slice into strips.

2. Trim ends off peas. Place in a large bowl along with pepper, green onion, mint, and carrot.

3. In a small bowl, whisk vinegar with olive oil, sesame oil, honey, garlic, ginger, and salt.

4. Toss with salad and beef and serve on top of a bed of leafy greens.

Makes 4 main servings or 6 appetizers.

POPPY SEED DRESSING

I like to alternate lemon juice and apple cider vinegar as the acidic component of my salad dressings. Both are great for your health, but they have very different flavors and provide the body with different benefits. Some small studies on apple cider vinegar have shown that it may help to lower blood sugar by increasing the body's response to insulin as well as helping to increase feelings of fullness after eating.

INGREDIENTS:

1 tsp poppy seeds

2 tbsp extra-virgin olive oil

1 tsp apple cider vinegar

1 tsp Dijon mustard

½ tsp raw honey

1 tbsp minced onion

⅛ tsp pink rock salt or gray sea salt, or to taste

DIRECTIONS:

1. Place all ingredients in a Mason jar and shake until blended. Store covered in the refrigerator.

Makes ¼ cup.

Note: If you have digestive problems, allow your raw salads to be pre-digested by the dressing. The acidity of the juice will go to work on the cellulose in the greens and make them easier to assimilate.

THE 4-C SALAD

Celery, carrots, cranberry, and cinnamon make this salad simply splendid. Crispy, crunchy celery is the perfect way to lighten up your menu. At only 10 calories per stalk, this veggie may be light in calories, but when it comes to nutrients, it's a heavyweight. It boasts good amounts of vitamins A, B, C, and K, as well as calcium, magnesium, and potassium. Its phytonutrient content is being studied for everything from cancer prevention to cardio-vascular health.

INGREDIENTS:

3 cups carrots, scrubbed and shredded

1½ cups sliced celery

¼ cup chopped cilantro or parsley

⅓ cup dried cranberries (apple juice sweetened)

¼ cup hemp seeds

3 tbsp extra-virgin olive oil

3 tbsp fresh lemon juice

¼ tsp pink rock salt or gray sea salt

1 tsp cinnamon

OPTIONAL ADDITION:

1 tsp raw honey

DIRECTIONS:

1. Place carrots, celery, and cilantro in a large mixing bowl. Add cranberries and hemp seeds and combine.

2. In a jar with a tight-fitting lid, add olive oil, lemon juice, salt, and cinnamon and shake vigorously.

3. Toss over salad and gently mix.

Makes 8 side servings.

DANDELION GREENS WITH BLUEBERRIES AND PINE NUTS

Dandelion greens are amazing for their nutrient-packed goodness and liver-cleansing properties, but it is tough to get folks hooked on their bitterness. This won't be a problem with this wilted salad! The blueberries add sweetness, the pine nuts lend richness to the dish, and the maple syrup brings it all together. It's easy and nutritious, and feels like a spring cleanse on a plate.

INGREDIENTS:

½ cup pine nuts

2 tbsp extra-virgin olive oil

¼ cup chopped purple onion

1 tbsp apple cider vinegar

1½ tsp maple syrup or 1 tsp raw honey

½ cup dried blueberries (or cranberries if you prefer)

5 cups dandelion greens, stems removed, washed, and cut into 3-inch lengths

DIRECTIONS:

1. Heat a small pan on stove top over medium heat. Add pine nuts and stir or toss until toasted gently. Remove from heat and set aside.

2. Heat olive oil over medium heat in a large pan. Add onion and sauté until soft. Add vinegar and maple syrup, and taste for balance. Add more oil or more vinegar, to taste.

3. Add blueberries and cook slightly until they soften, about 1 minute. Lower heat and stir dandelion greens into pan. Toss until just wilted.

4. Place all ingredients into a bowl, top with reserved pine nuts, and serve immediately.

Makes 4 side salads.

GRAIN-FREE TABOULI SALAD

Pulsing seeds in a food processor for a few seconds gives them the texture of tabouli grain. Fresh parsley is slimming and detoxifying and may help to modulate the immune system. Parsley contains essential oils that have been shown to suppress an over-stimulated immune response, making it a key player in the fight against allergies and autoimmune and chronic inflammatory disorders.

INGREDIENTS:
SALAD:
½ cup sunflower seeds, chopped

½ cup sesame seeds

½ cup pumpkin seeds

2 cups finely chopped fresh parsley

½ cup goji berries

DRESSING:
⅓ cup fresh lemon juice

2 tbsp extra-virgin olive oil

1 tsp toasted sesame oil

½ tsp pink rock salt or gray sea salt

1 tsp grated fresh ginger root

DIRECTIONS:
1. Put all seeds in blender and pulse a few times to create a crumbly texture.

2. Place seeds and parsley in a large mixing bowl and add goji berries.

3. Add all dressing ingredients to blender and blend well. Pour over salad and mix well to combine.

Makes 4 servings.

STARTERS, SOUPS, AND SIDES

"Our lives are not in the lap of the gods, but in the lap of our cooks." –Lin Yutang

220

ASPARAGUS AND SALMON ROLLS

I love to make these cool, fresh summer rolls for a light dinner when it's too hot to turn on the stove. Salmon is one of the richest sources of omega-3 fats, best known for reducing inflammation, boosting mood, and improving memory and concentration. Salmon also contains nerve-relaxing tryptophan, which can aid in getting a good night's sleep.

INGREDIENTS:

1 bunch thin asparagus, ends trimmed and spears cut in half

1 tbsp fresh lemon juice

1 tbsp all-natural, sugar-free mayonnaise, such as Vegenaise

2 tbsp prepared yellow mustard

5 oz (140 g) smoked salmon (sugar free), sliced into 2-inch by 3-inch by ¼-inch slices

½ cup fresh chives or dill sprigs

12 rice paper rounds (9-inch)

1 cup basil leaves

1½ cups pea or sunflower sprouts

DIRECTIONS:

1. Partially fill a large frying pan with water and bring to a boil over high heat. Boil asparagus until tender-crisp, about 2 minutes. Drain and rinse under cold running water to stop cooking.

2. In a small bowl, stir together lemon juice, mayonnaise, and mustard.

3. Fill a pie plate with lukewarm water and place beside a clean cutting board. Line up smoked salmon, mayo mixture, asparagus, and greens near the cutting board. Set a clean tea towel near the cutting board.

4. Dip one rice paper round at a time into water and soak until very pliable, about 30 seconds. Set wet rice paper round against a towel, gently dabbing it dry on both sides, and then lay on cutting board.

5. Place a slice of salmon along the bottom third of round. Spread a teaspoon of mayo mixture over salmon. With the tips in opposite directions, lay two asparagus spears on top of the salmon. Top with chives, basil, and sprouts.

6. Lift rice paper edge closest to you up and over filling, then roll tightly toward the center. When you reach the center, fold in sides. Continue rolling to form a log. Set roll, seam-side down, on a platter.

7. Repeat with remaining ingredients. As soaking water cools, replace with lukewarm water. Slice rolls in half diagonally to serve right away or leave whole and refrigerate up to 4 hours.

Makes 12 rolls.

FAR EAST BROCCOLI

It's no wonder broccoli is such a popular superfood. It is packed with vitamins, nutrients, and fiber but only has 44 calories per cup. This recipe is full of flavor and maximizes broccoli's nutritional benefits. Serve cold as an hors d'oeuvre or hot as a side dish.

INGREDIENTS:

4 cups broccoli florets

1 tbsp coconut vinegar

1 tbsp sesame oil

1 tsp wheat-free tamari or coconut aminos★

1 tsp prepared yellow mustard

1 tsp toasted sesame seeds

DIRECTIONS:

1. Steam broccoli until tender-crisp (about 6 to 8 minutes) and then drain.

2. Combine vinegar, oil, tamari, and mustard. Add broccoli and toss with mixture to coat.

3. Toast sesame seeds lightly in a nonstick pan and use as garnish.

Makes 4 servings.

★**Coconut aminos soy-free seasoning sauce:** Coconut aminos can be used anywhere you enjoy soy sauce, such as stir-frys, salads, and marinades.

BLENDER BROCCOLI SOUP

I came up with this ultra-simple but delicious recipe one day when I had a crown of broccoli in the fridge and a house full of hungry people. I just threw everything into the blender and out came a delicious healing soup that fed everyone! Broccoli is loaded with anti-inflammatory nutrients. It contains sulfur compounds, which help the liver to neutralize toxic chemicals, and it is rich in powerful antioxidants. The florets and the stems of broccoli have almost the same amounts of nutrients, and fiber, so remember when you are making this soup that you can use the whole vegetable.

INGREDIENTS:

4 cups broccoli

4 cups vegetable or chicken broth

2 tbsp dairy-free basil pesto

Pink rock salt or gray sea salt, to taste

2 tbsp fresh lemon juice

2 tbsp virgin coconut oil

IF PESTO IS UNAVAILABLE, ADD THE FOLLOWING:

½ clove garlic

2 tbsp extra-virgin olive oil

1 tbsp dried basil

¼–½ tsp pink rock salt or gray sea salt

2 tbsp fresh lemon juice

2 tbsp coconut oil

DIRECTIONS:

1. Cook broccoli in broth until tender (about 8 to 10 minutes). Let cool slightly to allow for safe transfer to blender.

2. Add all ingredients to blender and blend until smooth. Alternatively, you can use an immersion blender.

3. Taste and adjust seasonings.

Makes 3 to 4 servings.

BEET THE SCALE BORSCHT

This simple, low-calorie vegetable borscht showcases the flavor and color of beets and red cabbage with a backdrop of fresh dill. Phytonutrients known as anthocyanins are what give beets and red cabbages their deep magenta color. These nutrients are powerful antioxidants that repair and protect our DNA from the damaging effects of free radicals.

INGREDIENTS:

1½ tbsp virgin coconut oil

1½ cups diced onion

2 cloves garlic, chopped

6 cups chicken or vegetable stock

3 cups julienned beets

1 cup julienned carrot

1 cup green peas (frozen if fresh not available)

1 cup diced celery

2 bay leaves

¼ cup apple cider vinegar

½ tsp pink rock salt or gray sea salt

1½ cups shredded purple cabbage

¾ cup chopped dill weed

DIRECTIONS:

1. Place oil, onion, and garlic in large stockpot and cook until onions soften, about 5 minutes.

2. Add all remaining ingredients except for dill and bring to a boil.

3. Reduce heat, cover, and simmer for 40 minutes. Add dill just before serving.

If you want the soup to be authentic and are ready to test dairy in the last phase of the SMTH plan, consider topping each serving with a tablespoon of sheep or goat yogurt for a creamy contrast to the sour soup.

Makes 8 servings.

EZRA'S GAZPACHO

Perfect for a hot summer night, this recipe created by Chef Ezra Title is really tasty, and it couldn't be easier. Watermelon is high in natural sugar, but you can slow down the absorption and inevitable blood sugar spike it will cause by pairing it with oil and vinegar. Remember that the soup needs time to chill before serving. If you are avoiding nightshades, this soup tastes great without the red pepper but will be slightly thin. You can bump up the amount of cucumber by a cup.

INGREDIENTS:

½ cup diced red onion

8 cups large seedless watermelon, peeled and diced

1½ cups diced English cucumber

1 clove garlic, minced

¼ cup apple cider vinegar, divided

¼ cup extra-virgin olive oil, divided

Pink rock salt or gray sea salt, to taste

OPTIONAL ADDITION:

1 red pepper, seeded, peeled, and diced

DIRECTIONS:

1. Place all ingredients except oil, vinegar, and salt into a bowl and mix well.

2. Transfer half the recipe to a blender and blend at high speed. Add half the vinegar, and then slowly pour in half the olive oil. Salt to taste. Pour soup into a large bowl, then repeat the previous steps to make the second batch.

Makes 10 cups.

GINGER HONEY SALMON SOUP

The fantastically talented Hannah Arthurs created this rich, warming soup while doing her co-op placement with my practice, Daniluk Consulting. Salmon is one of nature's highest sources of vitamin D, the ultimate immune booster. A number of studies have found that fish oil helps reduce symptoms of rheumatoid arthritis, including joint pain and morning stiffness. If you suffer from arthritis pain, eating salmon regularly may allow you to lower your dose of non-steroidal anti-inflammatory drugs (NSAIDs). This soup will keep in Mason jars for a few days.

INGREDIENTS:

2 tbsp extra-virgin olive oil

3 tbsp honey

2 tbsp freshly grated ginger root

2 medium onions, thinly sliced

8 cups water

4 cups thinly sliced fennel (remove
    core first)

2 chicken boullion cubes

1 cup sliced shiitake mushrooms

1 tsp pink rock salt or gray sea salt

2 tsp cinnamon

3 tbsp fresh lemon juice

½ lb sockeye salmon fillets

1 cup chopped parsley

OPTIONAL ADDITION:

1 tbsp lemon-flavored fish oil

DIRECTIONS:

1. In a large pot over medium heat, add oil, honey, ginger, and onion, and sauté until onion is translucent.

2. Add water, fennel, boullion, and mushrooms, and bring to a boil. Add salt, cinnamon, and lemon juice. Reduce heat and allow soup to simmer, uncovered, for 15 minutes.

3. Add fish to pot, cover with lid, and poach for 10 minutes.

4. Serve soup, using ⅛ of the fish in each bowl, and garnish with parsley. For an extra anti-inflammatory boost, consider pouring fish oil into the soup as it cools.

Makes 8 servings.

CREAMY ASPARAGUS SOUP

No need for dairy in this soup! I have used coconut and cauliflower in this recipe to give it a thick and creamy texture. Asparagus is high in two classes of antioxidants called phenolics and flavonoids. These powerful antioxidants protect the heart and arterial walls from free-radical damage that causes the type of inflammation that can eventually lead to heart disease.

INGREDIENTS:

3 cups asparagus, ends trimmed

1 tbsp virgin coconut oil

1 clove garlic, crushed

3½ cups chopped leeks or white onion

4 cups vegetable or chicken broth

2 cups chopped cauliflower

½ cup coconut milk

1 tsp pink rock salt or gray sea salt

1 tbsp nutritional yeast

DIRECTIONS:

1. Cut stalks in ½-inch pieces and set tips aside.

2. In a large soup pot, over medium heat, sauté oil, garlic, leeks, and asparagus stalks until onions are slightly translucent, about 10 minutes.

3. Add broth and cauliflower. Bring to a boil, cover, and then lower heat and simmer for 30 minutes.

4. Add coconut milk, salt, and nutritional yeast, then purée soup with an immersion blender or food processor until smooth.

5. Steam asparagus tips for a few minutes until tender, and use as a garnish when serving the soup.

Makes 8 servings.

THE FASTEST SPINACH SOUP EVER

Sometimes when I am working, I get so focused on the task at hand that a few hours go by before I remember to nourish myself. Sound familiar? This soup is perfect for those moments when you want a healing meal but don't want to stop working! I kid you not, it takes literally three minutes to prepare. Hemp hearts add a good dose of essential fatty acids, which are a great inflammation buster! The optional cooked squash adds extra creaminess.

INGREDIENTS:

8 cups loosely packed baby spinach

3 tbsp fresh lemon juice

1 tbsp coconut butter (raw is best)

¼ cup green onions (white parts and greens)

2½–3 cups heated vegetable stock or boiling water with an organic bouillon cube
      dissolved in it★

Pink rock salt or gray sea salt (if using low-sodium stock or bouillon), to taste

½ cup hemp hearts, divided

OPTIONAL ADDITIONS:

1 cup cooked squash or pumpkin

Drizzle extra-virgin olive oil or hemp oil

DIRECTIONS:

1. Pack spinach and all other ingredients except hemp hearts into a blender and blend on high for 2 minutes. Use 2½ cups broth if not adding the optional ingredients.

2. Let soup cool slightly for about a minute. Reserving 1 tbsp of hemp hearts, add the rest to the blender and continue to blend until silky smooth.

3. Garnish with 1 tbsp hemp hearts and enjoy.

★Look for organic bouillon cubes that are free of sugar and artificial flavors (e.g., MSG).

Makes 6 cups.

HEALING GINGER GREEN SOUP

This soup is an excellent choice for those new to cleansing. Both avocado and tahini are rich in phytosterols that help to keep inflammation under control, while the ginger gives the soup a nice kick. Enjoy when freshly prepared, as avocado oxidizes quickly and does not keep long.

INGREDIENTS:

1 cup water

4 cups chopped broccoli

1 cup chopped red onion

1 cup chopped celery

4 cups vegetable broth

1 cup spinach (tightly packed)

2 tbsp finely chopped ginger root

1 tbsp wheat-free tamari or coconut aminos

½ tsp cumin

½ tsp turmeric

½ tsp pink rock salt or gray sea salt

1 tbsp lemon juice

½ avocado or 2 tbsp tahini

DIRECTIONS:

1. Lightly steam broccoli, onion, and celery in water for 10 minutes.

2. In a large pot, add steamed vegetables and all remaining ingredients except avocado and purée with an immersion blender until smooth. (Alternatively, use a large blender or food processor.) Add avocado at the end to prevent oxidation.

Makes 4 servings.

GARLIC BOK CHOY STIR-FRY

I struggle sometimes to get my father to eat enough cooked green vegetables. He resists my kale experiments, so I hoped that the delicate light flavor of bok choy would be a hit. When paired with shiitake mushrooms, a sweet Asian dressing, and lots of red pepper, this green veggie takes on sweetness without dominating. I was thrilled when my dad cleared his plate and uttered, "These greens I like, Julie. I am sad that there is none left or I would have had a second portion." Next time, I'll double the recipe!

INGREDIENTS:

1 tsp sesame oil

1 tbsp extra-virgin olive oil

1½ cups onion, coarsely chopped

2 cups chopped shiitake mushroom caps

2 cloves garlic, coarsely chopped

1 tbsp freshly grated ginger root

2 cups thinly sliced red pepper

6 cups baby bok choy, chopped into
    2-inch strips

2 tbsp wheat-free tamari or coconut
    aminos

1 tbsp fresh lemon juice

1 tsp maple syrup or honey

¼ cup cashews for garnish

DIRECTIONS:

1. Have all ingredients ready before beginning to cook. Heat sesame oil and olive oil in a large pot over medium heat.

2. Add onion and stir-fry for 2 minutes or until soft.

3. Add mushrooms and continue to stir-fry for 2 minutes.

4. Add garlic, ginger, and red peppers. Toss for a further 2 minutes until peppers are just beginning to soften.

5. Add remaining ingredients, and cover for 2 to 3 minutes to steam bok choy.

Makes 6 servings.

JICAMA FRIES

Jicama (pronounced HE-kuh-muh) is a root vegetable that is popular in Mexico. It tastes like a potato crossed with water chestnut and pear, and it is super-low in calories (1 cup contains 46 calories and a whopping 6 grams of fiber). It's high in B complex, vitamin C, calcium, iron, and potassium. The vegetable's sweet flavor comes from the fructo-oligosaccharide also known as inulin, a type of soluble fiber that feeds the healthy bacteria in our gut.

INGREDIENTS:

1 jicama, peeled and cut into French
     fry shapes
1 tsp extra-virgin olive oil
2 tbsp nutritional yeast
Pinch pink rock salt or gray sea salt

DIRECTIONS:

1. Place jicama sticks in a glass dish that has a tight-fitting lid. Top with oil, nutritional yeast, and sea salt.

2. Place lid on and shake well, until all jicama slices are coated.

Makes 6 servings.

LEMON-ROASTED GREEN BEANS WITH CHOPPED HAZELNUTS

If you are bored of plain old green beans, try this fresh twist on green beans amandine. Green beans possess strong anti-inflammatory properties due to their high levels of carotenoid phytonutrients beta-carotene, lutein and zeaxanthin. This recipe also works well when you substitute zucchini, asparagus, or Brussels sprouts for the beans.

INGREDIENTS:

1 tsp extra-virgin olive oil

6 cups green beans, trimmed

1 medium onion, peeled, cut into 8 wedges

6 fresh marjoram sprigs (or 2 tbsp dried)

2 tbsp extra-virgin olive oil

½ tsp pink rock salt or gray sea salt

1 tbsp fresh lemon juice

1 tsp finely grated lemon peel

½ cup coarsely chopped hazelnuts

DIRECTIONS:

1. Position oven racks so 1 is in the top third of the oven and 1 is in the bottom third. Preheat oven to 325°F.

2. Coat 2 large rimmed baking sheets with 1 tsp oil, using your fingers to evenly coat.

3. Combine green beans, onion wedges, and marjoram in large bowl. Add 2 tbsp olive oil, sprinkle with salt, toss, and divide between prepared sheets.

4. Roast vegetables for 15 minutes.

5. Reverse position of baking sheets in oven, and continue to roast for 10 minutes or until beans are tender and beginning to brown in spots.

6. Transfer vegetables to bowl. Add lemon juice, grated lemon peel, and half of chopped hazelnuts. Gently toss.

7. Serve sprinkled with remaining hazelnuts.

Makes 10 side servings or 5 meal-sized servings.

JAPANESE DEVILED EGGS

Hard-boiled eggs have never tasted so spicy or looked so lovely. Wasabi powder adds a flavorful Asian kick to these deviled eggs along with a few health benefits. The pungent flavor of wasabi is due to its biochemically active isothiocyanates (ITCs). Research suggests that these ITCs have anti-inflammatory, anti-microbial, anti-platelet and anti-cancer effects. Note: Hard-boil and stuff the eggs up to a day ahead, then garnish when ready to serve. Garnished eggs can be prepared up to two hours ahead, then lightly covered and refrigerated until needed.

INGREDIENTS:

6 hard-boiled eggs

2½ tbsp all-natural, sugar-free mayonnaise, such as Vegenaise

¼ tsp pink rock salt or gray sea salt

½ tsp sesame oil

1 tsp wasabi powder (or less, depending on your preference)

½ tsp ground ginger

2 tbsp pickled ginger, drained

12 small watercress or parsley sprigs

½ tsp black sesame seeds

DIRECTIONS:

1. Cut eggs in half, crosswise. Slice a small piece off rounded ends so eggs will lie flat on plate.

2. Scoop out yolks and mash with 2 tbsp mayonnaise, sea salt, and sesame oil. Pile back into egg hollows.

3. Combine remaining ½ tbsp mayonnaise with wasabi powder. Cover separately and chill until needed.

FOR GARNISH:

1. Curl a small piece of the pickled ginger to form a rosebud shape, then tuck into each egg.

2. Put a small dollop of wasabi-mayonnaise on top and add a watercress or parsley sprig. Sprinkle with sesame seeds.

Makes 12 appetizers.

SUPER-FAST BEET SOUP

This energizing yet detoxifying soup is super-fast and easy and yet it tastes gourmet! Celery contains a phytonutrient called polyacetylene, which has been shown to provide relief from inflammatory conditions such as rheumatoid arthritis and osteoarthritis.

INGREDIENTS:

2 cups chopped beets

1 cup chopped apple

2 cups chopped celery

2 cloves garlic, chopped

2 cups chopped carrots

4 cups vegetable broth or chicken broth

2 tbsp freshly grated ginger root

1 tbsp fresh thyme or 2 tsp dried thyme

½ tsp pink rock salt or gray sea salt

¼ cup apple cider vinegar

2 cups unsweetened coconut beverage (2% fat) or other unsweetened non-dairy milk
    (hemp, almond)

1 cup hemp or sunflower seeds

OPTIONAL ADDITION:

2 tbsp dairy-free basil pesto

DIRECTIONS:

1. Add all ingredients, except coconut beverage and seeds, to a large pot. Bring to a boil, then simmer for 10 minutes or until everything is very soft.

2. In a blender, process the soup with coconut beverage and seeds until smooth. Top with pesto if desired.

Makes 8 servings.

ROASTED APPLE AND PARSNIP SOUP

When you make this soup, you fill your home with the warm smell of baking apples. And the parsnips are excellent for your health, too. Studies show that the compound falcarindiol (FAD), found in parsnips, has the ability to stop dendritic (or immune) cells from reaching maturity. The ability to suppress the immune system gives parsnips great potential to be part of a new therapy for the treatment of autoimmune and allergic diseases.

INGREDIENTS:

4 cups chopped parsnips

4 cups chopped apples

1 tsp pink rock salt or gray sea salt, divided

5 tbsp virgin coconut oil, divided

1 cup diced onion

1 cup diced celery

1 tbsp Dijon mustard

2 tsp ground ginger

2 tbsp apple cider vinegar

2 bay leaves

2 tsp cinnamon

4 cups water

4 cups vegetable stock

1 cup coconut milk

½ cup pumpkin seeds

DIRECTIONS:

1. Preheat oven to 350°F. Place parsnips and apples on a cookie sheet. Drizzle with 2 tbsp of coconut oil and sprinkle with a pinch of sea salt. Roast for 45 minutes.

2. Melt 3 tbsp coconut oil in a large pan. Sauté onions and celery until tender, then add Dijon mustard, the rest of the salt, and ginger. Add apple cider vinegar and stir around to deglaze the pan.

3. Add roasted apple and parsnips along with bay leaves, cinnamon, water, and vegetable stock. Bring to a boil, then reduce heat and simmer for 30 minutes.

4. Remove from heat, add coconut milk, and purée soup in a blender or with an immersion blender until silky smooth. Taste and adjust seasoning if needed.

5. Garnish with pumpkin seeds.

Makes 12 servings.

KALE FLAT BREAD

This flat bread comes out a beautiful shade of deep green and is slightly tender on the inside and crisp on the outside. It is a tasty way to sneak a little bit more kale into your diet. Kale contains high levels of sulfur compounds such as sulforaphane and isothiocyanates. Both of these compounds help the liver to perform a series of important tasks, including fat metabolism. Sulfur compounds help the liver to produce bile, which breaks down fat. Bile also filters toxins out of our blood. Eating kale optimizes your liver health, which can help you increase energy, lose weight, and reach your goals.

INGREDIENTS:

4 cups chopped kale leaves, spine removed
    and tightly packed

1 cup red onion, chopped

1 cup ground flaxseeds

⅓ cup nutritional yeast

½–1 tsp pink rock salt or gray sea salt

1 clove garlic

⅓ cup fresh parsley or 2 tbsp dried parsley

¼ cup chopped green olives, pitted

¼ cup dried figs

1 tsp dried oregano

1 tsp dried basil

1 tsp dried rosemary

2 tbsp extra-virgin olive oil

½ cup hemp seeds

Note: This recipe requires a large-capacity food processor. If yours is smaller, you'll have to divide the recipe ingredients and process in 2 batches.

DIRECTIONS:

1. Preheat oven to 250°F.

2. Place all ingredients except hemp seeds in a food processer and process until smooth.

3. Stir in hemp by hand to avoid pulverizing the seeds.

4. Line a baking sheet with parchment paper. With a spatula, spread mixture out on baking sheet, to a layer of ¼-inch thick.

5. With a sharp knife, score mixture into 3-inch triangles and then bake for 20 minutes.

6. Remove baking sheet from oven. Place a separate parchment-lined baking sheet on top of the hot baking sheet and carefully flip over. Remove parchment paper from top of the crackers so they dry evenly. Bake for an additional 20 minutes.

7. Remove baking sheet from oven. Carefully lift parchment and transfer crackers to a wire rack. Allow to cool for 10 minutes.

Note: This recipe can also be made in a dehydrator at 120°F. Drying times will vary from 6 to 8 hours.

Makes 20 flat breads.

242

LEMONADE-MARINATED FENNEL

This is a "two for one" recipe because once you have marinated the fennel, you can reserve the marinade liquid, dilute it (add 2 cups of water), and enjoy it as a delicious lemonade. The fennel lends the lemonade a mild hint of licorice and some wonderful health benefits. Fennel is at the top of my list of anti-inflammatory foods, and you will see it in a lot of my recipes. This is because it contains a unique phytonutrient called anethole, which is both an antioxidant and anti-inflammatory compound.

INGREDIENTS:

1 large fennel bulb

3 tbsp fresh lemon juice

Pinch pink rock salt or gray sea salt

2 tbsp maple or coconut syrup or ¼ tsp stevia liquid or 2 grams stevia powder

⅓ cup water

DIRECTIONS:

1. Wash and trim fennel bulb. Remove core and quarter bulb, then slice it into long ½-inch-thick slices, lengthwise.

2. Mix lemon juice with salt, maple syrup, and water. Place in a large Mason jar and add fennel. Allow to marinate in the fridge for 30 minutes to a full day.

Makes 4 servings.

SMOKED SALMON TARTARE IN CUCUMBER CUPS

This is a great cocktail party appetizer. It is pleasing to the eye and easy to eat, and I love how the smoky, silky, and tangy salmon mixture complements the crisp and refreshing slice of cucumber. You may know that eating salmon is good for your heart—but did you know that it is good for the brain too? Studies have shown that eating salmon makes you smarter and happier! The brain is 60 percent fat, and most of that is the omega-3 fatty acid DHA. Eating salmon regularly has been shown to reduce the risk and incidence of depression and cognitive decline. This recipe may be made several hours ahead of serving.

INGREDIENTS:

4 oz smoked salmon (sugar free), finely chopped

3 tbsp finely chopped red onion

1 tbsp finely chopped capers

1 tbsp extra-virgin olive oil

2 tsp fresh lemon juice

1 tsp Dijon mustard

2 tsp chopped fresh dill

Pinch pink rock salt or gray sea salt

20 slices English cucumber, ½-inch thick

DIRECTIONS:

1. Place all ingredients, except for cucumber, in a bowl and combine gently.

2. Use a small spoon to scoop out some of the center portion of each cucumber slice.

3. Mound 2 tsp of the salmon tartare in the center of each cucumber slice.

4. Arrange on a serving tray.

5. Cover and store in fridge until ready to serve.

Makes 20 bites.

SKINNY ONION RINGS

Onions are anti-inflammatory powerhouses but not when they have been dipped in batter and deep-fried in toxic oil! I have come up with a light and crispy onion ring recipe that preserves all of the goodness of onions. Try using purple onions—they contain resveratrol, a phytonutrient that has been found to work on a cellular level, affecting macrophages, lymphocytes, and dendritic cells (your soldiers of immunity) to lower inflammation and boost your immune system. Amaranth is a tiny, yellow grain that is rich in magnesium and reduces painful muscle cramps. Apple cider vinegar slows the release of sugar (from foods) into the bloodstream. When your blood sugar is balanced, inflammation is reduced.

INGREDIENTS:

Olive oil for brushing

2 egg whites

¼ cup non-dairy milk

2 tbsp apple cider vinegar

½ cup brown rice flour

1 tsp dill weed

1 tbsp extra-virgin olive oil

1½ cups puffed amaranth

1 tsp nutritional yeast

¼ –½ tsp pink rock salt or gray sea salt

2 large purple onions, sliced into ¼-inch rings

OPTIONAL ADDITION:

½ tsp curry powder

DIRECTIONS:

1. Preheat oven to 350°F. Coat a baking sheet with light brush of olive oil.

2. Beat egg whites, non-dairy milk, vinegar, rice flour, dill weed, and oil in a bowl until light and foamy.

3. Combine puffed amaranth, nutritional yeast, and salt in a separate bowl.

4. Add separated onion rings to egg-white mixture and coat well. Drop a few onion rings at a time into the bowl with the amaranth mixture, gently coating the rings with the seasoning.

5. Spread evenly on the baking sheet and bake for 35 to 40 minutes or until crispy.

Makes 8 servings.

MAIN MEALS

"Act the way you want to be and soon you'll be the way you act." –Bob Dylan

AMAZING EASY STIR-FRY

The name of this recipe says it all—it really is easy and always tastes amazing. Fresh shiitakes are now a breeze to find at the supermarket, and dried ones are usually available in natural food stores. Shiitake mushrooms help in the production of white blood cells. Research is showing that they may make white blood cells act more aggressively against foreign bacteria. They have a meaty texture and tons of flavor, so feel free to omit the meat and make this a vegetarian dish along with some quinoa.

INGREDIENTS:

1 lb boneless skinless chicken breasts or beef strips or tempeh, cut into
    ½-inch by 2-inch strips

3 cloves garlic, minced

2 tsp extra-virgin olive oil

1 tbsp grated fresh ginger root

2 tbsp honey

2 tbsp wheat-free tamari or coconut aminos

3 cups broccoli florets

2 cups sliced shiitake mushroom caps

2 cups red pepper, sliced (or carrots if nightshade sensitive)

DIRECTIONS:

1. In a large nonstick skillet, stir-fry meat and garlic in oil for 1 minute. Add ginger, honey, and tamari. Stir until meat is cooked through, then remove with a slotted spoon, leaving sauce in pan.

2. Stir-fry vegetables in sauce for 4 to 5 minutes or until tender. Return meat to pan and stir gently. Serve immediately.

Makes 4 servings.

BUTTER ME CHICKEN

This is a better butter chicken because in this version olive oil and coconut milk replace the dairy you find in the Indian classic. If you are running short on time, use an organic rotisserie chicken in place of cooking from scratch. If sensitive to nightshades, you can enjoy an adapted recipe by removing the curry powder and tomatoes. The garlic, ginger, cinnamon, cumin, cloves, cardamom, and coriander all carry anti-inflammatory power!

INGREDIENTS:

2 lbs boneless, skinless chicken breast or
    thighs, cut into bite-sized pieces

MARINADE:

¼ cup coconut milk

2 tbsp fresh lemon juice

2 tsp minced garlic

1 tbsp grated fresh ginger root

Pinch pink rock salt or gray sea salt

BUTTER CHICKEN SAUCE:

1 tbsp extra-virgin olive oil

1½ cups thinly sliced yellow onion

2 cloves garlic, minced

2 tsp powdered ginger

1 tsp curry powder (omit if sensitive to
    nightshades)

1 tsp cinnamon

2 tsp cumin

⅛ tsp cloves

½ tsp cardamom

½ tsp coriander

28-oz can diced tomatoes, drained (or 3
    cups applesauce if sensitive to
    nightshades)

2 tbsp fresh lemon juice

½ tsp pink rock salt or gray sea salt

2 tbsp coconut sugar or honey

1 cup coconut milk

GARNISH:

2 cups minced fresh cilantro

DIRECTIONS:

1. Combine marinade ingredients in a glass bowl. Place chicken in marinade and refrigerate for 1 to 8 hours.

2. Mix all dry spices into a small mixing bowl and put aside. Once chicken has finished marinating, prepare sauce by sautéing oil, onion, garlic, and spices in a large saucepan over medium heat for 3 minutes, until onion is translucent. Add chicken with marinade and stir. Cook for 5 minutes until chicken has started to cook.

3. Add tomatoes, lemon juice, salt, and sweetener. Boil for 5 minutes. Reduce heat and simmer for 20 minutes uncovered until chicken is cooked through. Add coconut milk and taste to adjust seasoning.

4. Garnish with minced fresh cilantro.

Makes 6 servings.

SLIMMING SPRING ROLL-UPS

The salty taste of mackerel paired with the sweet apple and carrot creates a delicious flavor combination that will satisfy the most intense cravings, which intensify when we are stressed. Mackerel is a rich source of omega-3s, and the fish omegas docosahexanoic acid (DHA) and eicosanopentanoic acid (EPA) are especially important for helping to minimize the amount of cortisol and epinephrine released during stress.

INGREDIENTS:

2 cups unpeeled, julienned apple

1 cup grated carrot

1 cup very thin fennel slices, shaved on a mandoline

1 tbsp umeboshi vinegar or rice vinegar

1 tbsp sesame oil

9 rice paper sheets or nori sheets

5 oz canned mackerel or herring

OPTIONAL ADDITIONS:

¼ cup fresh chopped parsley

Great Gomasio, to taste (page 195)

DIRECTIONS:

1. Combine apple, carrot, fennel, vinegar, and oil in a mixing bowl and set aside.

2. Mash fish in a bowl to crush any small bones.

3. Fill a pie plate with lukewarm water and place beside a clean cutting board. Line up ingredients near cutting board, along with a clean towel.

4. Dip one rice paper round at a time into water and soak until very pliable, about 30 seconds. Gently set wet rice wrap against towel, dabbing it dry on both sides, then lay on cutting board. Place vegetable mixture along bottom third of the round. Spread fish over filling and sprinkle with parsley and gomasio, if desired.

5. Roll rice wrap tightly toward center and fold in sides. Continue rolling to form a log. Set roll, seam-side down, on a platter. Repeat with remaining ingredients. As soaking water cools, replace with lukewarm water.

6. Slice rolls in half diagonally to serve right away or leave whole and refrigerate up to 4 hours. If you want to skip the rice wrap, this also makes a sushi hand roll by placing the vegetable mixture in the middle of a nori sheet and wrapping it up into a cone shape.

Makes 9 rolls.

MOCK SOUR CREAM AND CHIVE DIP

The mock sour cream is made from soaked cashews, which are rich in inflammation-reducing nutrients, including monounsaturated fats, magnesium, and manganese. It is a great substitute for ranch dip, and way better for you. This dip will keep for five days if stored in a sealed container in the refrigerator.

INGREDIENTS:

1 cup raw cashews, soaked overnight

½ cup water

2 tbsp fresh lemon juice

½ tsp minced garlic

1 tsp nutritional yeast

½ tsp pink rock salt or gray sea salt

2 tbsp minced fresh chives or green onions

1 tbsp minced fresh basil or 1 tsp dried

1 tbsp minced fresh dill or 1 tsp dried

DIRECTIONS:

1. Soak cashews for 8 hours or overnight to ensure creaminess. You can skip this step if you don't mind a chunky texture.

2. Place cashews, water, lemon juice, garlic, nutritional yeast, and salt in a food processor and process until silky smooth, stopping occasionally to scrape down the sides with a spatula.

3. Add chives, basil, and dill and pulse briefly to mix them in.

4. Chill for at least 30 minutes before serving.

Makes 1 cup.

WARM WHITE BEANS WITH SUMMER VEGETABLES

This light and fresh dish bursts with color and flavor, especially when you use multi-colored, local heirloom tomatoes. This is an adaption from Ezra Title's recipe on our TV show, *Healthy Gourmet*. Tomatoes are full of vitamin C, the antioxidant that not only protects your adrenals from free-radical damage but also plays a role in the production of adrenal hormones and in the adrenals' stress response.

INGREDIENTS:

SALAD:

¼ cup minced red onion

1 cup chopped heirloom tomatoes

½ cup diced summer squash

½ cup diced cucumber

2–3 tbsp extra-virgin olive oil

1 lemon, juiced

¼ cup chopped fresh parsley

Pinch pink rock salt or gray sea salt

DRESSING:

1 tbsp extra-virgin olive oil

1 clove garlic, minced

2 14-oz cans cannellini beans, drained
   and rinsed

1 tsp fresh thyme

1 tsp fresh rosemary, chopped

½ lemon, juiced

2 tsp chopped fresh parsley

Pinch pink rock salt or gray sea salt

DIRECTIONS:

1. Mix salad ingredients together in a mixing bowl and set aside.

2. In a medium frying pan on medium heat, heat olive oil and sauté garlic for 30 seconds. Add beans, thyme and rosemary. Cook for 2 minutes or until beans are warm. Add lemon juice and parsley, and season with salt. Serve warm on top of salad.

Makes 4 servings.

CASHEW-CRUSTED CHICKEN

This easily prepared family dinner will please everyone at the table. The recipe calls for 2 cups of parsley, making it an ultimate anti-inflammatory meal! Parsley contains a volatile oil called eugenol that has been shown in studies to have strong anti-inflammatory, as well as anti-arthritic, properties and can significantly suppress swelling in the joints.

INGREDIENTS:

6 chicken thighs, boneless and skinless

2 cups sweet potatoes, cut into ¼-inch-thick half coins, well-packed

2 tbsp extra-virgin olive oil

1 tbsp fresh lemon juice

2 tbsp Italian seasoning

1 cup finely chopped fresh parsley

1 recipe Mock Sour Cream and Chive Dip (page 252)

DIRECTIONS:

1. Preheat oven to 350°F.

2. Place chicken and sweet potatoes in a large bowl and add oil, lemon juice, and Italian seasoning. Toss to coat. Place chicken pieces in the center of a large baking dish, surrounded by sweet potatoes.

3. Mix Mock Sour Cream and Chive Dip with parsley and spread across top of chicken and sweet potatoes.

4. Bake uncovered for 60 minutes.

Makes 6 servings.

LENTILS WITH GRAINY MUSTARD

Tangy mustard, tart vinegar, and the earthy flavor of lentils come together to create this well-rounded, satisfying dish from Chef Ezra Title. I love lentils because they are a quick and easy last-minute meal idea requiring less cooking time than beans but with all of the same benefits. They are packed with two kinds of fiber: insoluble and soluble. Insoluble fiber absorbs and removes bile from the body and helps us to get rid of excess cholesterol. Soluble fiber helps to keep the digestive system in working order and helps to prevent the development of disorders such as irritable bowel syndrome and diverticulosis.

INGREDIENTS:

1½ cups green lentils

2½ cups vegetable broth

1 tbsp extra-virgin olive oil

½ cup diced carrot

½ cup diced red onion

½ cup diced celery

½ cup diced fennel

½ tsp pink rock salt or gray sea salt

1 clove garlic, minced

3 tbsp whole-grain mustard

¼ cup apple cider vinegar

DIRECTIONS:

1. In a medium pot combine lentils and broth. Bring to a boil over medium heat, then reduce heat to a simmer. Cook for about 35 minutes or until lentils are soft. Remove pot from heat and let lentils sit for 10 to 15 minutes.

2. Meanwhile, place olive oil in a large sauté pan over medium heat. Add carrots. Cover and cook for 5 minutes, stirring occasionally. Add onions, celery, and fennel. Season with salt and cover again. Cook vegetables until soft and aromatic, about 3 minutes.

3. Add the garlic and sauté for another minute. Add the lentils to the vegetable mixture and stir until combined. Whisk mustard and vinegar in a small bowl and add to cooked lentils, stirring gently to avoid making the lentils mushy.

Makes 6 servings.

BUFFALO STRIP LOIN

Why buffalo? Buffalo are raised on open grassland and graze on omega-rich natural grasses. As a result, buffalo meat has 60 percent to 80 percent less fat compared to beef and, on average, 50 percent less cholesterol. Because buffalo are naturally resistant to disease and grow faster than domestic animals, they don't need the antibiotics and growth hormones that are typically given to beef cattle. The horseradish is wonderful for digestion, and the flax oil provides extra omega-3. Leftover slices make a great salad topping the next day.

INGREDIENTS:

3 lbs buffalo or beef strip loin

Pink rock salt or gray sea salt, to taste

1 tsp virgin coconut oil

1 clove garlic, minced

1 tbsp grated horseradish

Zest of 2 limes

OPTIONAL TOPPINGS:

1 tsp chili powder

Garlic-chili flaxseed oil, to taste

DIRECTIONS:

1. Preheat oven to 400°F.

2. Season meat with salt. In an ovenproof cast-iron pan, sear meat with coconut oil on medium-high heat and then place in oven.

3. Cook for 60 minutes (20 minutes per pound), or until internal temperature reaches 135°F for medium-rare. Allow to rest for 10 minutes before slicing.

4. Meanwhile, mix together garlic, horseradish, and lime zest. Serve on the side.

Makes 8 servings.

BEEF AND MUSHROOM STROGANOFF

If you are in the mood for comfort food, this rich and filling dish is for you. Try it as a savory filling for the Kasha Crepes on page 176 (double the recipe to make six crepes). You may have noticed that I use shiitake mushrooms in a lot of my recipes. When it comes to reducing inflammation and slimming down, shiitake mushrooms are great: low in calories, flavorful, high in fiber, and extremely versatile.

INGREDIENTS:

2 tbsp coconut oil, divided

1 lb flank steak, trimmed

4 cups halved and thinly sliced shiitake mushroom caps

2 cups sliced onion

1 tbsp dried basil

1 tsp dried oregano

1 tsp dried thyme

½ tsp pink rock salt or gray sea salt

2 tbsp arrowroot flour

1½ cups beef or chicken broth

1½ tbsp apple cider vinegar

½ cup coconut milk

GARNISH:

2 cups chopped fresh chives or fresh parsley

DIRECTIONS:

1. Heat 1 tbsp of oil in a large pot over medium-high heat until shimmering but not smoking.

2. Add steak and cook until browned on both sides, 3 to 4 minutes per side. Transfer to a cutting board and let rest for 5 minutes. Cut lengthwise into 2 long pieces, then crosswise, across grain, into ¼-inch-thick slices.

3. Heat remaining 1 tbsp of oil in pan over medium heat. Add mushrooms, onion, basil, oregano, thyme, and salt. Cook, stirring often, until vegetables are very tender, 8 to 10 minutes.

4. Sprinkle flour over vegetables; stir to coat. Stir in beef broth and vinegar and bring to a boil, stirring often. Reduce heat to a simmer and continue cooking, stirring often, until mixture is thickened, about 3 minutes.

5. Stir in coconut milk, sliced steak, and any accumulated juices. Bring to a simmer and cook, stirring, until heated through, 1 to 2 minutes more. Top with fresh parsley or chives and serve on kelp noodles or Kasha Crepes.

Makes 6 servings.

CHICKEN OR STEAK LETTUCE WRAPS

This is a fun and delicious way to share a meal with friends. Encourage your guests to make their own lettuce wraps with the toppings they prefer. Using lettuce instead of a wheat wrap will keep this a light, low-carbohydrate, slimming meal. I often pack these ingredients into small jars and make up wraps at work.

INGREDIENTS:

1 lb organic chicken breast or flank steak

Pink rock salt or gray sea salt, to taste

⅓ cup apple cider vinegar

1 tbsp prepared yellow mustard

1 tsp raw honey

¾ cup extra-virgin olive oil

2 medium Boston (aka bibb, butter) or
    romaine lettuce heads

1 pint cherry tomatoes

½ cup roasted red peppers

½ cup dill pickles, sliced into coins

1 large avocado, sliced

1 cup basil leaves

1 cup mint or extra basil leaves

1 cup chopped curly parsley

1 cup chopped green onion

DIRECTIONS:

1. Preheat grill pan using the broil setting on low.

2. Season meat with salt and place on grill pan. Low broil meat for 7 minutes for medium doneness and allow to rest for 10 minutes.

3. Combine vinegar, mustard, and honey in a mixing bowl. Slowly drizzle in olive oil while whisking constantly.

4. Wash and dry lettuce, leaving all leaves intact. Place cherry tomatoes, red peppers, pickles, and avocados in separate bowls and set aside. Combine herbs into a small bowl and set aside.

5. Slice meat across grain and place on a serving platter. Encourage guests to make hand rolls using lettuce as the wrap and filling with meat and assorted toppings.

Makes 12 wraps.

262

CHICKEN STEW À LA JULIE

Shiitake mushrooms contain lentinan, an active compound that can boost and strengthen your immune system, increasing your ability to fight various infections and diseases. Ginger and garlic are both powerful anti-inflammatory and immune-supportive spices. The extra spices in this recipe make it a potent, healing stew.

INGREDIENTS:

2 lbs chicken thighs, skinless and boneless

1 tbsp extra-virgin olive oil

2 large onions, diced

1 cup sliced shiitake mushroom caps

⅓ cup apple cider vinegar

2½ cups sliced carrots

2 tbsp stone-ground mustard

1 inch fresh ginger root, minced

3 tbsp chopped fresh sage or 1½ tbsp dried

2 tbsp chopped fresh rosemary or 1 tbsp dried

2 cups unsweetened applesauce or peach- or berry-flavored applesauce

½ tsp pink rock salt or gray sea salt

2 cups chicken or vegetable broth

8 cups Swiss chard or kale leaves, cut into ribbons

OPTIONAL TOPPINGS:

2 tbsp dairy- and nut-free pesto

¼ cup hemp hearts

½ cup chopped cilantro

DIRECTIONS:

1. Cut chicken into chunks and set aside.

2. In large saucepan over medium-high heat, cook oil, onions, mushrooms, and vinegar for 5 minutes or until onions soften.

3. Add chicken and cook, stirring occasionally, for another 15 minutes.

4. Add carrots, mustard, ginger, sage, rosemary, applesauce, salt, and broth and cook 5 minutes longer.

5. Add Swiss chard and cook another 5 minutes. Stir in pesto if desired.

6. Serve immediately in large bowls. Sprinkle with hemp hearts and cilantro if desired.

Makes 6 servings.

CURRIED SLOPPY JOES

This is my version of the messy, kid-friendly classic. Sloppy joes are traditionally made by cooking ground beef with onions and spices and then adding ketchup and brown sugar. The meat is then served on a squishy, nutrient-void, refined, white hamburger bun. My version is much healthier; I removed the ketchup and sugar and added pumpkin purée and spinach. Those avoiding nightshades can remove the tomatoes and add more broth—the recipe still tastes great.

INGREDIENTS:

1 cup vegetable broth or tomato juice (drained from diced tomatoes)

½ tsp pink rock salt or gray sea salt

1 tbsp curry powder

1 tsp garam masala

1 tsp turmeric

2 tsp ground ginger

1 lb ground turkey or chicken, or crumbled tempeh

1 tbsp fresh ginger root, minced

28-oz can diced tomatoes

1½ cups squash purée or pumpkin purée

2 cups onion, diced

1 clove garlic, minced

3 cups sliced celery

4 cups baby spinach, loosely packed

¾ cup coconut milk

DIRECTIONS:

1. Add broth, salt, and spices to a large pot on medium heat and cook ground poultry (or tempeh) for 5 minutes, stirring occasionally.

2. Add ginger root, diced tomatoes, and squash purée and cook another 10 minutes.

3. Add onion, garlic, and celery and simmer until vegetables are tender but crisp (approximately 5 minutes).

4. Remove from heat and mix in the spinach and coconut milk. Serve on a Kasha Crepe (page 176) or bed of greens.

Makes 6 to 8 servings.

GRAIN-FREE SUSHI

My favorite type of sushi is futomaki—the large, colorful rolls packed with pickled radish, egg, vegetables, and rice. Replacing the sweet, refined sushi rice with cauliflower lowers the glycemic index and calories of this dish significantly, and you won't believe how convincing it tastes.

INGREDIENTS:

2 cups cauliflower florets broken into small pieces (do not include stem)

1 tsp coconut syrup or raw honey

2 tsp apple cider vinegar

¼ tsp pink rock salt or gray sea salt

1 tbsp dairy- and nut-free pesto

1 tbsp prepared yellow mustard

3-oz can herring or mackerel, or 1 cup black beans, drained and rinsed

3 large nori sheets

½ cup cucumber, sliced vertically into match sticks

½ cup carrot, sliced vertically into match sticks

DIRECTIONS:

1. Combine cauliflower, syrup, vinegar, and salt in a food processor and pulse until mixture is rice-like in texture. Place into a bowl and set aside.

2. Place pesto, mustard, and fish in a bowl and mash into a paste.

3. Lay nori sheet on top of a sushi roller. Place a thin layer of "rice" mixture across the nori sheet, leaving 2 inches at bottom clear to allow for effective rolling. Using a spoon, smooth a layer of fish paste across "rice"-covered nori sheet. Place cucumber and carrots in a row across center of nori sheet. Roll firmly and seal end of nori with a wet finger. Repeat with other 2 nori sheets.

4. Cut with a sharp knife into 1-inch coins. Serve immediately.

Makes 3 rolls or 24 pieces.

RAINBOW TROUT WITH TOMATO-FENNEL RAGOUT

This is a spectacular recipe by Chef Ezra Title created for *Healthy Gourmet*. The rainbow trout is full of decadent flavor and looks divine on the colorful bed of slimming Tomato-Fennel Ragout. Fennel contains a wealth of phytonutrients like quercetin and rutin that give it a strong standing in the antioxidant department. Antioxidants provide us with anti-inflammatory benefits because they help prevent the oxidation of fatty acids in our bodies. When we have lower levels of oxidized fatty acids, our bodies produce fewer pro-inflammatory messaging molecules, and our level of inflammation is kept in check.

266

TOMATO-FENNEL RAGOUT INGREDIENTS:

1 tbsp extra-virgin olive oil

1 cup chopped red onion

1 bulb fennel, trimmed, cored and chopped

2 cloves garlic, minced

4 cups chopped Roma tomatoes

Pink rock salt or gray sea salt, to taste

1 tsp apple cider vinegar

½ cup fish or chicken broth

1 tbsp fresh basil, chopped

1 tbsp fresh thyme leaves

DIRECTIONS:

1. Over medium heat in a large sauté pan, add olive oil and sauté red onion until translucent, approximately 5 minutes.

2. Add fennel and garlic and sauté for 5 minutes. Add tomatoes and season with salt. Cook for 15 to 20 minutes on medium-low heat until mixture has thickened.

3. Add vinegar and broth and cook for another 10 minutes. Stir in fresh herbs. Check for seasoning and adjust to taste.

RAINBOW TROUT INGREDIENTS:

2 large trout fillets (approx. 2½ lbs)

4 tbsp nut- and dairy-free pesto

¼ tsp fresh thyme

6 cloves garlic, crushed

⅛ tsp pink rock salt or gray sea salt

DIRECTIONS:

1. Preheat oven to 350°F.

2. Coat fish with pesto, thyme, and garlic. Bake for 14 minutes. When trout is cooked through, serve on a platter with Tomato-Fennel Ragout.

Makes 8 servings.

HEALTHY "CHEESE" SAUCE

This sauce can be served over your favorite gluten-free pasta but is really delicious and slimming served over steamed broccoli or cauliflower. Its zesty flavor comes from nutritional yeast—which is loaded with B vitamins—and from iron-rich tahini. Its bright orange color comes from the puréed carrots and reminds me of those good old macaroni-and-cheese-in-a-box days! If you want to double the recipe, the sauce can be stored in the fridge for a week.

INGREDIENTS:

1½ cups carrots, cut into ½-inch-thick coins

¼ cup coconut milk

¾ cup nutritional yeast

2 tsp prepared yellow mustard

1 tsp pink rock salt or gray sea salt

¼ cup extra-virgin olive oil

2 tbsp tahini

1½ cups navy beans

DIRECTIONS:

1. Bring pot of water to a boil. Add carrots and cook for 10 minutes until mushy, then drain and add to blender or food processor. Purée until smooth.

2. Add coconut milk and blend on low. Increase speed gradually until mixture becomes silky smooth. Add remaining ingredients and continue to blend until mixture reaches a cheese-sauce consistency.

3. Adjust seasonings to taste. Thin out sauce to your desired thickness using additional coconut milk.

Makes 2 cups.

HEARTY VENISON-PARSNIP STEW

This is one of my husband's favorite recipes because it reminds him of the stew his mother used to make on crisp fall days when he was growing up in northern Ontario. She was a teacher and would assemble these ingredients quickly in the morning and then place them in a slow cooker. When Alan arrived home from school, the house would smell simply delicious. I have used parsnips in this version, but feel free to use sunchokes if they are available. Parsnips are particularly high in soluble fiber (7 grams a cup), which lowers cholesterol levels and regulates blood sugar.

INGREDIENTS:

2 tbsp extra-virgin olive oil

2 cups chopped red onions

3 cloves garlic, minced

2 cups chopped parsnip (or sunchokes, if available)

2 cups chopped carrots

1 tsp pink rock salt or gray sea salt

1 lb venison or beef stew meat

4 cups vegetable broth

1 cup water or 28-oz can diced tomatoes

2 tbsp fresh rosemary, minced

¼ cup rolled quinoa flakes

DIRECTIONS:

1. In a large pot over medium-high heat, sauté oil, onion, garlic, parsnips, carrots, and salt for 5 to 7 minutes.

2. Add meat, broth, water (or tomatoes, if you can tolerate them—if you are using tomatoes, omit the 1 cup of water), and rosemary. Bring to a light boil, then reduce heat to low.

3. Add quinoa flakes and cover and simmer for 45 minutes or longer.

Makes 6 servings.

HAPPY WRAPS

These extraordinary wraps are perfect fast food when on the run. A great new product to hit the market recently is a wrap made from coconut meat. With each wrap containing just 70 calories, this gluten-free option is a great alternative to wheat- or corn-based tortillas. And the best part is that coconut contains medium-chain triglycerides, a type of fat that likes to be burned as energy! If you can't find coconut wraps, nori sheets or other gluten-free wraps make a lovely substitute.

INGREDIENTS:

1 cup fermented or freshly grated beet

1 cup kelp noodles or brown rice noodles or sweet potato noodles

1 tbsp toasted sesame oil

Pinch pink rock salt or gray sea salt

1 large apple, thinly sliced

4 oz smoked salmon, sugar-free, or 4 oz seasoned, cooked tempeh

2 tbsp nut- and dairy-free pesto

4 coconut or soft flax grain–free wraps or nori sheets

DIRECTIONS:

1. Mix beet, noodles, oil, and salt and set aside. (If you are using freshly grated beets, consider splashing them with a squeeze of lemon juice to give them a tangy taste.)

2. Layer beet-noodle mixture with apple, salmon, and pesto inside wrap. Fold over once and eat like a soft taco.

Makes 4 wraps.

ANTI-INFLAMMATORY FISH CHOWDER

Job's tears look and taste like barley but don't contain the inflammatory protein gluten. They are a popular allergy remedy in Asia, and studies on mice show that they can suppress allergic reactions and balance the immune system. Quinoa is rich in magnesium that helps to relax blood vessels and thereby to alleviate migraines. Magnesium also may reduce type 2 diabetes by promoting healthy blood sugar control. Spinach and mushrooms are an amazing source of folate (vitamin B9). Folate deficiency can contribute to atherosclerosis and dementia.

INGREDIENTS:

2 cups chopped leeks or onions

2 cloves garlic, chopped

8 cups vegetable stock

1 cup Job's tears (yi yi ren), soaked in water overnight and drained, or quinoa

1 cup sliced fresh shiitake mushroom caps

2 cups cubed celeriac root or turnip

2 tbsp finely chopped fresh ginger root

14 oz white fish (e.g., halibut, black cod, pollock)

6 cups baby spinach, loosely packed

1 cup chopped basil or cilantro, loosely packed

½ tsp pink rock salt or gray sea salt

1 cup coconut milk

2 green onions, finely chopped

OPTIONAL ADDITION:

1 tsp flaxseed, ground

Dash sustainable fish oil

DIRECTIONS:

1. In a stockpot, place leeks, garlic, stock, Job's tears, mushrooms, celeriac root, and ginger and bring to a rolling boil. Reduce heat to low, cover, and simmer for 45 minutes.

2. Place fish on top of ingredients, cover again, and simmer for an additional 15 minutes.

3. Add all remaining ingredients except green onion. Simmer for 5 minutes, then remove from heat. If using quinoa instead of Job's tears, add optional flaxseed to create a thicker soup.

4. Ladle into individual serving bowls. If desired, add a dash of fish oil to each bowl before serving (make sure soup has cooled for a minute or two to prevent damaging the omega-3 fatty acids in the fish oil). Garnish with green onion.

Note: This recipe can also be made in a slow cooker. Throw all ingredients except greens, herbs, and coconut milk into the slow cooker and cook for a minimum of 2 hours. Add the greens, herbs, and coconut milk just before serving. Combine well and enjoy!

Makes 8 to 10 servings.

MOCK FRIED CHICKEN

These tasty morsels are packed with the flavor inspiration of Chef Ezra Title. They have a crunch that kids (of all ages) will love, combined with hidden nutrition that the grown-up side of you will appreciate. I have included a sweet-and-sour dipping sauce that is sure to please. This recipe is the anti-inflammatory answer to that ultimate comfort food—fried chicken.

INGREDIENTS:

1 tsp virgin coconut oil

¾ cup finely crushed whole-grain gluten-free crackers

1 lb chicken breast (skinless and boneless), cut into 3-inch strips

1 tbsp chopped fresh basil leaves

½ tsp dried oregano

½ tsp dried thyme

2 tsp dried parsley

2 cloves garlic, minced

⅔ cup squash purée or pumpkin purée

Pinch pink rock salt or gray sea salt

DIPPING SAUCE:

¼ cup apple cider vinegar

¼ cup apple butter (no added sugar)

1 tbsp pumpkin purée

Pinch pink rock salt or gray sea salt

DIRECTIONS:

1. Preheat oven to 375°F. Lightly coat a baking sheet with coconut oil.

2. Place crackers in a plastic bag and crush with a rolling pin until the size of bread crumbs. Alternatively, place crackers in a blender and use ice-crush setting until finely crushed. Place crumbs in a bowl and set aside.

3. In a medium bowl, combine basil, oregano, thyme, parsley, garlic, purée, and salt and mix well. Place chicken pieces into purée and mix well with your hands to coat. Transfer one piece at a time to crumb bowl to coat evenly. Place on prepared baking sheet.

4. Bake for 12 minutes, then turn chicken and bake for another 10 minutes, or until no longer pink. Meanwhile, combine dipping sauce ingredients in a small bowl.

Makes 4 to 6 servings.

KELP NOODLES WITH RAW TOMATO SAUCE

You will love the fresh, zesty Mediterranean flavor created by Chef Ezra Title in this versatile raw tomato sauce. I have paired it with kelp noodles—at only 7 calories a cup, they are a fantastic, low-carbohydrate, wheat-free alternative to pasta and other noodles. One of the great benefits of kelp noodles is that they contain iodine. Iodine is a trace mineral and essential nutrient that plays a key role in metabolism and thyroid function. If you can't locate kelp noodles, you can substitute the zucchini noodles from the Pesto Pasta Salad recipe on page 210.

INGREDIENTS:

3 cups chopped Roma tomatoes

3 tbsp apple cider vinegar

3 Medjool dates, chopped

1 cup fresh basil leaves

½ cup fresh oregano leaves, loosely packed

½ cup sun-dried tomatoes

½ clove garlic, chopped

1 tsp Faux Parmesan Cheese (page 186)

1 tsp nutritional yeast

1 tsp pine nuts

12 oz kelp noodles

DIRECTIONS:

1. Place tomatoes, vinegar, dates, basil, oregano, sun-dried tomatoes, and garlic in a food processor and blend until smooth.

2. Place faux Parmesan, nutritional yeast, and pine nuts in a smaller food processor or blender and blend until mixed.

3. Combine some tomato sauce with kelp noodles to coat, then pour the rest on top. Sprinkle with faux cheese mixture.

Makes 8 servings.

LOW-CAL TURKEY CHILI

We all know that when you are feeling stressed and overwhelmed, there is nothing better than coming home to a hearty dinner simmering away on the stove. This is a great recipe to throw into the slow cooker in the morning before work. Turkey is a great source of the amino acid tryptophan, which is necessary for serotonin production, the hormone that keeps us relaxed and happy. It is also high in the amino acid tyrosine, which is needed to make other hormones, including dopamine, the pleasure hormone.

INGREDIENTS:

1 cup vegetable or chicken broth

1 lb ground turkey, ground chicken, or
   crumbled tempeh

1 cup diced onion

28-oz can diced tomatoes

2 cups diced carrot

3 cups diced zucchini

19-oz can kidney beans or adzuki beans, rinsed

19-oz can chickpeas or navy beans, rinsed

1–2 tsp chili powder

½ tsp nutmeg

1 tsp mustard powder

⅛ tsp ground cloves

1 tsp ground ginger

1 tsp pink rock salt or gray sea salt

1½ cups red pepper

DIRECTIONS:

1. Heat broth in a large pot over medium heat. Place ground turkey in pot and cook until slightly brown. Stir in onion and cook until tender, approximately 3 minutes.

2. Mix in tomatoes, carrot, and zucchini. Add beans.

3. Season with chili powder, nutmeg, mustard, cloves, ginger, and salt.

4. Bring to a boil. Reduce heat to low, cover, and simmer 30 minutes.

5. Add red pepper a few minutes before serving to add a fresh element to the dish.

Makes 8 servings.

NORI-WRAPPED DOUBLE-GINGER CHICKEN

This dish is just like sushi but without all the high-glycemic white rice. I have used two different kinds of ginger, adding plenty of flavor to the chicken without the need for sugary sauces or piles of sodium. The avocado in this recipe is rich in vitamin B6, a critical nutrient for happy hormones. If you want to make these rolls ahead, cook up the chicken, chop ingredients, and then assemble the rolls at the last minute, as nori loses its crispness quickly.

INGREDIENTS:

½ cup fresh ginger root, chopped

1½ cups water

1 large boneless, skinless chicken breast, sliced lengthwise into 1-inch strips

2 tbsp fresh lemon juice

Pink rock salt or gray sea salt, to taste

6 large sheets nori

2 oz pickled ginger

1 large ripe avocado, sliced

½ large red bell pepper or apple, thinly sliced

DIRECTIONS:

1. In a saucepan, bring ginger, water, chicken, lemon juice, and salt to a boil. Reduce heat and simmer gently for about 15 minutes, or until cooked. Turn chicken once during this time. Remove from heat and let cool in cooking liquid.

2. When cool, remove chicken and ginger from liquid.

3. To make rolls, place one nori sheet on a flat surface. Put two slices of chicken end to end and some drained ginger on nori about 1 inch from bottom of sheet. Top with about 1 tbsp drained pickled ginger, two thin wedges of avocado, and bell pepper slices (substitute with apple if intolerant of nightshades). Roll tightly, then seal by brushing end of sheet with cold water.

Makes 6 wraps.

SAAG CHICKEN

If you want to maximize your spinach intake, few dishes can outdo Saag Chicken. Spinach is one of the highest dietary sources of magnesium. Magnesium is important for hormone development in our adrenal glands, and strong adrenals keep stress levels in check.

INGREDIENTS:

4 cups onion, minced or chopped extremely finely

6 cloves garlic, minced

2 tbsp extra-virgin olive oil

1 lb chicken pieces, skinned and cubed

5 cups spinach, thawed from frozen

1 cup coconut milk

1–2 tbsp fresh lime juice

1 tbsp coconut nectar or honey

3 tbsp fresh ginger root, grated and divided★

½ tsp ground coriander

½ tsp turmeric

½ tsp cardamom

½ tsp cinnamon

2 cups crushed tomatoes★★

1 tsp pink rock salt or gray sea salt

★ If you want to make the curry spicier and increase the health benefits, add 1 tablespoon of grated ginger while cooking and 1 tablespoon right before serving.

★★ If you are avoiding nightshade vegetables, substitute tomatoes with the same amount of applesauce and add an extra teaspoon of fresh lime juice or of lemon juice to replace the acidity.

DIRECTIONS:

1. In a large pot, sauté onion and garlic in olive oil for 3 to 4 minutes until translucent. Add chicken and reduce to medium heat, cooking with lid on for 10 minutes until chicken is tender. Stir occasionally to prevent sticking.

2. Put spinach, coconut milk, lime juice, coconut nectar, ginger root, and spices into a food processor and blend until smooth.

3. Add spinach mixture, tomatoes, and salt to chicken mixture and cook for an additional 20 minutes on a low heat to blend flavors and ensure chicken is well cooked. If using, add extra grated ginger. Enjoy as a main dish on top of brown rice or quinoa.

Makes 6 servings.

280

SEA SCALLOPS WITH HARVEST VEGETABLES

Sea scallops contain selenium and zinc to boost your immune function and omega-3 fats that directly decrease inflammation. Umeboshi plums are traditionally used in Japan as a natural antibiotic, antiseptic, and digestive aid. The rainbow of harvest vegetables in this dish provides dozens of different antioxidants that have been shown to reduce inflammation.

INGREDIENTS:

HARVEST VEGETABLES:

2 tsp avocado oil

2 cups cauliflower florets or sunchokes
（sliced very thin)

¼ tsp pink rock salt or gray sea salt

1 cup butternut squash, diced into ½-inch
cubes

1 cup thinly sliced shiitake mushrooms caps

2 cups purple cabbage, thinly sliced
lengthwise

2 cups coarsely chopped spinach

1 tsp umeboshi vinegar or apple cider
vinegar

¼ cup pumpkin purée

½ cup vegetable stock

½ cup sugar snap peas

SEA SCALLOPS:

12 sea scallops

Pink rock salt or gray sea salt, to taste

1 lemon, juiced

1 tsp avocado oil

1 tsp coconut butter

1 tsp dried thyme

1 clove garlic, minced

¼ cup pumpkin seeds

DIRECTIONS:

HARVEST VEGETABLES:

1. Heat pan on medium-high heat and add avocado oil. Add cauliflower and salt and stir-fry until golden, about 10 minutes.

2. Add butternut squash and cook 5 minutes with lid on. Add shiitakes and cook for 2 minutes more.

3. Add cabbage and cook for 2 minutes. Stir in spinach and cook until wilted.

4. Remove vegetables from pan, deglaze with vinegar, then add pumpkin purée and stock to make a thickened sauce right in pan. Return vegetables to pan and coat with sauce. Add sugar snap peas and check for seasoning. Keep warm on low heat until scallops are ready.

SCALLOPS:

1. Place a pan on medium heat. Meanwhile, season scallops with salt and lemon juice. Add oil to pan and place scallops and lemon juice in pan. Do not touch scallops.

2. After 2 minutes, turn scallops over. Add coconut butter, thyme, and garlic and baste scallops.

3. When scallops are cooked, remove them from pan. Spoon vegetables onto a platter; top with scallops and coconut butter sauce from pan. Garnish with pumpkin seeds.

Makes 6 servings.

SPICED BLACK COD

Fish is one of the easiest proteins for our bodies to break down, making it a good choice for people with sensitive digestive tracts. Fish is best poached in a barely simmering liquid. Sustainably caught black cod, sole, or halibut all poach well. This light cooking method imparts the flavor of the liquid, so always use stock instead of water. If stock is in short supply, consider using a natural bouillon cube dissolved into water before starting the rest of the recipe. Delicious, easy, and satisfying!

INGREDIENTS:

4 cups vegetable stock

1 tbsp grated fresh ginger root

½ cup chopped cilantro

2 cloves garlic, minced

2 tbsp rice vinegar

1 tsp grated lemon zest

1 tsp honey

1 cup shiitake mushrooms, quartered

2 tbsp wheat-free tamari or coconut aminos

4 6-oz fillets of black cod or sustainable halibut

Pink rock salt or gray sea salt, to taste

4 bok choy, halved, or 2 cups green kale

2 cups thinly sliced fennel

Cilantro (for garnish)

DIRECTIONS:

1. Combine stock, ginger, cilantro, garlic, vinegar, zest, honey, shiitakes, and tamari in a skillet large enough to hold fish in one layer.

2. Bring to boil on medium heat, reduce heat, and simmer gently for 3 minutes to blend flavors.

3. Season fish lightly with salt and add to broth. Cover skillet and poach fish for 8 to 10 minutes or until opaque throughout. Add bok choy and fennel at the 5-minute mark to ensure greens stay fresh.

4. Center each piece of fish in a rimmed soup plate and surround with vegetables. Drizzle with broth and garnish with cilantro.

Makes 4 servings.

Tip: We all know the health benefits of fish, but we need to be aware of the hazards as well. Choose your fish carefully and make sure to buy wild or organically farmed fish to avoid any pesticides and fungicides found in conventionally farmed fish.

STEWED MAPLE BEANS WITH DANDELION

This bean dish was created with Chef Ezra Title for my favorite episode of *Healthy Gourmet*, called "Raw Hide." We were hanging out with real cowboys and decided it was fitting to invent a sophisticated version of tinned baked beans without the high levels of sodium and sugar. Beans are packed with fiber and nutrients, so when you pair them with a good source of vitamin C like tomatoes, you are sure to absorb all of the goodness they have to offer. The addition of dandelion greens boosts the nutritional value of this dish tenfold. Not only are they packed with vitamins and minerals, they also have strong diuretic properties and have been used for centuries to support liver, gallbladder, and kidney health.

INGREDIENTS:

¼ cup extra-virgin olive oil

2 cups chopped onion

3 cloves garlic, finely chopped

¼ cup maple syrup

2 cups crushed tomatoes

1 tsp ground ginger

2 cups canned cannellini beans, drained and rinsed★

1 cup chicken stock

4 cups dandelion greens, washed and dried

1 tsp chopped fresh oregano

2 tbsp fresh lemon juice

½ tsp pink rock salt or gray sea salt

OPTIONAL PROTEIN BOOST:

½ lb blade or round steak, cubed

★ If you prefer to use dried beans, consult the bean-cooking guide in *Meals That Heal Inflammation*.

DIRECTIONS:

1. Heat large pot on medium-high heat. Add olive oil, steak (if using), onions, and garlic, and cook approximately 5 minutes.

2. Add maple syrup, tomatoes, and ginger and cook for another 5 minutes.

3. Add beans to pot. Cover with chicken stock. Bring to a simmer, turn heat down to low, cover with a lid, and cook for approximately 30 minutes.

4. For the last 5 minutes of cooking, add dandelion greens and cook until they are wilted. Add oregano and lemon juice and season with salt.

Makes 6 to 8 servings.

TURKEY BURGERS ON PORTOBELLO "BUNS"

Try this twist on the standard hamburger and you won't be disappointed. By using delicious baked portobello mushrooms in place of the traditional hamburger bun, Chef Ezra Title and I transformed this burger into a slimming meal. His recipe included cheese—I made it dairy free by using calcium-rich tahini. Mushrooms play a key role in slowing down the production of pro-inflammatory molecules that can be responsible for the development of many chronic inflammatory diseases like type 2 diabetes and cardiovascular disease.

INGREDIENTS:

12 portobello mushrooms (or 6 if you prefer open-face burgers)

1 tbsp coconut vinegar

1 tbsp extra-virgin olive oil

1 lb ground turkey

½ cup grated sweet potato

1 egg or flax or chia substitute★

¼ cup finely chopped green onions

1 tbsp grainy mustard

½ tsp pink rock salt or gray sea salt

½ tsp ground ginger

1 tbsp tahini

1 tsp nutritional yeast

★Flax or chia egg substitute (to replace 1 egg): Mix 1 tbsp ground flax or chia with 3 tbsp water until it takes on an egg white texture.

DIRECTIONS:

1. Preheat over to 350°F.

2. Snap stems off each mushroom. Using a spoon, scrape gills off underside of each mushroom. Place on a baking sheet, topside down.

3. Season mushrooms with drizzles of vinegar and olive oil. Bake for 30 minutes.

4. To make burgers, mix remaining ingredients in a large bowl and blend, using your hands. Form into patties (½-inch thick) and place on a cookie sheet.

5. Bake for 10 minutes, then flip. Bake another 6 minutes. (Burgers can bake alongside mushrooms.)

6. Lay out mushrooms in pairs, underside up. Place a patty on one mushroom and then cover with another. (Omit the second mushroom if preparing open-face burgers.)

Makes 6 burgers.

WORLD'S HEALTHIEST GLUTEN-FREE LASAGNA

My husband, Alan, went to Italy with an exchange program when he was in high school. While he was there, his surrogate Italian mother taught him how to make the best lasagna you can imagine. I re-created that famous recipe, keeping the flavor but cutting the carbs and high-fat cheese. I use zucchini in place of wheat pasta and the result is not only delicious, it's healthy! The presence of carotenoids like lutein, zeaxanthin, and beta-carotene in the skin of the zucchini makes it a perfect anti-inflammatory vegetable. Shop for dark-skinned mushrooms like portobello due to their higher anti-inflammatory vitamin D content. If you are sensitive to nightshades, you may omit the tomatoes and serve the recipe as a casserole.

INGREDIENTS:

28-oz can diced tomatoes, drained

1 tbsp extra-virgin olive oil

1 lb ground turkey

2 cups diced red onion

½ tsp pink rock salt or gray sea salt

3 tbsp Italian seasoning

2 cups thinly sliced portobello mushrooms

4 cloves garlic, minced

⅓ cup chopped pitted olives

1 cup chopped basil, divided

1½ cups thinly sliced red pepper

4 cups zucchini (sliced ⅛-inch thick lengthwise on a mandoline)

4 cups spinach, loosely packed

1 8-oz package Daiya cheese (tapioca cheese)

1 cup Faux Ricotta Cheese (page 187)

DIRECTIONS:

1. Drain tomatoes; set aside. Preheat oven to 350°F.

2. In a large pot, sauté olive oil, turkey, onions, salt, Italian seasoning, and mushrooms over medium heat.

3. Once turkey is cooked, about 8 minutes, add reserved tomatoes, garlic, olives, and ¼ cup basil and cook until most of the liquid has evaporated, approximately 5 minutes. Remove from heat and set aside.

4. In a 9 x 13–inch baking dish, layer a quarter of the zucchini strips, then ⅓ each of turkey mixture, peppers, cheeses, fresh basil, and spinach. Repeat with two more layers. Top with a thin layer of zucchini strips and Daiya cheese. (The uncooked lasagna will be very high because of the raw spinach. It will cook down to half its size.)

5. Bake for 45 minutes. Let rest for 20 minutes before serving.

Makes 10 to 12 servings.

TREATS AND SNACKS

"There's a crack in everything. That's how the light gets in." –Leonard Cohen

PEPPERMINT PATTIES

These refreshing treats make your mouth tingle with the taste of peppermint. The cocoa provides a great lift before or after any workout. Mesquite is high in protein and soluble fiber and has a nice molasses flavor that works very well in raw sweet treats. Most important, though, it has been known to help stabilize glucose levels in the blood.

INGREDIENTS:

½ cup hemp 70% protein powder★

¼ cup mesquite powder or tiger nut powder or coconut flour

½ cup cocoa or carob powder

1 tsp pure vanilla extract

¼ cup raw honey or coconut syrup

2–3 tsp peppermint extract (depending on how minty you like it)

¼ cup coconut butter, soft

DIRECTIONS:

1. Run powders through a sieve into a bowl to combine evenly.

2. Place all ingredients into the bowl and stir together. Place in refrigerator for about 3 or 4 minutes to firm up slightly.

3. Using your hands, form into small patties and place on parchment paper inside of a container with a lid. The butter may heat up and become more liquid as you work, but the patties will harden again once cool. These patties must be stored in the fridge or freezer—they do not travel well due to their melting factor.

★ Other dairy-free protein powders will work but may be gritty.

Makes 16 cookies.

ANTI-INFLAMMATORY TRAIL MIX

You don't need to be trekking through the forest to enjoy a good trail mix. It is a great snack to have on hand anytime you need an energy boost, whether you are on the go in the city or on a hike in the woods. The main recipe for this trail mix is savory, with the anti-inflammatory spices turmeric, coriander, and cumin, while the variation is a sweet one, with cinnamon, cacao, and coconut sugar.

INGREDIENTS:

2 tbsp ground flaxseeds

2 tbsp water

1 cup cashews

1 cup hazelnuts

1 cup pumpkin seeds

1 cup sunflower seeds

2 tsp turmeric

½ tsp coriander

1 tbsp ground ginger

1 tsp cumin

1 tsp cardamom

1 tsp pink rock salt or gray salt (or to taste)

½ cup dried cranberries (apple juice–sweetened)

½ cup dried cherries

FOR OPTIONAL SWEET-AND-SPICY FLAVOR:

Replace turmeric, coriander, and cumin with:

1 tbsp cinnamon

2 tsp raw cacao powder

1 tsp coconut sugar

DIRECTIONS:

1. Preheat oven to 200°F. Mix flaxseeds in water until you create a slurry. Set aside.

2. Mix nuts and seeds in a medium mixing bowl and stir in flax mixture.

3. Mix spices and salt in a small bowl and sprinkle evenly over mix.

4. Place on a pan in oven and dehydrate for 1 hour until dry and crunchy.

5. Place into a large mixing bowl, add dried fruit, and store in a Mason jar until ready to enjoy.

Makes 16 servings.

CAROB SUPER SQUARES

I created this recipe after traveling through Virginia for a friend's wedding. We stopped for gas in a small town and, miraculously, I stumbled upon a health food store. I popped in to look around for some healthy snacks and found these tasty squares. As good as they were, I managed to save one so that I could make my own version when I got home. I promise you that this nutritious treat tastes just like chocolate! Consider doubling the recipe and freezing some.

INGREDIENTS:

⅓ cup raw honey or rice syrup

¼ cup tahini

¾ cup carob powder

½ tbsp pure vanilla extract

½ tbsp spirulina

½ tsp pink rock salt or gray sea salt

½ cup hemp seeds

½ cup sunflower seeds

½ cup pumpkin seeds

OPTIONAL SUPERFOOD BOOSTERS:

1 tsp maca powder or ashwagandha powder

DIRECTIONS:

1. Blend honey and tahini in a large mixing bowl until well combined. Add carob one tablespoon at a time until mixture becomes stiff and has a smooth consistency.

2. Add vanilla, spirulina, maca powder (if using), and salt, and mix to combine.

3. Stir in hemp and sunflower seeds, then evenly roll out the mixture onto a parchment-lined cookie tray to a ½-inch thickness. Sprinkle pumpkin seeds on top and press down with a cutting board to ensure they stick.

4. Cut into squares and cool in the fridge for 30 minutes before serving.

5. Wrap squares individually and store in the fridge or freezer.

Makes 30 1-inch squares.

COCO KALE CHIPS

These raw, vegan, gluten- and soy-free snacks beat anything you would find on a supermarket shelf. Dehydrating the kale in a low-temperature oven not only retains all the vitamins and minerals, it transforms it into a crispy chip that answers the craving for a crunch while the chocolaty coating satisfies a sweet tooth.

INGREDIENTS:

12 cups kale leaves, washed and
    thoroughly dried

½ cup hemp seeds or sunflower seeds

¼ cup raw cacao powder

1 tsp pure vanilla extract

¼ tsp pink rock salt or gray sea salt

1 tsp cinnamon

¾ cup unsweetened coconut beverage (2%
    fat) or unsweetened non-dairy milk
    (hemp, almond)

5–6 large pitted Medjool dates, chopped

DIRECTIONS:

1. Cut kale into 3-inch strips and pat down with a dry, clean dish towel to remove moisture. (It is important that the kale is thoroughly dried after washing or it will take too long to dehydrate.) Place kale in a large mixing bowl and set aside.

2. In a blender add seeds, cacao, vanilla, salt, cinnamon, and non-dairy milk and blend until smooth. Add dates one at a time until a smooth paste forms.

3. Pour mixture over kale and mix with hands until kale is evenly coated.

4. Spread evenly over two baking sheets and, ensuring pieces do not overlap, place in a 170°F oven for 2 to 2 ½ hours. Crack open the oven door to allow steam to escape. If using a dehydrator, place on nonstick sheets at 155°F for 3 hours. Flip kale chips over after 1 hour. Every oven is different, so check to ensure all the kale is crispy before removing from oven, but be careful to avoid burning.

5. Allow chips to cool completely and store in a tightly sealed container to keep them crisp. This treat has a long shelf life if kept dry.

Makes 6 servings.

BANANA BREAD BARS

I know that banana bread is a comfort food for many, so I cut the sugar and enriched white flour and came up with these bars that give you all the indulgence without the painful ingredients! Flaxseeds are high in fiber and omega-3 fatty acids as well as phytochemicals called lignans, all of which have powerful anti-inflammatory benefits. Make sure you grind the seeds yourself and store them in the freezer to preserve these nutrients. This treat is best made in a dehydrator, but the oven method works well too.

INGREDIENTS:

3 large ripe bananas

1½ cups Medjool dates, pitted and
   chopped

2 cups flaxseeds

1 tsp cinnamon

1 tsp vanilla powder or pure vanilla
   extract

1½ cups pumpkin seeds

1½ cups sunflower seeds

1 cup hemp hearts

OPTIONAL ADDITIONS:

½ tsp pink rock salt or gray sea salt

1 tsp maca powder or ashwagandha powder

DIRECTIONS:

1. In a food processor, blend bananas and dates to create a thick paste.

2. Grind flaxseeds, then add to banana mixture along with the cinnamon and vanilla. Mix until blended (about 10 seconds) and then transfer into a large mixing bowl.

3. Add pumpkin seeds, sunflower seeds, hemp hearts, and maca and salt (if using) to mixture until well combined. Don't hesitate to use your clean hands to combine.

4. Scoop mixture onto parchment paper sheets on a dehydrator tray or cookie sheet and spread to ½-inch thick. Cut and separate into bar shapes 2 x 3 inches. Leave space around each bar to speed up drying time. Dehydrate at 145°F for 6 hours or in oven at 170°F for 5 hours. Flip bars halfway through the drying process.

Makes 24 bars.

FRUIT FUNDUE WITH COCONUT CARAMEL SAUCE

This recipe works well at a cocktail party or an event as part of a buffet, but I think that it is most fun served as an after-dinner treat when everyone is sitting around the table socializing. The caramel sauce gets its "melt in your mouth," creamy, rich consistency from raw coconut butter, which you can find in most local health food stores. Coconut butter is different from coconut oil in that the meat of the coconut, including its natural oils, is puréed into a creamy butter. Eating coconut has been shown to increase metabolism and energy, which helps to maintain a healthy body weight. The sauce lasts in the fridge for over two weeks, so enjoy on fruit anytime.

CARAMEL SAUCE:

1 cup raw honey

½ cup coconut butter

½ cup coconut milk

¼ tsp pink rock salt or
    gray sea salt

1 tbsp pure vanilla extract

½ cup tahini

DIPPING FOOD IDEAS:

Chunks of bananas, apples, and pears; clementine orange sections; whole strawberries

TOPPING IDEAS:

Finely chopped nuts (e.g., pecans, almonds, and/or hazelnuts), ground cocoa nibs, black sesame seeds

DIRECTIONS:

1. Place all caramel sauce ingredients in a blender and blend until smooth. Transfer to a fondue pot or medium bowl.

2. Serve fruit on a sectioned platter and arrange each topping in a separate bowl.

3. Arrange fruit and toppings around the fondue pot or bowl containing the dipping sauce. Using a wooden or metal spear, pierce fruit and dip into the caramel sauce and then into the topping of your choice.

Makes 20 servings.

SPICED HARVEST APPLESAUCE

For a delicious, healing, and balanced snack, mix half a cup of harvest applesauce with one tablespoon hemp protein powder and/or sprinkle with hemp seeds.

INGREDIENTS:

10 cups Ambrosia apple slices

1–2 tsp ground ginger (or to taste)

2 tsp cinnamon

1 tsp cardamom

½ tsp ground cloves

1 cup apple juice

1 cup blueberries or cranberries

DIRECTIONS:

1. Add all ingredients to a pot and bring to a boil.

2. Turn down to a simmer and cook until fruit is soft, about 12 minutes.

3. Mash fruit with a fork or blend with an immersion blender. Add the sauce to heat-safe glass containers (wide-mouth Mason jars are ideal) while hot. Stores well in refrigerator for up to a week.

Tip: For a low-carbohydrate version, replace 1 cup of juice with water and add ½ tsp of stevia powder or 10 drops of stevia liquid.

Makes 8 cups.

HAZELNUTTY HOT CHOCOLATE

Coconut butter and cocoa powder make this creamy, chocolaty treat a great drink that will be beneficial before or after your workout. Cocoa powder contains caffeine, which has been shown to delay the onset of muscle fatigue by helping the body use its fat stores as energy. Coconut butter is high in medium-chain triglycerides (MCTs), which are rapidly absorbed by the body and immediately converted into fuel for the organs and muscles to use during a workout. This treat is also great for after a workout because the body is primed to absorb these calories and use them to replace the glycogen in the liver.

INGREDIENTS:

3 cups unsweetened coconut beverage (2% fat)

1 tbsp coconut butter

2 tbsp hazelnut butter

¼ cup raw cocoa powder

¼ cup raw honey

1 tbsp pure vanilla extract

Pinch pink rock salt or gray sea salt

⅛ tsp ground ginger

OPTIONAL SUPERFOOD BOOSTER:

2 tbsp lacuma powder or tiger nut powder or mesquite powder or 1 tbsp extra honey

DIRECTIONS:

1. Place coconut beverage in a medium pot and heat until hot but not boiling.

2. Add remaining ingredients to a blender, finishing with hot coconut beverage, and blend until well combined. If not using the sweet superfoods listed, be sure to add the extra honey, or taste and adjust sweetness to personal preference.

Makes 4 cups.

LOW-CARB VANILLA COCONUT COOKIES

If you ever find yourself craving something sweet to go alongside a cup of herbal tea in the afternoon, these cookies will come in handy. They are made with low-carb coconut flour, an exceptionally good source of the mineral manganese, which is crucial to a healthy nervous system and thyroid and balanced blood sugar levels.

WET INGREDIENTS:

½ cup melted virgin coconut oil

1 cup unsweetened coconut beverage
     (2% fat)

6 eggs, preferably free range and organic

2 tsp pure vanilla extract

½ cup xylitol crystals (or ⅔ cup coconut
     sugar or ¾ tsp liquid stevia)

FOR OPTIONAL LEMON FLAVOR, ADD IN STEP 2:

½ tbsp vitamin C crystals (ascorbic acid)

DRY INGREDIENTS:

1 cup coconut flour

¼ tsp pink rock salt or gray sea salt

½ cup shredded unsweetened coconut

DIRECTIONS:

1. Preheat oven to 350°F.

2. Whisk wet ingredients until xylitol is partially dissolved.

3. Add flour, salt, and shredded coconut to wet ingredients. Whisk until the mixture forms a thick paste.

4. On a parchment-lined baking sheet, place 1-inch dough balls 2 inches apart. Using a fork, push into the ball. Turn the fork 90 degrees and press into the ball again, making a cross pattern on the cookie.

5. Bake for 24 minutes for stevia cookies, 25 minutes for xylitol cookies, or 28 minutes for coconut sugar cookies. Store in airtight container in the fridge for up to a week. These cookies freeze well.

Makes 34 cookies.

PEACHY KEEN CRISP

This great gluten-free summer treat is perfect for a potluck BBQ or outdoor dinner party. The combination of sweet juicy peaches and tart summer berries is delicious and satisfying. Give your guests the gift of great taste and nutritional healing power all in one. Besides being packed full of fiber and water, peaches are also very high in beta-carotene. Recent studies have suggested that beta-carotene plays a role in regulating some aspects of the fat-burning process.

INGREDIENTS:

FILLING:

4 cups organic fresh or frozen berries

3 cups sliced apples

6 cups sliced fresh organic peaches

⅓ cup unsweetened berry or apple juice

2 tbsp fresh lemon juice

½ tsp ground cloves

½ tsp ground nutmeg

1 tsp cinnamon

OPTIONAL SUPERFOOD BOOSTER:

½ cup organic goji berries

TOPPING:

1 cup rolled quinoa flakes

½ cup almonds or hazelnuts, chopped

1 cup pumpkin seeds

1 cup sunflower seeds

½ cup raw honey

2 tsp cinnamon

½ tsp ground ginger

¼ tsp pink rock salt or gray sea salt

4 tbsp coconut butter or chilled coconut oil, cut into 8 pieces

OPTIONAL ADDITION:

2 tsp maca powder

FILLING DIRECTIONS:

1. Preheat oven to 350°F.

2. In a medium bowl combine berries, apples, peaches, and goji berries (if using). Add the berry juice, lemon juice, and spices.

3. Toss thoroughly and transfer to a 9 x 13–inch baking dish.

TOPPING DIRECTIONS:

1. In a large bowl, combine quinoa flakes, nuts, pumpkin seeds, sunflower seeds, honey, cinnamon, ginger, and salt. Place coconut butter on top of flour mixture. Using your hands, blend until mixture looks like coarse meal.

2. Sprinkle topping evenly and loosely over fruit mixture, leaving fruit visible in a few spots for the juices to bubble up.

3. Bake crisp for 35 minutes or until top is brown and fruit juices are bubbling at the edges. If using maca powder, sprinkle on top when crisp comes out of the oven.

Makes 12 servings.

303

HORMONE HEAVEN PUDDING

Send your hormones into orbit with this perfect pudding. Ashwagandha is an adaptogen that has the ability to maintain homeostasis and combat stress. It balances your thyroid gland to improve metabolism and works with your hormones to energize or calm you, depending on what you need.

INGREDIENTS:

6 tbsp raw cacao powder (or ⅔ cup carob powder)

6 tbsp raw honey

⅛ tsp pink rock salt or gray sea salt

3 tbsp hemp hearts

2 ripe avocados

½ cup unsweetened coconut beverage (2% fat)

OPTIONAL ADDITION:

2 tsp maca powder or ashwagandha powder

DIRECTIONS:

1. Add all ingredients to food processor and blend until smooth. Enjoy immediately or store in fridge for up to 3 days.

Makes 6 servings.

THE BEST NO-BAKE APPLE CRUMBLE

Never mind baking an apple pie—the nutrient value is so much higher if you keep it raw! Make sure that you leave the skin on the apples, since the quercetin content in the apple skin has the ability to reduce the histamine response, a cause of painful inflammation.

INGREDIENTS:

FILLING:

5 large organic Ambrosia apples

1 lemon, juiced

¼ cup dried cranberries

2 tbsp cinnamon

½ tsp ground nutmeg

½ tsp ground ginger

2 tbsp raw honey

CRUST:

1 cup hazelnuts

1 cup cashews or pecans

½ cup chopped Medjool dates

1 tsp pure vanilla extract

1 tsp cinnamon

½ tsp virgin coconut oil

TOPPING:

¼ cup hazelnuts

¼ cup cashews

¼ cup rolled quinoa flakes

¼ cup dried cranberries

Pinch pink rock salt or gray sea salt

Note: For a nut-free version, substitute dried coconut and hemp hearts for hazelnuts and cashews.

DIRECTIONS:

1. Slice the apples with a mandoline on the thin setting and put them in a bowl with the lemon juice, cranberries, cinnamon, nutmeg, ginger, and honey for 30 minutes. If you don't own a mandoline, slice apples as thinly as possible.

2. To make the crust, place nuts in a food processor with dates, vanilla, and cinnamon. Pulse until mixture sticks together and is the texture of crumbs. Use coconut oil to coat a 9 x 13–inch lasagna pan, then press in crust ingredients. Put pan in freezer for 20 minutes. Drain apples and place inside crust.

3. For topping, put hazelnuts, cashews, quinoa flakes, and cranberries into a food processor and pulse until fine. Spread topping ingredients over apples.

Makes 12 servings.

RED, WHITE, AND BLUE PIE

This sweet and subtly tart dessert is the perfect thing to bring to a summer BBQ. You can use strawberries or raspberries in this recipe, or both if you prefer. Berries are at the top of every superfood list because they are low in sugar, high in fiber, and absolutely bursting with antioxidant and anti-inflammatory nutrients—not to mention flavor!

INGREDIENTS:

CRUST:

1½ cups unsweetened shredded coconut, dried

10 pitted Medjool dates

¼ tsp whole vanilla bean powder or ½ tsp pure vanilla extract

1 tbsp virgin coconut oil

FILLING:

3 cups blueberries

1½ cups sliced strawberries or raspberries or combination

10 pitted Medjool dates

2 tbsp fresh lemon juice

2 cups unsweetened shredded coconut, dried

DIRECTIONS:

1. In a food processor, combine all crust ingredients until well blended. Press into a 10-inch pie dish and set aside.

2. In food processor, combine filling ingredients until well mixed, but avoid liquefying ingredients. Spread into crust and let pie set in the fridge for 2 hours before slicing.

Makes 12 servings.

ROCKET MACA TRUFFLES

Maca is an adaptogenic root whose B vitamins help your body handle stress. I call the truffles my rockets because when I need a boost before a TV segment, I enjoy a huge jolt of energy from one or two of these treats. Cocoa is great for energy and mood, and is high in antioxidants. Maca is known for increasing libido and nourishing the adrenals. Try it in smoothies, baked goods, and treats.

INGREDIENTS:

2 tbsp maca powder

Pinch pink rock salt or gray sea salt

1 tsp cinnamon

⅔ cup cocoa or raw cacao or carob powder

1 cup nut butter, stirred well

¼ cup raw honey

1 tsp pure vanilla extract

TOPPING CHOICES:

1 tbsp cocoa or carob powder

1 tbsp dried shredded coconut or sesame seeds

DIRECTIONS:

1. In a bowl, stir together maca powder, salt, cinnamon, and cocoa until well mixed.

2. Slowly add nut butter, honey, and vanilla and mix by hand.

3. Roll into 1-inch balls and dust with cocoa or carob powder, or shredded coconut or sesame seeds. Keep chilled in fridge until serving.

Makes 24 balls.

SALAD BARS

I had my very own "aha" moment when I created these bars. Let's face it—with our busy lives sometimes a "salad to go" can be difficult. This tasty recipe made me realize I can be running out the door and still have time to grab a salad to go. Using a dehydrator would be best but is not strictly necessary for this recipe. With a list of ingredients like this, it's hard to spotlight just one. The synergy of the nutrients in the foods listed below makes these salad bars a handheld package of tasty, anti-inflammatory goodness.

INGREDIENTS:

1 cup ground flaxseeds

¾ cup water

2 cups grated carrots

2 cups grated beet

1 cup kale leaves or collard greens, tightly packed

1 cup parsley leaves, tightly packed

1 tsp pink rock salt or gray sea salt

1 tbsp umeboshi paste or 6 pitted black olives (kalamata is best)

1 cup hemp seeds

1 cup sunflower seeds

OPTIONAL ADDITION:

1 tbsp apple cider vinegar (if using black olives)

DIRECTIONS:

1. Soak ground flaxseeds with water in a bowl for 10 minutes. Meanwhile, grate carrots and beets in a food processor and transfer to a mixing bowl.

2. Add soaked ground flaxseeds, kale, parsley, salt, and umeboshi paste or olives, and vinegar (if using) to the food processor. Using an S-blade, blend to paste consistency. Scrape down the sides as needed.

3. Transfer to mixing bowl with carrots and beets. Add hemp seeds and sunflower seeds.

4. Mix all ingredients together and spread smoothly onto parchment sheets to a thickness of ¼ inch.

5. Dehydrate in 200°F oven (or 155°F dehydrator) for 4 hours. (If using oven, create a tinfoil ball and prop the door open slightly to vent the moisture.) Remove from oven, place another piece of parchment paper on top, flip over and remove the paper. Cut and separate into 2 x 3–inch bars and return to oven or dehydrator to dry for another 1 to 2 hours.

You can also spread the mixture out more and increase drying time by another hour to make a hard cracker that will keep in an airtight container for 2 weeks out of the fridge.

Note: If you don't have ground flax, this recipe will work with whole flax by increasing soaking time to 20 minutes. Start with the flax in the food processor, pulsing until flax creates a paste.

Makes 24 bars.

LYNN'S "NO-BAKE" PUMPKIN PIE!

Pumpkin pie is a favorite in our house at Thanksgiving, so my sister, Lynn Daniluk, came up with a version that tastes as good as the original but doesn't contain all that sugar and fat. This no-bake pie will be a hit at your dinner table, and it won't take up any prime real estate in the oven of a busy holiday kitchen! Consider making it in 8 individual ramekins for easy serving.

INGREDIENTS:

CRUST:

2 cups pecans

2 tbsp raw honey

⅛ tsp pink rock salt or gray sea salt

½ tsp cinnamon

FILLING:

¾ cup coconut butter

3 cups cooked puréed pumpkin

¼ tsp pink rock salt or gray sea salt

½ cup raw honey

1 tsp pure vanilla extract

1 tbsp cinnamon

½–1 tsp nutmeg

¼ tsp ground cloves

1 tsp ginger

½ cup agar-agar

DIRECTIONS:

1. Put pecans in a food processor and process until it becomes a meal. Add honey, salt, and cinnamon and pulse until well combined. Press mixture into a 10-inch pie plate.

2. In a large pot on medium-low heat add coconut butter, cooked pumpkin, salt, honey, vanilla, and spices. Stir until well blended. Add agar-agar and continue to stir until mixture begins to thicken.

3. If mixture is too chunky, let cool slightly, transfer to a food processor, and mix until smooth.

4. Pour pumpkin mixture into crust. Chill in fridge for 3 hours to let pie set.

Makes 8 servings.

RESOURCES

Acropolis Organics

Organic olive oil

6 Curity Avenue, Unit 6

Toronto, ON

M4B 1X2

1-416-429-5111

www.acropolisorganics.com

Ascenta Health Ltd.

Sustainable omega-3 oils

4-15 Garland Avenue

Dartmouth, NS

B3B 0A6

1-866-224-1775

www.ascentahealth.com

Bio-K International Inc.

Scientifically proven probiotics

Parc Scientifique

495 boul. Armand-Frappier

Laval, QC

H7V 4B3

1-450-978-2465

www.biokplus.com

Bob's Red Mill

Organic gluten-free grains and beans

13521 SE Pheasant Court

Milwaukie, OR

97222

1-503-654-3215

www.bobsredmill.com

Caldwell Bio Fermentation Inc.

Organic raw cultured vegetables
579 chemin de la Rivière
Saint-Edwidge, QC
J0B 2R0
Tel: 1-802-323-1785
www.caldwellbiofermentation.com

Daiya Foods Inc

Dairy-free cheese
2768 Rupert Street
Vancouver, BC
V5M 3T7
1-604-569-0530
www.daiyafoods.com

Eden Foods Inc.

Noodles, beans, sauces, seeds, rice
    syrup, dried fruit
701 Tecumseh Road
Clinton, MI
49236
1-517-456-7854
www.edenfoods.com

Follow Your Heart

Supplier of Vegenaise egg-free and
    dairy-free mayonnaise
21825 Sherman Way
Canoga Park, CA
91303
1-818-348-3240
www.followyourheart.com

Food For Life

Gluten-free bread and tortilla
P.O. Box 1434
Corona, CA
92878
1-951-279-5090
www.foodforlife.com

Fresh Hemp Foods Ltd.

Top-quality hemp seed products and
    organic hemp protein shake
    powder
69 Eagle Drive
Winnipeg, MB
R2R 1V4
1-204-953-0233
www.manitobaharvest.com

Green Health Inc.

Pressing juicers, dehydrators,
 spiralizers
5350 Concession 3
New Lowell, ON
L0M 1N0
1-888-481-7739
www.greenhealthcanada.com

Kate Kent

Experiential Dynamic Counseling
348 Danforth Avenue, Suite 209
Toronto, ON
M4K 1N8
416-466-5849
www.katekentTCM.com

Mary's Organic Crackers

Gluten-free products
P.O. Box 965
Gridley, CA
95948
1-530-846-5100
www.marysorganiccrackers.com

**Natural Factors Nutritional
 Products Ltd.**

PGX ™ fiber
1550 United Boulevard
Coquitlam, BC
Canada V3K 6Y2
1-800-663-8900
www.pgx.com

Preferred Nutrition Inc.

Hormone-, inflammation-, and
 immune-balancing supplements
153 Perth Street
Acton, ON
L7J 1C9
1-888-826-9625
www.pno.ca

Raincoast Trading

Sustainable fish products
9398 Alaska Way
Delta, BC
V4C 4R8
1-604-582-8268
www.raincoasttrading.com

Sahana Ayurvedic Products

Top-quality organic herbs and spices

5764 Monkland Avenue

Suite 471

Montreal, QC

H4A 1E9

1-514-369-8175

www.arayuma.com

SaunaRay

Far-infrared saunas

P.O. Box 188

Collingwood, ON

L9Y 3Z5

1-877-992-1100

www.saunaray.com

Sea Tangle Noodle Company

Kelp noodles

San Diego, CA

1-408-966-3109

www.kelpnoodles.com

Sunbiotics

Raw probiotic chocolate

P.O. Box 328

Glenview, IL

60025

1-800-925-0577

www.sunbiotics.com

TallGrass Distribution Ltd.

Food-based supplements and body care

40 East 5th Avenue

Vancouver, BC

V5T 1G8

1-604-709-0101

www.tallgrass.ca

Weleda

Organic skin care

1 Closter Road

P.O. Box 675

Palisades, NY

10964

1-800-241-1030

www.weleda.com

Look for a regional food co-op in your area where you can buy healthy food choices directly. For example:

Ontario Natural Food Co-op

Organic food manufacturer and distributor

5685 McLaughlin Road

Mississauga, ON

L5R 3K5

1-905-507-2021

www.onfc.ca

Look for a local health food store in your area with great staff who can guide you to healthy choices. For example:

The Big Carrot Natural
  Food Market
348 Danforth Avenue
Toronto, ON
M4K 1N8
1-416-466-2129
www.thebigcarrot.ca

To learn more about my TV show, *Healthy Gourmet*, visit www.ownca. oprah.com/Shows/Healthy-Gourmet.aspx.

To learn more about co-host Ezra Title, visit www.chezvousdining.ca.

For a detailed glossary, extended reference section, and further information about how to heal inflammation, check out www.juliedaniluk.com. The Anti-inflammatory Quick Start program explores in depth the concepts outlined in this book.

REFERENCES

The complete list of the scientific references for *Slimming Meals That Heal* may also be found on my website, www.juliedaniluk.com.

Chapter 1: Why Diets Don't Work

Mann, T., et al. 2007. "Medicare's Search for Effective Obesity Treatments—Diets Are Not the Answer." *American Psychologist* 62(3): 220–33.

Shepherd, R. 1999. "Social Determinants of Food Choice." *Proceedings of the Nutrition Society* 58: 807–12.

Taylor, K., et al. 1983. *Clinical Nutrition*. New York, NY: McGraw-Hill.

Chapter 2: How Allergies Cause Weight Gain

Adams, S. 1996. "What is gluten? What is gliadin?" Celiac.com, July 26. http://www.celiac.com/articles/8/1/What-is-gluten-What-is-gliadin/Page1.html.

AllergyExpert.US. 2013. "Lactose Intolerance." http://www.allergyexpert.us/food/lactoseintolerance.html.

AllergyExpert.US. 2013. "What are food allergy symptoms?" http://www.allergyexpert.us/food/foodallergysymptoms.html.

Allergy UK. 2013. "Fish/Seafood Allergy." http://www.allergyuk.org/fish-and-seafood-allergy/fish-and-seafood-allergy.

Allergy UK. 2013. Peanut and Tree Nut Allergy. http://www.allergyuk.org/peanut-and-tree-nut-allergy/peanut-and-tree-nut-allergy

Amar, J., et al. 2008. "Energy Intake is Associated with Endotoxemia in Apparently Healthy Men." *American Journal of Clinical Nutrition* 87(5): 1219–23.

Atkinson, W., et al. 2004. "Food Elimination Based on IgG Antibodies in Irritable Bowel Syndrome: A Randomised Controlled Trial." *Gut* 53(10): 1459–64.

Baenkler, H. 2008. "Salicylate Intolerance: Pathophysiology, Clinical Spectrum, Diagnosis and Treatment." *Deutsches Arzteblatt International* 105(8): 137–42.

Barrett, J., et al. 2012. "Fermentable Oligosaccharides, Disaccharides, Monosaccharides and Polyols (FODMAPs) and Nonallergic Food Intolerance: FODMAPs or Food Chemicals?" *Therapeutic Advances in Gastroenterology* 5(4): 261–68.

Biesiekierski, J., et al. 2011. "Gluten Causes Gastrointestinal Symptoms in Subjects Without Celiac Disease: A Double-Blind Randomized Placebo-Controlled Trial." *American Journal of Gastroenterology* 106(3): 508–14.

Bolin, T. 2009. "IBS or Intolerance?" *Australian Family Physician* 38(12): 962–65.

Bray, G., et al. 2002. "The Influence of Different Fats and Fatty

Acids on Obesity, Insulin Resistance and Inflammation." *Journal of Nutrition* 132(9): 2488–91.

Buttriss, J., ed. 2008. *Adverse Reactions to Food: The Report of a British Nutrition Foundation Task Force.* Hoboken, NJ: Wiley-Blackwell.

California Department of Public Health. 2013. "Scomboid Fish Poisoning. http://www.cdph.ca.gov/HEALTHINFO/DISCOND/Pages/ScombroidFishPoisoning.aspx.

Campbell-McBride, N. 2010. *Gut and Psychology Syndrome: Natural Treatment for Autism, Dyspraxia, A.D.D., Dyslexia, A.D.H.D., Depression and Schizophrenia.* Cambridge, UK: Medinform Publishing.

Cani, P., 2012. "Gut Microbiome and Energy Metabolism: The Concept of MicrObesity." 15th International Congress of Endocrinology. Florence, Italy.

Cani, P., et al. 2007. "Metabolic Endotoxemia Initiates Obesity and Insulin Resistance." *Diabetes* 56(7): 1761–72.

Carroccio, A., et al. 2012. "Non-celiac wheat sensitivity diagnosed by double-blind placebo-controlled challenge: exploring a new clinical entity." *American Journal of Gastroenterology* 107(12):1898–906.

Dalla Pellegrina, C., et al. 2009. "Effects of Wheat Germ Agglutinin on Human Gastrointestinal Epithelium: Insights from an Experimental Model of Immune/Epithelial Cell Interaction." *Toxicology and Applied Pharmacology* 237(2): 146–53.

Fasano, A. 2011. "Zonulin and Its Regulation of Intestinal Barrier Function: The Biological Door to Inflammation, Autoimmunity, and Cancer." *Physiological Reviews* 91(1): 151–75.

Goldstein, D. 2006. *Adrenaline and the Inner World: An Introduction to Scientific Integrative Medicine.* Baltimore, MD: Johns Hopkins University Press.

Goodman, H. 2003. *Basic Medical Endocrinology.* San Diego, CA: Academic Press.

Greenstein, B., et al. 2011. *At a Glance: Endocrine System at a Glance, 3rd Edition.* Hoboken, NJ: Wiley-Blackwell.

Guo, H., et al. 2012. "The Value of Eliminating Foods According to Food-Specific Immunoglobulin G Antibodies in Irritable Bowel Syndrome with Diarrhea." *Journal of International Medical Research* 40(1): 204–10.

Herman, P., et al. 2004. "Evaluating the Clinical Relevance of Food Sensitivity Tests: A Single Subject Experiment." *Alternative Medicine Review* 9(2): 198–207.

Heyman, M. 2000. "Effect of Lactic Acid Bacteria on Diarrheal Diseases." *Journal of the American College of Nutrition* 19(2 Suppl): 137S–146S.

Holt, R., et al. 2011. *Endocrine Aspects of Metabolic Syndrome. Metabolic Syndrome: Science and Clinical Practice.* Hoboken, NJ: Wiley-Blackwell. 120–38.

Karlsson, A. 1999. "Wheat Germ Agglutinin Induces NADPH-oxidase Activity in Human Neutrophils by Interaction with Mobilizable Receptors." *Infection and Immunity* 67(7): 3461–68.

Kitts, D., et al. 2003. "Bioactive Proteins and Peptides from Food Sources. Applications of Bioprocesses Used in Isolation and Recovery." *Current Pharmaceutical Design* 9(16): 1309–23.

Lavine, E. 2012. "Blood Testing for Sensitivity, Allergy or Intolerance to Food." *Canadian Medical Association Journal* 184(6): 666–68.

Liu, W., et al. 2004. "Wheat Germ Lectin Induces G2/M Arrest in Mouse L929 Fibroblasts." *Journal of Cellular Biochemistry* 91(6): 1159–73.

Maintz, L., et al. 2007. "Histamine and Histamine Intolerance." *American Journal of Clinical Nutrition* 85(5): 1185–96.

Mason, J. 2013. "Mechanisms of Nutrient Absorption and Malabsorption." *UpToDate.com.* http://www.uptodate.com/contents/mechanisms-of-nutrient-absorption-and-malabsorption.

Mayo Clinic. 2013. "Shellfish allergy." Mayoclinic.com. http://www.mayoclinic.com/health/shellfish-allergy/DS00987

Mercer, M., et al. 1997. "Food Cravings, Endogenous Opioid Peptides, and Food Intake: A Review." *Appetite* 29(3): 325–52.

Misra, M., et al. 2008. "Lower Growth Hormone and Higher Cortisol are Associated with Greater Visceral Adiposity, Intramyocellular Lipids, and Insulin Resistance in Overweight Girls." *American Journal of Physiology, Endocrinology and Metabolism* 295(2): E385–92.

Mitchell, N., et al. 2011. "Randomised Controlled Trial of Food Elimination Diet Based on IgG Antibodies for the Prevention of Migraine Like Headaches." *Nutrition Journal* 10:85. doi: 10.1186/1475-2891-10-85.

Montgomery, R., et al. 2013. Lactose Intolerance. *UpToDate.com.* http://www.uptodate.com/contents/lactose-intolerance.

Mosby's Medical Dictionary. 2009. s.v. "food allergy."

Myers, M., et al. 2010. "Obesity and Leptin Resistance: Distinguishing Cause from Effect." *Trends in Endocrinology and Metabolism: TEM* 21(11): 643–51.

Ovelgonne, J., et al., 2000. "Decreased Levels of Heat Shock Proteins in Gut Epithelial Cells After Exposure to Plant Lectins." *Gut* 46(5): 679–87.

Pessione, E. 2012. "Lactic Acid Bacteria Contribution to Gut Microbiota Complexity: Lights And Shadows." *Frontiers in Cellular Infection Microbiology* 2:86. doi: 10.3389/fcimb.2012.00086.

Praag, H., et al. 2004. *Stress, The Brain and Depression*. West Nyack, NY: Cambridge University Press.

Purnell, J., et al. 2009. "Enhanced Cortisol Production Rates, Free Cortisol, and 11beta-HSD-1 Expression Correlate with Visceral Fat and Insulin Resistance in Men: Effect of Weight Loss." *American Journal of Physiology, Endocrinology and Metabolism* 296(2): E351–7.

Pusztai, A., et al. 1993. "Antinutritive Effects of Wheat-Germ Agglutinin and Other N-Acetylglucosamine-Specific Lectins." *British Journal of Nutrition* 70(1): 313–21.

Ratliff, J., et al. 2010. "Association of Prescription H1 Antihistamine Use with Obesity: Results from the National Health and Nutrition Examination Survey." *Obesity* 18(12): 2398–400.

Sapone, A., et al. 2011. "Divergence of Gut Permeability and Mucosal Immune Gene Expression in Two Gluten-Associated Conditions: Celiac Disease and Gluten Sensitivity." *BMC Medicine* 9:23. doi: 10.1186/1741-7015-9-23.

Sapone, A., et al. 2012. "Spectrum of Gluten-Related Disorders: Consensus on New Nomenclature and Classification." *BMC Medicine* 10:13. doi: 10.1186/1741-7015-10-13.

Siebler, J., et al. 2008. "The Gut-Liver-Axis: Endotoxemia, Inflammation, Insulin Resistance and NASH." *Journal of Hepatology* 48(6): 1032–34.

Takahashi, M., et al. 2000. "Behavioral and Pharmacological Studies on Gluten Exorphin A5, A Newly Isolated Bioactive Food Protein Fragment, In Mice." *Japanese Journal of Pharmacology* 84(3): 259–65.

Teschemacher, H. 2003. "Opioid Receptor Ligands Derived from Food Proteins." *Current Pharmaceutical Design* 9(16): 1331–44.

Tillin, T. et al. 2011. "Metabolic Syndrome and Ethnicity" in *Metabolic Syndrome: Science and Clinical Practice*. Hoboken, NJ: Wiley-Blackwell. 19–44.

Tortora, G., et al. 2004. *Introduction to the Human Body: Essentials of Anatomy and Physiology*. Hoboken, NJ: John Wiley & Sons.

U.S. Department of Health and Human Services. 2008. "Celiac Disease." National Digestive Diseases Information Clearinghouse. http://digestive.niddk.nih.gov/ddiseases/pubs/celiac.

U.S. Department of Health and Human Services. 2010. "Food Allergy: Food Intolerance." National Institute of Allergy and Infectious Diseases. http://www.niaid.nih.gov/topics/foodallergy/understanding/pages/foodintolerance.aspx.

U.S. Department of Health and Human Services. 2010. "Guidelines for the Diagnosis and Management of Food Allergy in the United States: Report of the NIAID-Sponsored Expert Panel." *The Journal of Allergy and Clinical Immunology* 126(6): S1–S58.

U.S. Department of Health and Human Services. 2010. "Irritable Bowel Syndrome." National Digestive Diseases Information Clearinghouse. http://digestive.niddk.nih.gov/ddiseases/pubs/ibs.

Vaidya, V. 2006. "Advances in Psychosomatic Medicine, Volume 27." *Health and Treatment Strategies in Obesity*. Karger Publishers.

Venter, C., et al. 2009. "Classification and Prevalence of Food Hypersensitivity" in *Food Hypersensitivity: Diagnosing and Managing Food Allergies and Intolerance*. Hoboken, NJ: Wiley-Blackwell. 3–114.

Vojdani, A. 2009. "Detection of IgE, IgG, IgA and IgM antibodies against raw and processed food antigens." *Nutr Metab* 6(22). doi: 10.1186/1743-7075-6-22.

Weber-Hamann, B., et al. 2002. "Hypercortisolemic Depression Is Associated with Increased Intra-Abdominal Fat." *Psychosomatic Medicine* 64(2): 274–77.

Yarnell, E. 2003. *Exorphins, Food Cravings, and Schizophrenia*. East Wanatchee, WA: Healing Mountain Publishing.

Zioudrou, C., et al. 1979. "Opioid Peptides Derived from Food Proteins. The Exorphins." *The Journal of Biological Chemistry* 254(7): 2446–49.

Chapter 3: The Hormone Heist

Adlercreutz, H. 2007. "Lignans and Human Health." *Critical Reviews in Clinical Laboratory Sciences* 44(5–6): 483–525.

Agil, A., et al. 2011. "Beneficial Effects of Melatonin on Obesity and Lipid Profile in Young Zucker Diabetic Fatty Rats." *Journal of Pineal Research* 50(2): 207–12.

Ahmadieh, H. 2011. "Vitamins and Bone Health: Beyond Calcium and Vitamin D." *Nutrition Reviews* 69(10): 584–98.

Atoum, M., et al. 2012. "Endogenous Estradiol, Estrogen and Progesterone Receptors Increase Benign and Breast Cancer Risk among Non-Familial Postmenopausal Females." *Health Science Journal* 6(10): 693–702.

Aubertin-Leheudre, M. 2011. "Diets and Hormonal Levels in Postmenopausal Women With or Without Breast Cancer." *Nutrition & Cancer* 63(4): 514–24.

Badria, F. 2002. "Melatonin, Serotonin, and Tryptamine in Some Egyptian Food and Medicinal Plants." *Journal of Medicinal Food* 5(3): 153–57.

Blask, D., et al. 2004. "Melatonin Uptake and Growth Prevention in Rat Hepatoma 7288CTC in Response to Dietary Melatonin: Melatonin Receptor-Mediated Inhibition of Tumor Linoleic Acid Metabolism to the Growth Signaling Molecule 13-Hydroxyoctadecadienoic Acid and the Potential Role of Phytomelatonin." *Carcinogenesis* 25(6): 951–60.

Bornstein, S., et al. 2002. "The Adrenal Hormone Metabolism in the Immune/Inflammatory Reaction." *Endocrine Research* 28(4): 719–28.

Bowden, J. 2011. "Healthy Solutions DEEP Cleaning: Natural Solutions for Hepatitis C and Liver Health." *Better Nutrition* 73(10): 28–30.

Burkhardt, S., et al. 2001. "Detection and quantification of the antioxidant melatonin in Montmorency and Balaton tart cherries (Prunus cerasus)." *Journal of Agricultural and Food Chemistry* 49(10): 4898–902.

Capeau, J. 2005. "Insulin Signaling: Mechanisms Altered in Insulin Resistance." *International Journal of Medical Sciences* Spec No: 34–39.

Chen, M., et al. 2000. "Zinc May Be a Mediator of Leptin Production in Humans. *Life Sciences* 66(22): 2143–49.

Eaton, N., et al. 1999. "Endogenous Sex Hormones and Prostate Cancer: A Quantitative Review of Prospective Studies." *British Journal of Cancer* 80(7): 930–34.

Frye, C., et al. 2012. "Endocrine Disrupters: A Review of Some Sources, Effects, and Mechanisms of Actions on Behavior and Neuroendocrine Systems." *Journal of Neuroendocrinology* 24(1): 144–59.

Fucic, A., et al. 2012. "Environmental Exposure to Xenoestrogens and Oestrogen-Related Cancers: Reproductive System, Breast, Lung, Kidney, Pancreas, and Brain. *Environmental Health: A Global Access Science Source* 11(Supp l): S8.

Fink, H., et al. 1998. "Major biological actions of CCK – a critical evaluation of research findings." *Experimental Brain Research* 123(1–2): 77–83.

Galluzzi, F., et al. 2005. "Reversible Weight Gain and Prolactin Levels-Long-Term Follow-up in Childhood." *Journal of Pediatric Endocrinology and Metabolism* 18(9): 921–24.

Gann, P., et al. 1996. "Prospective Study of Sex Hormone Levels and Risk of Prostate Cancer." *Journal of the National Cancer Institute* 88(16): 1118–26.

Harvey, P. 2006. "Hyperprolactinaemia as an Adverse Effect in Regulatory and Clinical Toxicology: Role in Breast and Prostate Cancer." *Human & Experimental Toxicology* 25(7): 395–404.

2009. "Health is REAL WEALTH." *Alive: Canada's Natural Health & Wellness Magazine.* 102.

Heaney, R. 1998. "Toward Optimal Health: The Experts Respond to Osteoporosis. Interview by Jodi G. Meisler." *J Women's Health Gend Based Med* 9(2): 89–96.

Hietala, M., et al. 2008. "Prolactin Levels, Breast-Feeding and Milk Production in a Cohort of Young Healthy Women from High-Risk Breast Cancer Families: Implications for Breast Cancer Risk." *Familial Cancer* 7(3): 221–28.

Holzer, P. 1998. "Neural Injury, Repair, and Adaptation in the GI Tract: The Elusive Action of Capsaicin on the Vagus Nerve." *American Journal of Physiology* 275(1 Pt 1): G8–13.

Huang, X., et al. 2011. "Simultaneous Analysis of Serotonin, Melatonin, Piceid and Resveratrol in Fruits Using Liquid Chromatography Tandem Mass Spectrometry." *Journal of Chromatography* 1218(25): 3890–99.

Ionkova, I. 2011. "Anticancer Lignans—from Discovery to Biotechnology." *Mini Reviews in Medicinal Chemistry* 11(10): 843–56.

Jie, L. 2011. "Improvement in Chewing Activity Reduces Energy Intake in One Meal and Modulates Plasma Gut Hormone Concentrations in Obese and Lean Young Chinese Men." *American Journal of Clinical Nutrition* 94(3): 709–16.

Keller, C., et al. 2010. "Perimenopausal Obesity." *Journal of Women's Health* 19(5): 987–96.

Koretz, R. 2012. "Nutritional Support for Liver Disease." *Cochrane Database of Systematic Reviews.*

Kroner, J. 2005. "Optimal Liver Health." *Better Nutrition* 67: 36–38.

Laumann, E., et al. 1999. "Sexual Dysfunction in the United States: Prevalence and Predictors." *Journal of the American Medical Association* 281(6): 537–44.

Lindstad, T. 2010. "STAMPs at the Crossroads of Cancer and Nutrition." *Nutrition & Cancer* 62(7): 891–95.

Little, T., et al. 2005. "Role of Cholecystokinin in Appetite Control and Body Weight Regulation." *Obesity Reviews* 6(4): 297–306.

Ma, R., et al. 2009. "A Systematic Review of the Effect of Diet in Prostate Cancer Prevention and Treatment." *Journal of Human Nutrition and Dietetics* 22(3):187–99.

Massé, P., et al. 2004. "Dietary Macro- and Micronutrient Intakes of Nonsupplemented Pre- and Postmenopausal Women with a Perspective on Menopause-Associated Diseases." *Journal of Human Nutrition and Dietetics* 17(2): 121–32.

Morrison, C. 2007. "Neurobiology of Nutrition and Obesity." *Nutrition Reviews* 65(12 Pt 1): 517–34.

Nielsen, F. H. 2010. "Magnesium, inflammation, and obesity in chronic disease." *Nutrition Reviews* 68(6): 333–40.

Panda, S., et al. 1998. "Changes in Thyroid Hormone Concentrations After Administration of Ashwagandha Root Extract to Adult Male Mice." *Journal of Pharmacy and Pharmacology* 50(9): 1065–68.

Panda, S., et al. 1999. "Gugulu (Commiphora mukul) Induces Triiodothyronine Production: Possible Involvement of Lipid Peroxidation." *Life Sciences* 65(12): PL137–41.

Pasman, W., et al. 2008. "The Effect of Korean Pine Nut Oil on In-Vitro CCK Release, on Appetite Sensations and on Gut Hormones in Post-Menopausal Overweight Women." *Lipids in Health and Disease* 7(10).

Pastore, L. 2012. "Beta-Endorphins." *Journal of Endocrinology and Metabolism* 2(1): 11–20.

Peters, E., et al. 2001. "Vitamin C Supplementation Attenuates the Increases in Circulating Cortisol, Adrenaline and

Anti-inflammatory Polypeptides Following Ultramarathon Running." *International Journal of Sports Medicine* 22(7): 537–43.

Peterson, J. 2010. "Dietary Lignans: Physiology and Potential for Cardiovascular Disease Risk Reduction." *Nutrition Reviews* 68(10): 571–603.

Reinholz, J., et al. 2008. "Compensatory Weight Gain Due to Dopaminergic Hypofunction: New Evidence and Own Incidental Observations." *Nutrition & Metabolism* 1(5): 35.

Reiter, R. 2005. "Melatonin in Walnuts: Influence on Levels of Melatonin and Total Antioxidant Capacity of Blood Nutrition." 21(9): 920–24.

Saad, Farid, et al. 2012. "Testosterone therapy in treatment of obesity in men: a review." *Current diabetes reviews* 8(2):131.

Setright, R. 2012. "The Use of Nutritional and Herbal Supplements in the Maintenance of Prostate Health: An Independent Review of Complementary Medicine Evidence." *The Setright Letter*. 02:12:1–15. *Journal of the Australian Traditional-Medicine Society* 18:199–209.

Stege, P., et al. 2010. "Determination of Melatonin in Wine and Plant Extracts by Capillary Electrochromatography with Immobilized Carboxylic Multi-Walled Carbon Nanotubes as Stationary Phase." *Electrophoresis* 31(13): 2242–48.

Tripathi, Y., et al. 1984. "Thyroid Stimulating Action of Z-Guggulsterone Obtained from Commiphora Mukul." *Planta Medica* 50(1): 78–80.

Vitalini, S., et al. 2011. "The Presence of Melatonin in Grapevine (Vitis Vinifera L.) Berry Tissues." *Journal of Pineal Research* 51(3): 331–37.

Webb, A. 2005. "Dietary Lignans: Potential Role in Cancer Prevention." *Nutrition & Cancer* 51(2): 117–31.

Chapter 4: The Nutrition of Weight Loss

Ball, S.D., et al. 2003. "Prolongation of Satiety After Low Versus Moderately High Glycemic Index Meals in Obese Adolescents." *Pediatrics* 111(3): 488–94.

Basu, A., et al. 2006. "Dietary Factors that Promote or Retard Inflammation." *Arteriosclerosis, Thrombosis, and Vascular Biology* 26(5): 995–1001.

Calder, P.C. 2011. "Fatty Acids and Inflammation: The Cutting Edge Between Food and Pharma." *European Journal of Pharmacology* 688(Suppl 1): S50–S58.

de Rougemont, A., et al. 2007. "Beneficial Effects of a 5-Week Low-Glycemic Index Regimen on Weight Control and Cardiovascular Risk Factors in Overweight Non-Diabetic Subjects." *British Journal of Nutrition* 98(6): 1288–98.

Gunnarsdottir, J., et al. 2008. "Inclusion of Fish or Fish Oil in Weight-Loss Diets for Young Adults: Effects on Blood Lipids." *International Journal of Obesity* (London) 32(7): 1105–12.

Jenkins, D.J., et al. 1981. "Glycemic Index of Foods: A Physiological Basis for Carbohydrate Exchange." *The American Journal of Clinical Nutrition* 34(3): 362–66.

Johnson, G.H., et al. 2012. "Effect of Dietary Linoleic Acid on Markers of Inflammation in Healthy Persons: A Systematic Review of Randomized Controlled Trials." *Journal of the Academy of Nutrition and Dietetics* 112(7): 1029–41.

Kondo, T., et al. 2009. "Acetic Acid Upregulates the Expression of Genes for Fatty Acid Oxidation Enzymes in Liver to Supress Body Fat Accumulation." *Journal of Agricultural and Food Chemistry* 57(13): 5982–86.

Ostman, E., et al. 2005. "Vinegar Supplementation Lowers Glucose and Insulin Responses and Increases Satiety After a Bread Meal in Healthy Subjects." *European Journal of Clinical Nutrition* 59(9): 983–88.

Rallidis, L.S., et al. 2003. "Dietary a-Linolenic Acid Decreases C-Reactive Protein, Serum Amyloid A and Interleukin-6 in Dyslipidemic Patients." *Atherosclerosis* 167(2): 237–42.

Salbe, A.D., et al. 2009. "Vinegar Lacks Antiglycemic Action on Enteral Carbohydrate Absorption in Human Subjects." *Nutrition Research* 29(12): 846–49.

Tai, C.C., et al. 2009. "Docosahexaenoic Acid Enhances Hepatic Serum Amyloid A Expression Via Protein Kinase A-Dependent Mechanism." *The Journal of Biological Chemistry* 284(47): 32239–47.

Vasickova, L., et al. 2011. "Possible Effect of DHA Intake on Body Weight Reduction and Lipid Metabolism in Obese Children." *Neuroendocrinology Letters* 32 (Suppl 2): 64–67.

Veldhorst, M., et al. 2008. "Protein-Induced Satiety: Effects and Mechanisms of Different Proteins." *Physiology & Behaviour* 94(2): 300–07.

Wall, R., et al. 2010. "Fatty Acids from Fish: The Anti-inflammatory Potential of Long-Chain Omega-3 Fatty Acids." *Nutrition Reviews* 68(5): 280–89.

Westerterp-Plantenga, M.S., et al. 2012. "Dietary Protein: It's Role in Satiety, Energetics, Weight Loss and Health." *British Journal of Nutrition* 108(Suppl 2): S105–S112.

Wilde, P.J. 2009. "Eating For Life: Designing Foods for Appetite Control." *Journal of Diabetes and Science Technology* 3(2): 336–70.

Zorzanelli Rocha, V., et al. 2011. "Inflammatory Concepts of Obesity." *International Journal of Inflammation*. 1–14.

Chapter 5: The Live-It Tool Kit

Bishop, B. Personal Training. http://www.iambishop.com.

Carr, K. April 17, 2011. Lecture Q and A with Kris Carr. Cancer Summit for Young Adults. New York.

Craig, G. 2011. *The EFT Manual.* Fulton, CA: Energy Psychology Press.

Driver, J. July 12, 2012. Interview with Josie Driver. (J. Daniluk, Interviewer).

Freud, S. 1991. *On Metapsychology–The Theory of Psychoanalysis.* Edited by A. Dickson. London: Penguin.

Genuis, S.J., et al. 2010. "Blood, Urine, and Sweat (BUS) Study: Monitoring and Elimination of Bioaccumulated Toxic Elements." *Archives of Environmental Contamination and Toxicology* 61(2): 9611–15.

Genuis, S.J., et al. 2012. "Human Elimination of Phthalate Compounds: Blood, Urine, and Sweat (BUS) Study." *The Scientific World Journal.* Article ID 615068, 10 pages.

Genuis, S.J. 2012. "Human Excretion of Bisphenol A: Blood, Urine, and Sweat (BUS) Study." *Journal of Environmental and Public Health* 2012:185731:1–10.

Hanh, T.N. 2010. *Savor.* San Francisco, CA: HarperOne.

Kent, K. June 2010. Interview with Therapist Kate Kent. (J. Daniluk, Interviewer).

Meeker, J.D., et al. 2011. "Relationship between Urinary Phthalate and Bisphenol A Concentrations and Serum Thyroid Measures in U.S. Adults and Adolescents from the National Health and Nutrition Examination Survey (NHANES) 2007-2008." *Environmental Health Perspectives* 119(10): 1396–1402.

Natural Resources Defense Council. 2011. Neglect at Your Own Risk: Your Thyroid and Environmental Toxins. NRDC.org. http://www.nrdc.org/living/healthreports/thyroid.asp.

Ortner, N. 2013. *The Tapping Solution.* Carlsbad, CA: Hay House.

Roizen, M.F. 2009. *YOU: On a Diet, Revised Edition.* New York: Scribner.

Shambunata. Yoga. http://www.shambunata.com.

Spiegel, K., et al. 2004. "Leptin Levels are Dependent on Sleep Duration: Relationships with Sympathovagal Balance, Carbohydrate Regulation, Cortisol, and Thyrotopin." *The Journal of Clinical Endocrinology & Metabolism* 89(11): 5762–71.

Chapter 6: The 5-Step Plan

Beauchamp, G.K., et al. 2005. "Phytochemistry: Ibuprofen-Like Activity in Extra-Virgin Olive Oil." *Nature* 437(7055): 45–46.

Benbrook, C., et al. 2008. "New evidence confirms the nutritional superiority of plant-based organic foods." *State of Science Review.* March: 1–8.

Bondesson, M., et al. 2009. "A CASCADE of Effects of Bisphenol A." *Reproductive Toxicology* 28(4): 563–67.

Belleme, J., et al. 2007. *Japanese Foods That Heal: Using Traditional Japanese Ingredients to Promote Health, Longevity, and Well-Being.* North Clarendon, VT: Tuttle Publishing.

Borek, C. 2006. "Garlic Reduces Dementia and Heart-Disease Risk." *Journal of Nutrition* 136(Suppl. 3): 810S–812S.

Breaky, J., et al. 2001. "The Role of Food Additives and Chemicals in Behavioral Learning, Activity, and Sleep Problems in Children." In *Food Additives, 2nd ed.* Edited by Larry Brenan. New York: Marcel Dekker. 87–97.

Brien, S., et al. 2004. "Bromelain as a Treatment for Osteoarthritis: A Review of Clinical Studies." *Evidence-Based Complementary and Alternative Medicine* 1(3): 251–57.

Bukovská, A., et al. 2007. "Effects of a Combination of Thyme and Oregano Essential Oils on TNBS-Induced Colitis in Mice." *Mediators of Inflammation* 23296. doi: 10.1155/2007/23296.

Chainy, G.B., et al. 2000. "Anethole Blocks Both Early and Late Cellular Responses Transduced By Tumor Necrosis Factor: Effect on NF- kb, AP-1, JNK, MAPKK and Apoptosis." *Oncogene* 19(25): 2943–50.

Chen, J., et al. 2008. "Expression Profiling of Genes Targeted by Bilberry (Vaccinium Myrtillus) in macrophages Through DNA Microarray." *Nutrition and Cancer* 60(1): 43–50.

Cherng, J.M., et al. 2008. "Immunomodulatory Activities of Common Vegetable and Spices of Umbelliferae and Its Related Coumarins and Flavonoids." *Food Chemistry* 106(3): 944–50.

Chobotova, K., et al. 2010. "Bromelain's Activity and Potential as an Anti-Cancer Agent: Current Evidence and Perspectives." *Cancer Letters* 290(2): 148–56.

Choi, D.W., et al. 1990. "The Role of Glutamate Neurotoxicity in Hypoxic-Ischemic Neuronal Death." *Annual Review of Neuroscience* 13(1): 171–82.

Conrad, K. 2006. *Eat Well, Feel Well.* New York, NY: Random House.

Das, U.N. 2002. "Essential Fatty Acids as Possible Enhancers of the Beneficial Actions of Probiotics." *Nutrition* 18(9): 786–89.

Deutsch, L. 2007. "Evaluation of the Effect of Neptune Krill Oil on Chronic Inflammation and Arthritic Symptoms. *Journal of the American College of Nutrition* 26(1): 39–48.

Environmental Working Group. Shopper's Guide to Pesticides. www.foodnews.org.

Ezz El-Arab, A.M., et al. 2006. "Effect of Dietary Honey on Intestinal Microflora and Toxicity of Mycotoxins in Mice." *BMC Complementary and Alternative Medicine* 6: 6.

Farkas, D., et al. 2008. "Influence of Fruit Juices on Drug Disposition: Discrepancies Between In Vitro and Clinical Studies." *Expert Opinion on Drug Metabolism and Toxicology* 4(4): 381–93.

Feingold, B.F. 1975. "Hyperkinesis and Learning Disabilities Linked to Artificial Food Flavors and Colors." *The American Journal of Nursing* 75(5): 797–803.

321

Food and Nutrition Board, Institute of Medicine. 2005. *Dietary Reference Intakes for Energy, Carbohydrate, Fiber, Fat, Fatty Acids, Cholesterol, Protein, and Amino Acids.* Washington, DC: National Academy Press.

Gilliland, F.D., et al. 1996. "Serum Perfluorooctanoic Acid and Hepatic Enzymes, Lipoproteins, and Cholesterol: A Study of Occupationally Exposed Men. *American Journal of Industrial Medicine* 29(5): 560–68.

Gottschall, E.G. 1994. *Breaking the Vicious Cycle.* Kirkton, ON: Kirkton Press.

Grzanna, R., et al. 2005. "Ginger—An Herbal Medicinal Product with Broad Anti-inflammatory Actions." *Journal of Medicinal Food* 8(2): 125–32.

Haenlein, G.F.W. 2004. "Goat Milk in Human Nutrition." *Small Ruminant Research* 51(2): 155–63.

Hidaka, M., et al. 2004. "Potent Inhibition by Star Fruit of Human Cytochrome P450 3A (CYP3A) Activity." *Drug Metabolism and Disposition* 32(6): 581–83.

Hidaka, M., et al. 2006. "Transient Inhibition of CYP3A in Rats by Star Fruit Juice." *Drug Metabolism and Disposition* 34(3): 343–45.

Holt, P.R., et al. 2005. "Curcumin Therapy in Inflammatory Bowel Disease: A Pilot Study." *Digestive Diseases and Science* 50(11): 2191–93.

Jandal, J.M. 1996. "Comparative Aspects of Goat and Sheep Milk." *Small Ruminant Research* 22(2): 177–85.

Jeppesen, P.B., et al. 2002. "Stevioside Induces Antihyperglycaemic, Insulinotropic and Glucagonostatic Effects In Vivo: Studies in the Diabetic Goto-Kakizaki (GK) Rats." *Phytomedicine* 9(1): 9–14.

Kharazmi, A., et al. 1999. "Rose Hip Inhibits Chemotaxis and Chemiluminescence of Human Peripheral Blood Neutrophils In Vitro and Reduces Certain Inflammatory Parameters In Vivo." *Immunopharmacology* 7(4): 377–86.

Kim, H., et al. 2006. "Inhibitory Effects of Fruit Juices on CYP3A Activity." *Drug Metabolism and Disposition* 34(4): 521–23.

Kochhar, K.P. 1999. "Effects of Dietary Herbs and Spices." *Journal of Orthomolecular Medicine* 14(4): 210–18.

Krop, J.J. 2002. *Healing the Planet, One Patient at a Time.* Toronto, ON: Kos Publishing.

Kultétyová, I., et al. 1998. "Neurotoxic Lesions Induced by Monosodium Glutamate Result in Increased Adenopituitary Proopiomelanocortin Gene Expression and Decreased Corticosterone Clearance in Rats." *Neuroendocrinology* 67(6): 412–20.

Lee, S.W., et al. 2010. "Effects of Roasting Conditions of Sesame Seeds on the Oxidative Stability of Pressed Oil during Thermal Oxidation." *Food Chemistry* 118(3): 681–85.

Lugasi, A., et al. 2003. "The Role of Antioxidant Phytonutrients in the Prevention of Diseases." *Acta Biologica Szegediensis* 47(1–4): 119–25.

Malanin, G., et al. 1989. "The Results of Skin Testing with Food Additives and the Effect of an Elimination Diet in Chronic and Recurrent Urticaria and Recurrent Angiodema." *Clinical and Experimental Allergy* 19(5): 539–43.

Manthey, F.A., et al. 2002. "Processing and Cooking Effects on Lipid Content and Stability of a Linolenic Acid in Spaghetti Containing Ground Flaxseed." *Journal of Agricultural and Food Chemistry* 50(6): 1668–71.

McCall, A., et al. 1979. "Monosodium Glutamate Neurotoxicity, Hyperosmolarity, and Blood-Brain Barrier Dysfunction." *Neurobehavioral Toxicity* 1(4): 279–83.

McDowell, L.R. 2003. *Minerals in Animal and Human Nutrition.* Philadelphia, PA: Elsevier Science B.V.

Mitchell, A.E., et al. 2007. "Ten-Year Comparison of the Influence of Organic and Conventional Crop Management Practices on the Content of Flavonoids in Tomatoes." *Journal of Agricultural and Food Chemistry* 55(15): 6154–59.

Mozaffarin, D., et al. 2004. *"Dietary Intake of Trans Fatty Acids and Systemic Inflammation in Women." American Journal of Clinical Nutrition* 79(4): 606–12.

Munro, I.C., et al. 1998. "Erythritol: An Interpretive Summary of Biochemical, Metabolic, Toxicological and Clinical Data." *Food and Chemical Toxicology* 36(12):1139–74.

Murkovic, M. et al. 2000. "Stability of Pumpkin Seed Oil." *European Journal of Lipid Science and Technology* 102(10): 607–11.

Murray, M.T. 1995. *The Healing Power of Herbs.* New York, NY: Random House.

Murray, M.T. 1998. *Encyclopedia of Natural Medicine. Revised 2nd ed.* Roseville, CA: Prima Publishing.

Nagao, T., et al. 2005. "Ingestion of a Tea Rich in Catechins Leads to a Reduction in Body Fat and Malondialdehyde-Modified LDL in Men." *American Journal of Clinical Nutrition* 81(1): 122–29.

Nair, M.K., et al. 2005. "Antibacterial Effect of Caprylic Acid and Monocaprylin on Major Bacterial Mastitis Pathogens." *Journal of Dairy Science* 88(10): 3488–95.

Nicoll, R., et al. 2009. "Ginger (Zingiber officinale Roscoe): A Hot Remedy For Cardiovascular Disease?" *International Journal of Cardiology* 131(3): 408–9.

Olney, J.W., et al. 1969. "Brain Lesions in an Infant Rhesus Monkey Treated with Monosodium Glutamate." *Science* 166(3903): 386–88.

Park, Y.W., et al. 2007. "Physico-Chemical Characteristics of Goat and Sheep Milk." *Small Ruminant Research* 68(1–2): 88–113.

Pastorello, E.A., et al. 1989. "Role of the Elimination Diet in Adults With Food Allergy." *Journal of Allergy and Clinical Immunology* 84(4, Pt. 1): 475–83.

Pravst, I., et al. 2010. "Coenzyme Q10 Contents in Foods and Fortification Strategies." *Critical Reviews in Food Science and Nutrition* 50(4): 269–80.

Prentice, J. 2006. *Full Moon Feast: Food and the Hunger for Connection.* White River Junction, VT: Chelsea Green Publishing.

Rangan, C., et al. 2009. "Food Additives and Sensitivities." *Disease-a-Month* 55(5): 292–311.

Rimando, A.M., et al. 2004. "Resveratrol, Pterostilbene, and Piceatannol in Vaccinium Berries." *Journal of Agriculture and Food Chemistry* 52(15): 4713–19.

Said, H.M. 2009. "Cell and Molecular Aspects of Human Intestinal Biotin Absorption." *The Journal of Nutrition* 139(1): 158–62.

Sarjeant, D. 1999. *Hard to Swallow: The Truth About Food Additives.* Burnaby, BC: Alive Books.

Schlosser, E. 2001. *Fast Food Nation: The Dark Side of the All-American Meal.* Boston, MA: Houghton Mifflin.

SeaChoice. Canada's Sustainable Seafood Guide. www.seachoice.org.

Singh S. M., et al. 2007. "Biological Activities of Ocimum Sanctum L. Fixed Oil—An Overview." *Indian Journal of Experimental Biology* 45(5): 403–12.

Spolaore, P., et al. 2006. "Commercial Applications of Microalgae." *Journal of Bioscience and Bioengineering* 101(6): 201–11.

Staggs, G., et al. 2004. "Determination of the Biotin Content of Select Foods Using Accurate and Sensitive HPLC/Avidin Binding." *Journal of Food Composition and Analysis* 17(6): 767–76.

Stuchl'k, M., et al. 2002. "Vegetable Lipids as Components of Functional Foods." *Biomedical Papers* 146(2): 3–10.

Takaki, I., et al. 2008. "Anti-inflammatory and Antinociceptive Effects of Rosmarinus officinalis L. Essential Oil in Experimental Animal Models." *Journal of Medicinal Food* 11(4): 741–46.

Thomson, M., et al. 2002. "The Use of Ginger (Zingiber officinale Rosc.) as a Potential Anti-inflammatory and Antithrombotic Agent." *Prostaglandins, Leukotrienes, and Essential Fatty Acids* 67(6): 475–78.

Torbergsen, A.C., et al. 2000. "Recovery of Human Lymphocytes from Oxidative DNA Damage: The Apparent Enhancement of DNA Repair by Carotenoids Is Probably Simply an Antioxidant Effect." *European Journal of Nutrition* 39(2): 80–85.

Tsai, P.J., et al. 2007. "Evaluation of NO-Suppressing Activity of Several Mediterranean Culinary Spices." *Food and Chemical Toxicology* 45(3): 440–47.

Tsai, T.H., et al. 2005. "Antioxidant and Anti-inflammatory Activities of Several Commonly Used Spices." *Journal of Food Science* 70(1): C93–C97.

Vaclavik, V., et al. 2007. *Essentials of Food Science, 3rd ed.* New York, NY: Springer Science.

Varzakas, T.H., et al. 2010. "Food Additives and Contaminants." In *Applied Food Chemistry.* Edited by F. Yildiz. Boca Raton, FL: CRC Press. 409–56.

Wannamethee, G., et al. 2006. "Associations of Vitamin C Status, Fruit and Vegetable Intakes, and Markers of Inflammation and Hemostasis." *American Journal of Clinical Nutrition* 83(3): 567–74.

Winther, K., et al. 1999. "The Anti-inflammatory Properties of Rose-Hip." *Immunopharmacology* 7(1): 63–68.

Zhang, J-W., et al. 2007. "Inhibition of Human Liver Cytochrome P450 by Star Fruit Juice." *Journal of Pharmacy and Pharmaceutical Sciences* 10(4): 496–503.

Chapter 7: Focus on Foods

Abdullah, T. H., et al. 1988. "Garlic Revisited: Therapeutic for the Major Diseases of Our Times?" *Journal of the National Medical Association* 80(4): 439–45.

Abraham, G. E. 1983. "Nutritional Factors in the Etiology of the Premenstrual Tension Syndromes." *The Journal of Reproductive Medicine* 28(7): 446–64.

Ahmed, S., et al. 2005. "Punica Granatum L. Extract Inhibits IL-1beta–Induced Expression of Matrix Metalloproteinases by Inhibiting the Activation of MAP Kinases and NF-kappaB in Human Chondrocytes In Vitro." *The Journal of Nutrition* 135(9): 2096–2102.

Alves-Rodrigues, A., et al. 2004. "The Science Behind Lutein." *Toxicology Letters* 150(1): 57–83.

Anderson, R. "Fats for Maximum Brain Potential." *Pharmacol Research* 40(3): 211–25.

Atkinson, Meghan. 2013. "Hemp Replaces Common Food Allergens." *Manitoba Harvest.* http://manitobaharvest.com/articles_studies/3816/Hemp-Replaces-Common-Food-Allergens.html.

Ayturk, S., et al. 2009. "Metabolic Syndrome and Its Components Are Associated with Increased Thyroid Volume and Nodule Prevalence in a Mild-to-Moderate Iodine-Deficient Area." *European Journal of Endocrinology* 161(4): 599–605.

Baba, N., et al. 1982. "Enhanced Thermogenesis and Diminished Deposition of Fat in Response to Overfeeding with Diet Containing Medium Chain Triglyceride. *The American Journal of Clinical Nutrition* 35(4): 678–82.

Bahadoran, Z., et al. 2011. "Broccoli Sprouts Reduce Oxidative Stress in Type 2 Diabetes: A Randomized Double-Blind Clinical Trial." *European Journal of Clinical Nutrition* 65(8): 972–77.

Ballot, D., et al. 1987. "The Effects of Fruit Juices and Fruits on the Absorption of Iron from a Rice Meal." *British Journal of Nutrition* 57(3): 331–43.

323

Beauchamp, G.K., et al. 2005. "Phytochemistry: Ibuprofen-Like Activity in Extra-Virgin Olive Oil." *Nature* 437 (7055): 45–46.

Body Ecology. 2007. "The Body Ecology Diet; The Quick and Easy Guide to Improving Your Health on the Body Ecology Program Part I: The First 7 Steps to Great Health." http://bodyecology.com/articles/7_steps_to_great_health.php#.UoFmMo5OTdk.

Brown, C.S., et al. 1998. "An Update on the Treatment of Premenstrual Syndrome." *Am J Managed Care* 4: 266–74.

Choi, E. M., et al. 2004. "Anti-inflammatory, Analgesic and Antioxidant Activities of the Fruit of *Foeniculum vulgare*." *Fitoterapia* 75(6): 557–65.

Comai, S., et al. 2007. "The Content of Proteic and Nonproteic (Free and Protein-Bound) Tryptophan in Quinoa and Cereal Flours." *Food Chemistry* 100(4): 1350–55.

D'Angelo, E.K., et al. 1992. "Magnesium Relaxes Arterial Smooth Muscle by Decreasing Intracellular Ca2+ without Changing Intracellular Mg2+." *Journal of Clinical Investigation* 89(6): 1988–94.

Detopoulou, P., et al. 2008. "Dietary Choline and Betaine Intakes in Relation to Concentrations of Inflammatory Markers in Healthy Adults: The ATTICA study." *The American Journal of Clinical Nutrition* 87(2): 424–30.

Di Giuseppe, R., et al. 2008. "Regular Consumption of Dark Chocolate Is Associated with Low Serum Concentrations of C-Reactive Protein in a Healthy Italian Population." *The Journal of Nutrition* 138(10): 1939–45.

Ding, H., et al. 2007. "Chemopreventive Characteristics of Avocado Fruit." *Seminars in Cancer Biology* 17(5): 386–94. Academic Press.

Dröge, W., et al. 2000. "Glutathione and Immune Function." *Proceedings of the Nutrition Society* 59(04): 595–600.

Drury, D.R., et al. 1924. "Observations on Some Causes of Gall Stone Formation III. The Relation of the Reaction of the Bile to Experimental Cholelithiasis." *The Journal of Experimental Medicine* 39(3): 403–23.

Eden, A.N. 2005. "Iron Deficiency and Impaired Cognition in Toddlers: An Underestimated and Undertreated Problem." *Pediatric Drugs* 7(6): 347–52.

Ekiz, C., et al. 2005. "The Effect of Iron Deficiency Anemia on the Function of the Immune System." *The Hematology Journal* 5(7): 579–83.

Emendörfer, F., et al. 2005. "Antispasmodic Activity of Fractions and Cynaropicrin from Cynara Scolymus on Guinea-Pig Ileum." *Biological and Pharmaceutical Bulletin* 28(5): 902–4.

Estruch, R., et al. 2009. "Effects of Dietary Fibre Intake on Risk Factors for Cardiovascular Disease in Subjects at High Risk." *Journal of Epidemiology and Community Health* 63(7): 582–88.

Fausto, Nelson, C. 2006. "Cell Injury, Cell Death." Course syllabus, University of Washington. http://courses.washington.edu/hubio520/print/syllabus_cellinjurydeath.pdf

Felgines, C., et al. 2003. "Strawberry Anthocyanins Are Recovered in Urine as Glucuro- and Sulfoconjugates in Humans." *The Journal of Nutrition* 133(5): 1296–1301.

Foss, Y.J. 2009. "Vitamin D Deficiency Is the Cause of Common Obesity." *Medical Hypotheses* 72(3): 314–21.

Gates, D., et al. 2011. *The Body Ecology Diet: Recovering Your Health and Rebuilding Your Immunity*. Carlsbad, CA: Hay House.

Geng, H., et al. 2008. "Cartilage Oligomeric Matrix Protein Deficiency Promotes Early Onset and the Chronic Development of Collagen-Induced Arthritis." *Arthritis Research and Therapy* 10(6): R134.

Grassi, D., et al. 2008. "Blood Pressure Is Reduced and Insulin Sensitivity Increased in Glucose-Intolerant, Hypertensive Subjects after 15 Days of Consuming High-Polyphenol Dark Chocolate." *The Journal of Nutrition* 138(9): 1671–76.

Guerrera, M.P., et al. 2009. "Therapeutic Uses of Magnesium." *American Family Physician* 80(2): 157.

Handayani, D., et al. 2011. "Dietary Shiitake Mushroom (Lentinus Edodes) Prevents Fat Deposition and Lowers Triglyceride in Rats Fed a High-Fat Diet." *Journal of Obesity*. doi: 10.1155/2011/258051.

Hartmann, E. 1983. "Effects of L-tryptophan on Sleepiness and on Sleep." *Journal of Psychiatric Research* 17(2): 107–13.

Holick, M.F. 2004. "Sunlight and Vitamin D for Bone Health and Prevention of Autoimmune Diseases, Cancers, and Cardiovascular Disease." *The American Journal of Clinical Nutrition* 80(6): 1678S–88S.

Holtmann, G., et al. 2003. "Efficacy of Artichoke Leaf Extract in the Treatment of Patients with Functional Dyspepsia: A Six Week Placebo Controlled, Double Blind, Multicentre Trial." *Alimentary Pharmacology & Therapeutics* 18(11–12): 1099–105.

Horrocks, L.A., et al. 1999. "Health Benefits of Docosahexaenoic Acid (DHA)." *Pharmacological Research* 40(3): 211–25.

Hunt, R., et al. 1993. "Therapeutic Role of Dietary Fibre." Division of Gastroenterology, McMaster University, Hamilton, Ont. Canadian Family Physician Médecin de Famille Canadien (impact factor: 1.41). 05/1993; 39: 897–900, 903–10.

Ishikawa, N.K., et al. 2001. "Antibacterial Activity of Lentinula Edodes Grown in Liquid Medium." *Brazilian Journal of Microbiology* 32(3): 206–10.

Kaplan, B.J., et al. 2007. "Vitamins, Minerals, and Mood." *Psychological Bulletin* 133(5): 747–60.

Kapoor, Rakesh, et al. 2006. "Gamma Linolenic Acid: An Antiinflammatory Omega-6 Fatty Acid." *Current Pharmaceutical Biotechnology* 7 (6): 531–34.

324

Kasai, M., et al. 2003. "Effect of Dietary Medium- and Long-Chain Triacylglycerols (MLCT) on Accumulation of Body Fat in Healthy Humans." *Asia Pacific Journal of Clinical Nutrition* 12(2): 151–60.

Kelley, D.S., et al. 2013. "Sweet Bing Cherries Lower Circulating Concentrations of Markers for Chronic Inflammatory Diseases in Healthy Humans." *The Journal of Nutrition* 143(3): 340–44.

Kim, M., et al. 2010. "Relationship Between Vitamin K Status, Bone Mineral Density, and hs-CRP in Young Korean Women." *Nutrition Research and Practice* 4(6): 507–14.

Liau, K. M., et al. 2011. "An Open-Label Pilot Study to Assess the Efficacy and Safety of Virgin Coconut Oil in Reducing Visceral Adiposity." *ISRN pharmacology.* doi: 10.5402/2011/949686.

Lee, Y.M., et al. 2009. "Antioxidant Effect of Garlic and Aged Black Garlic in Animal Model of Type 2 Diabetes Mellitus." *Nutrition Research and Practice* 3(2): 156–61.

Mejia Meza, E.I., et al. 2010. "Effect of Dehydration on Raspberries: Polyphenol and Anthocyanin Retention, Antioxidant Capacity, and Antiadipogenic Activity." *Journal of Food Science* 75(1): H5–H12.

Meydani, M., et al. 2010. "Dietary Polyphenols and Obesity." *Nutrients* 2(7): 737–51.

Mofidi, S. 2003. "Nutritional Management of Pediatric Food Hypersensitivity." *Pediatrics* 111(Supp 3): 1645–53.

Moghe, S.S., et al. 2012. "Effect of Blueberry Polyphenols on 3T3-F442A Preadipocyte Differentiation." *Journal of Medicinal Food* 15(5): 448–52.

Nielsen, F.H. 2010. "Magnesium, Inflammation, and Obesity in Chronic Disease." *Nutrition Reviews* 68 (6): 333–40.

Nurtjahja-Tjendraputra, E., et al. 2003. "Effective Anti-Platelet and COX-1 Enzyme Inhibitors from Pungent Constituents of Ginger." *Thrombosis Research* 111(4): 259–65.

Ogbolu, D.O., et al. 2007. "In Vitro Antimicrobial Properties of Coconut Oil on Candida Species in Ibadan, Nigeria." *Journal of Medicinal Food* 10(2): 384–87.

Paiva, S., et al. 1999. "β-Carotene and Other Carotenoids as Antioxidants." *Journal of the American College of Nutrition* 18(5): 426–33.

Pan, S.Y., et al. 2011. "Antioxidants and Breast Cancer Risk—A Population-Based Case-Control Study in Canada." *BMC Cancer* 11(1): 372.

Paola, C., et al. "Effects of n-3 PUFAs on Breast Cancer Cells Through their Incorporation in Plasma Membrane." *Lipids in Health and Disease* 10. doi: 10.1186/1476-511X-10-73.

Percival, M. 1997. "Phytonutrients and Detoxification." *Clinical Nutrition Insights* 5(2): 1–4.

Peters, B. S. E., et al. 2010. "Nutritional Aspects of the Prevention and Treatment of Osteoporosis." *Arquivos Brasileiros de Endocrinologia & Metabologia* 54(2): 179–85.

Phipps, W.R., et al. 1993. "Effect of Flax Seed Ingestion on the Menstrual Cycle." *Journal of Clinical Endocrinology & Metabolism* 77(5): 1215–19.

Raiten, D.J., et al. 2004. "Vitamin D and Health in the 21st Century: Bone and Beyond. Executive summary." *The American Journal of Clinical Nutrition* 80(6): 1673S–1677S.

Remer, T., et al. 1995. "Potential Renal Acid Load of Foods and Its Influence on Urine pH." *Journal of the American Dietetic Association* 95(7): 791–97.

Ritter, A., et al. 2013. "Antihypernociceptive Activity of Anethole in Experimental Inflammatory Pain." *Inflammopharmacology* 21(2): 187–97.

Ritz, B., et al. 2006. "Supplementation with Active Hexose Correlated Compound Increases the Innate Immune Response of Young Mice to Primary Influenza Infection." *The Journal of Nutrition* 136(11): 2868–73.

Romero, C., et al. 2007. "In Vitro Activity of Olive Oil Polyphenols Against Helicobacter Pylori." *Journal of Agricultural and Food Chemistry* 55(3): 680–86.

Sahyoun, N.R., et al. 2006. "Whole-Grain Intake is Inversely Associated with the Metabolic Syndrome and Mortality in Older Adults." *The American Journal of Clinical Nutrition* 83(1): 124–31.

Schwalfenberg, G.K. 2012. "The Alkaline Diet: Is There Evidence That an Alkaline pH Diet Benefits Health?" *Journal of Environment and Public Health.* 727630. doi: 10.1155/2012/727630.

Seaman, D.R. 1998. *Clinical Nutrition For Pain, Inflammation and Tissue Healing.* Santa Barbara, CA: NutrAnalysis, Inc.

Self. Nutrition Data. 2013. Nutrition Facts: Broccoli. http://nutritiondata.self.com/facts/vegetables-and-vegetable-products/2357/2

Serraino, M., et al. 1991. "The Effect of Flaxseed Supplementation on Early Risk Markers for Mammary Carcinogenesis." *Cancer Letters* 60(2): 135–42.

Sheila, T., et al. 2011. "Dietary Supplementation with Phytosterol and Ascorbic Acid Reduces Body Mass Accumulation and Alters Food Transit Time in a Diet-Induced Obesity Mouse Model." *Lipids in Health and Disease* 10. doi: 10.1186/1476-511X-10-107.

Shuvy, M., et al. 2008. "Intrahepatic CD8+ Lymphocyte Trapping During Tolerance Induction Using Mushroom Derived Formulations: A Possible Role for Liver In Tolerance Induction." *World Journal of Gastroenterology: WJG* 14(24): 3872–78.

Sicilia, T., et al. 2003. "Identification and Stereochemical Characterization of Lignans in Flaxseed and Pumpkin Seeds." *Journal of Agricultural and Food Chemistry* 51(5): 1181–88.

Sohn, E.H., et al. 2011. "Anti-Allergic and Anti-inflammatory Effects of Butanol Extract from Arctium Lappa L." *L. Clin. Mol. Allergy* 9(1): 1–11.

Sondergaard, B.C., et al. 2010. "Investigation of the Direct Effects of Salmon Calcitonin on Human Osteoarthritic Chondrocytes." *BMC Musculoskeletal Disorders* 11(1): 62.

Takeuchi, H., et al. 2008. "The Application of Medium-Chain Fatty Acids: Edible Oil with a Suppressing Effect on Body Fat Accumulation." *Asia Pac J Clin Nutr* 17(S1): 320–23.

Talbott, S., et al. 2007. *The Cortisol Connection: Why Stress Makes You Fat And Ruins Your Health–and What You Can Do About It*. Newport, RI: Hunter House.

Tsai, J.T., 2010. "Suppression of Inflammatory Mediators by Cruciferous Vegetable-Derived Indole-3-Carbinol and Phenylethyl Isothiocyanate in Lipopolysaccharide-Activated Macrophages." *Mediators of Inflammation.* doi: 10.1155/2010/293642.

Wang, Y.P., et al. 2010. "Effect of Blueberry on Hepatic and Immunological Functions in Mice." *Hepatobiliary Pancreat Dis Int* 9(2): 164–68.

Yousofi, A., et al. 2012. "Immunomodulatory Effect of Parsley (Petroselinum crispum) Essential Oil On Immune Cells: Mitogen-Activated Splenocytes And Peritoneal Macrophages." *Immunopharmacology and Immunotoxicology* 34(2): 303–8.

Vasey, C. 2006. *The Acid-Alkaline Diet for Optimum Health: Restore Your Health by Creating pH Balance in Your Diet, 2nd Edition*. Rochester, VT: Healing Arts Press.

Yu, B.S., et al. 2009. "Polyphenols of Rubus Coreanum Inhibit Catecholamine Secretion from the Perfused Adrenal Medulla of SHRs." *The Korean Journal of Physiology & Pharmacology* 13(6): 517–26.

Zhang, L., et al. 2005. "Efficacy of Cranberry Juice on Helicobacter Pylori Infection: A Double Blind, Randomized Placebo Controlled Trial." *Helicobacter* 10(2): 139–45.

Part 3: The Recipes

Alzoreky, N.S., et al. 2003. "Antibacterial Activity of Extracts from Some Edible Plants Commonly Consumed in Asia." *International Journal of Food Microbiology* 80(3): 223–30.

Amengual, J., et al. 2011. "Beta-Carotene Reduces Body Adiposity of Mice Via BCMO1." *PLoS One* 6(6):e20644.

Balance Ph Diet. "pH Scale, pH Level, ph Balance." http://www.balance-ph-diet.com/ph_scale.html.

Chawla, A.S., et al. 1987. "Anti-inflammatory Action of Ferulic Acid and its Esters in Carrageenan Induced Rat Paw Oedema Model." *Indian Journal of Experimental Biology* 25(3): 187–89.

Christensen, L.P., et al. "Bioactive Polyacetylenes in Food Plants of the Apiaceae Family: Occurrence, Bioactivity and Analysis." *Journal of Pharmaceutical and Biomedical Analysis* 41(3): 683–93.

Davis, D.R. 2009. "Declining Fruit and Vegetable Nutrient Composition: What Is the Evidence?" *HortScience* 44(1): 15–19.

Ganio, M.S., et al. 2009. "Effect of Caffeine on Sport-Specific Endurance Performance: A Systematic Review." *The Journal of Strength & Conditioning Research* 23(1): 315–24.

Grespan, R., et al. 2012. "Anti-Arthritic Effect of Eugenol on Collagen-Induced Arthritis Experimental Model." *Biological and Pharmaceutical Bulletin* 35(10): 1818–20.

Guardia, T., et al. 2001. "Anti-inflammatory Properties of Plant Flavonoids. Effects of Rutin, Quercetin and Hesperidin on Adjuvant Arthritis in Rat." *Il farmac* 56(9): 683–87.

Halley, F.M. 1991. "Self-Regulation of the Immune System through Biobehavioral Strategies." *Biofeedback and Self-Regulation* 16(1): 55–74.

Hlebowicz, J., et al. 2007. "Effect of Apple Cider Vinegar on Delayed Gastric Emptying in Patients with Type 1 Diabetes Mellitus: A Pilot Study." *BMC Gastroenterology* 7(1): 46.

Horrocks, L.A., et al. 1999. "Health Benefits of Docosahexaenoic Acid (DHA)." *Pharmacological Research* 40(3): 211–25.

Jeukendrup, A., et al. 1995. "Metabolic Availability of Medium-Chain Triglycerides Coingested with Carbohydrates During Prolonged Exercise." *Journal of Applied Physiology* 79(3): 756–62.

Johnston, C.S., et al. 2006. "Vinegar: Medicinal Uses and Antiglycemic Effect." *Medscape General Medicine* 8(2): 61.

Kawa, J.M., et al. 2003. "Buckwheat Concentrate Reduces Serum Glucose in Streptozotocin-Diabetic Rats." *Journal of Agricultural and Food Chemistry* 51(25): 7287–91.

Kim, N.Y., et al. 2010. "Comparison of Methods for Proanthocyanidin Extraction from Pine (Pinus densiflora) Needles and Biological Activities of the Extracts." *Nutrition Research and Practice* 4(1): 16–22.

Komura, D.L., et al. 2010. "Structure of Agaricus spp. Fucogalactans and Their Anti-inflammatory and Antinociceptive Properties." *Bioresource Technology* 101(15): 6192–99.

Lohachoompol, V., et al. 2004. "The Change of Total Anthocyanins in Blueberries and Their Antioxidant Effect after Drying and Freezing." *BioMed Research International* 2004(5): 248–52.

Papoulias, E., et al. 2009. "Effects of Genetic, Pre- and Post-Harvest Factors on Phenolic Content and Antioxidant Capacity of White Asparagus Spears." *International Journal of Molecular Sciences* 10(12): 5370–80.

Prasad, A.S., et al. 1996. "Zinc Status and Serum Testosterone Levels of Healthy Adults." *Nutrition* 12(5): 344–48.

Rennard, B.O., et al. 2000. "Chicken Soup Inhibits Neutrophil Chemotaxis In Vitro." *Chest* 118(4): 115–17.

Saketkhoo, K., et al. 1978. "Effects of Drinking Hot Water, Cold Water, and Chicken Soup on Nasal Mucus Velocity and Nasal Airflow Resistance." *Chest* 74(4): 408–10.

Seo, J.S., et al. 2005. "Extraction and Chromatography of Carotenoids from Pumpkin." *Journal of Chromatography A* 1073(1): 371–75.

Sondergaard, B.C., et al. 2010. "Investigation of the Direct Effects of Salmon Calcitonin on Human Osteoarthritic Chondrocytes." *BMC Musculoskeletal Disorders* 11(1): 62.

Tsai, J.T., et al. 2010. "Suppression of Inflammatory Mediators by Cruciferous Vegetable-Derived Indole-3-Carbinol and Phenylethyl Isothiocyanate in Lipopolysaccharide-Activated Macrophages." *Mediators of Inflammation*. doi: 10.1155/2010/293642.

Walston, J., et al. 2006. "Serum Antioxidants, Inflammation, and Total Mortality in Older Women." *American Journal of Epidemiology* 163(1): 18–26.

Yonezawa, T., et al. 1969. "Effects of Pyridoxine Deficiency in Nervous Tissue Maintained in Vitro." *Annals of the New York Academy of Sciences* 166(1): 146–57.

Young, H.Y., et al. 2005. "Analgesic and Anti-inflammatory Activities of [6]-Gingerol." *Journal of Ethnopharmacology* 96(1): 207–10.

Yousofi, A., et al. 2012. "Immunomodulatory Effect of Parsley (Petroselinum crispum) Essential Oil on Immune Cells: Mitogen-Activated Splenocytes and Peritoneal Macrophages." *Immunopharmacology and Immunotoxicology* 34(2): 303–8.

Yu, S., et al. 2009. "The Effects of Whole Mushrooms during Inflammation." *BMC Immunology* 10(1): 12.

CONVERSION CHARTS

The recipes in this book use the standard United States method for measuring liquid and dry or solid ingredients (teaspoons, tablespoons, and cups). The following charts are provided to help cooks outside the U.S. successfully use these recipes. All equivalents are approximate.

Standard Cup	Fine Powder (e.g., flour)	Grain (e.g., rice)	Granular (e.g., sugar)	Liquid Solids (e.g., butter)	Liquid (e.g., milk)
1	140 g	150 g	190 g	200 g	240 ml
¾	105 g	113 g	143 g	150 g	180 ml
⅔	93 g	100 g	125 g	133 g	160 ml
½	70 g	75 g	95 g	100 g	120 ml
3	47 g	50 g	63 g	67 g	80 ml
¼	35 g	38 g	48 g	50 g	60 ml
⅛	18 g	19 g	24 g	25 g	30 ml

Useful Equivalents for Liquid Ingredients by Volume					
¼ tsp				1 ml	
½ tsp				2 ml	
1 tsp				5 ml	
3 tsp	1 tbsp		½ fl oz	15 ml	
	2 tbsp	⅛ cup	1 fl oz	30 ml	
	4 tbsp	¼ cup	2 fl oz	60 ml	
	5⅓ tbsp	⅓ cup	3 fl oz	80 ml	
	8 tbsp	½ cup	4 fl oz	120 ml	
	10⅔ tbsp	⅔ cup	5 fl oz	160 ml	
	12 tbsp	¾ cup	6 fl oz	180 ml	
	16 tbsp	1 cup	8 fl oz	240 ml	
	1 pt	2 cups	16 fl oz	480 ml	
	1 qt	4 cups	32 fl oz	960 ml	
			33 fl oz	1000 ml	1 l

Useful Equivalents for Dry Ingredients by Weight

(To convert ounces to grams, multiply the number of ounces by 30.)

1 oz	1/16 lb	30 g
4 oz	1/4 lb	120 g
8 oz	1/2 lb	240 g
12 oz	3/4 lb	360 g
16 oz	1 lb	480 g

Useful Equivalents for Cooking/Oven Temperatures

Process	Fahrenheit	Celsius	Gas Mark
Freeze Water	32° F	0° C	
Room Temperature	68° F	20° C	
Boil Water	212° F	100° C	
Bake	325° F	160° C	3
	350° F	180° C	4
	375° F	190° C	5
	400° F	200° C	6
	425° F	220° C	7
	450° F	230° C	8
Broil			Grill

Useful Equivalents for Length

(To convert inches to centimeters, multiply the number of inches by 2.5.)

1 in			2.5 cm	
6 in	1/2 ft		15 cm	
12 in	1 ft		30 cm	
36 in	3 ft	1 yd	90 cm	
40 in			100 cm	1 m

SUBJECT INDEX

RECIPE INDEX

340

ABOUT THE AUTHOR

Julie Daniluk, R.H.N., is the bestselling author of *Meals That Heal Inflammation,* and the co-host of *Healthy Gourmet,* a reality cooking show on the Oprah Winfrey Network (OWN) in Canada. Julie has appeared on *The Dr. Oz Show* and is a resident expert on *The Marilyn Denis Show* and for *Reader's Digest.*

To learn more about Julie and Daniluk Consulting:
info@juliedaniluk.com
www.juliedaniluk.com
Facebook: Julie Daniluk Nutrition
Twitter: @JulieDaniluk
Instagram: Julie Daniluk

HAY HOUSE TITLES OF RELATED INTEREST

YOU CAN HEAL YOUR LIFE, the movie, starring Louise Hay & Friends
(available as a 1-DVD program and an expanded 2-DVD set)
Watch the trailer at: **www.LouiseHayMovie.com**

THE SHIFT, the movie, starring Dr. Wayne W. Dyer
(available as a 1-DVD program and an expanded 2-DVD set)
Watch the trailer at: **www.DyerMovie.com**

• • •

CRAZY SEXY KITCHEN:
150 Plant-Empowered Recipes to Ignite a Mouthwatering Revolution,
by Kris Carr, with Chef Chad Sarno

CULTURED FOOD FOR LIFE:
How to Make and Serve Delicious Probiotic Foods for Better Health and Wellness,
by Donna Schwenk

EATING IN THE LIGHT:
Making the Switch to Veganism on Your Spiritual Path,
by Doreen Virtue and Becky Black, M.F.T., R.D.

THE LOONEYSPOONS COLLECTION:
Good Food, Good Health, Good Fun!,
by Janet and Greta Podleski

THE MYSTIC COOKBOOK:
The Secret Alchemy of Food,
by Denise Linn and Meadow Linn

All of the above are available at your local bookstore,
or may be ordered by contacting Hay House (see next page).

• • •

We hope you enjoyed this Hay House book.
If you'd like to receive our online catalog featuring additional information on
Hay House books and products, or if you'd like to find out
more about the Hay Foundation, please contact:

Hay House, Inc., P.O. Box 5100, Carlsbad, CA 92018-5100
(760) 431-7695 or (800) 654-5126
(760) 431-6948 (fax) or (800) 650-5115 (fax)
www.hayhouse.com® • www.hayfoundation.org

• • •

Published and distributed in Australia by:
Hay House Australia Pty. Ltd., 18/36 Ralph St., Alexandria NSW 2015 •
Phone: 612-9669-4299 • *Fax:* 612-9669-4144 • www.hayhouse.com.au

Published and distributed in the United Kingdom by:
Hay House UK, Ltd., Astley House, 33 Notting Hill Gate, London W11 3JQ •
Phone: 44-20-3675-2450 • *Fax:* 44-20-3675-2451 • www.hayhouse.co.uk

Published and distributed in the Republic of South Africa by:
Hay House SA (Pty), Ltd., P.O. Box 990, Witkoppen 2068 •
Phone/Fax: 27-11-467-8904 • www.hayhouse.co.za

Published in India by:
Hay House Publishers India, Muskaan Complex, Plot No. 3, B-2, Vasant Kunj, New Delhi 110 070 •
Phone: 91-11-4176-1620 • *Fax:* 91-11-4176-1630 • www.hayhouse.co.in

• • •

Take Your Soul on a Vacation

Visit www.HealYourLife.com® to regroup, recharge, and reconnect
with your own magnificence. Featuring blogs, mind-body-spirit news,
and life-changing wisdom from Louise Hay and friends.

Visit www.HealYourLife.com today!

Free e-newsletters
from Hay House, the Ultimate
Resource for Inspiration

Be the first to know about Hay House's dollar deals, free downloads, special offers, affirmation cards, giveaways, contests, and more!

Get exclusive excerpts from our latest releases and videos from **Hay House Present Moments**.

Enjoy uplifting personal stories, how-to articles, and healing advice, along with videos and empowering quotes, within **Heal Your Life**.

Have an inspirational story to tell and a passion for writing? Sharpen your writing skills with insider tips from **Your Writing Life**.

Sign Up Now!

Get inspired, educate yourself, get a complimentary gift, and share the wisdom!

http://www.hayhouse.com/newsletters.php

Visit www.hayhouse.com to sign up today!

HAYHOUSE
RADIO
radio for your soul

HealYourLife.com

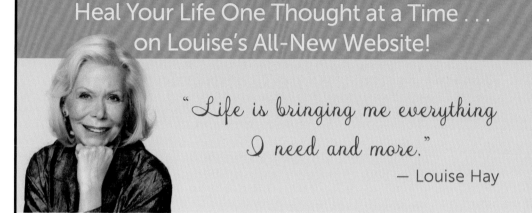

MEALS THAT HEAL!

Three-Lesson Online Companion Course
with Julie Daniluk

LESSON 1: *The Anti-Inflammatory Live-It Plan*
Learn how to create a "Live-It" lifetime eating plan.

LESSON 2: *Hormone and Weight Balance*
Discover the right way to maintain nutritional balance.

LESSON 3: *Eating for Bliss*
Embrace the superfoods that work with your brain chemistry.

REPORTED RESULTS INCLUDE:

- Dramatic reduction in inflammatory pain
- Controlled cravings and emotional eating
- Balanced hormones
- Elevated mood
- Increased energy
- Natural weight balance

AS AN ADDED BONUS, WHEN YOU PURCHASE THIS COURSE, YOU'LL RECEIVE:

- A 21-day "Live-It" plan that includes daily healing affirmations
- An anti-inflammatory food chart
- A food-choice guide to put directly on your fridge
- An anti-inflammatory supplement guide
- Julie's recipe for hormone balance and stress reduction

Visit www.hayhouse.com to sign up today!